THE POLITICS OF ECONOMIC ACTIVITY

The Politics of Economic Activity

ANDY SMITH

OXFORD
UNIVERSITY PRESS

OXFORD
UNIVERSITY PRESS

Great Clarendon Street, Oxford, OX2 6DP,
United Kingdom

Oxford University Press is a department of the University of Oxford.
It furthers the University's objective of excellence in research, scholarship,
and education by publishing worldwide. Oxford is a registered trade mark of
Oxford University Press in the UK and in certain other countries

First Edition published in 2016

Published in the United States of America by Oxford University Press
198 Madison Avenue, New York, NY 10016, United States of America

British Library Cataloguing in Publication Data
Data available

Library of Congress Control Number: 2016935486

ISBN 978–0–19–878815–7

To Caitríona

Acknowledgements

This book is the cumulative result of twenty-five years of research into different aspects of political economy. I therefore owe a considerable debt to the colleagues who have accompanied me in parts of this journey during a variety of projects and studies. Each are thanked specifically in the relevant chapters. Consequently, at this stage I would just like to acknowledge four sources of financial support that have made these collaborations possible and sustainable: the French *Agence Nationale de la recherche* and Ministry of Research, Aquitaine's Regional Council and the *Union Patronale de la Charente*. In blanket fashion, I would also like to thank the roughly 500 businessmen and women, politicians, civil servants, and interest group representatives who have granted me interviews over this period.

A second series of thanks goes to the organizations and people in Bordeaux who have constituted my workplace for the last twenty years. Sciences Po Bordeaux and, more recently, the University of Bordeaux as a whole, have provided invaluable structures and financial assistance. But naturally it is my research centre, *le Centre Émile Durkheim*, its political scientists, sociologists, and administrative staff that have provided the most daily support and intellectual nourishment. Indeed, this interdisciplinary adventure, shared by a small but stimulating group of neighbouring economists, has been a key source of the approach to political economy developed and advocated in the pages that follow. Particular thanks go to four colleagues who have commented in depth on parts of the manuscript: Matthieu Ansaloni, Cyril Benoît, Nicolas Charles, and Vincent Tiberj.

Gratitude of a similar nature is also owed to Oxford University Press's excellent reviewers of this book's first draft. In reacting to their perceptive criticisms, comments, and suggestions I have hopefully made its arguments sharper and removed a number of distracting passages that cluttered the initial manuscript. At the Press itself, I would also like to thank Dominic Byatt for his rapid endorsement of the book's aims and ceaseless encouragement regarding its realization.

A final round of thanks goes to a select group of colleagues from around the world who have been a constant source of inspiration, ideas, energy, and laughter throughout my career to date: Pierre Muller, Peter Hall, Bernard Jullien, Craig Parsons, Colin Hay, and, above all, my wife Caitríona Carter.

Contents

Figures and Tables

Abbreviations

ANT	Actor Network Theory
EU	European Union
GI	Geographical Indication
GVCs	Global Value Chains
HTA	Health Technology Assessment
IPE	International Political Economy
IR	Institutionalized Relationship
IO	Institutional Order
LEEM	*Les Entreprises du Médicament*
NICE	National Institute for Health and Care Excellence
NIE	New Institutionalist Economics
OECD	Organisation for Economic Co-operation and Development
TR	Trans-industry Regulation
WTO	World Trade Organization

Introduction

A Fresh Look at the Politics of the Economic

We are constantly told, be it by journalists, businessmen and women, or politicians, that 'economic reality' determines what companies and industries 'must do' and how public authorities should behave to enable them to achieve their goals. For example, throughout Western Europe this 'reality' is constantly invoked to justify the externalization of productive activities to countries with lower wages and less costly welfare systems, or reforms of European labour markets to make employees more 'flexible' and 'employable'. However, when examined more closely, it quickly becomes obvious that no single vision of 'economic reality' actually exists, just as there is never only one means of reacting to it. One might have thought that these multiple 'realities' and proposals for action would lead actors and observers to embrace the possibilities it opens up for diagnosing the economic and planning ways out from difficult situations. Indeed, across Europe and North America, the economic crisis of 2008 and its continuing fall-out seemed, for a couple of years, to create a space for such thinking and therefore heterodox challenges to neo-liberal recipes for running businesses and economies. Unfortunately, though, even a cursory look at any newspaper today reveals instead the 'resilience' not only of neo-liberalism in Western economic thought and practice (Schmidt & Thatcher, 2013; Crouch, 2011), but also of simplistic visions of economic reality and instant dismissal of deeper thought and action. Indeed, as Wolfgang Streeck has underlined in his ferocious critique of the European Union's reaction to the 2008 economic crisis, many powerful actors have sought to build a 'firewall' between the economy and politics 'which will permit the markets to assert their version of justice undisturbed by discretionary political intervention' (2014a: 117). In short, this overwhelmingly dominant viewpoint on the one hand considers the economic to be structured by purely material determinants and self-correcting markets whilst, on the other, denigrating politics as meddling with business, or just a channel for the pursuit of self-interest.

This book fundamentally challenges these widespread and deeply-rooted understandings of both the economic and politics. But it also refuses to simply set out, as others have already effectively done (Fourcade, 2009; Blyth, 2013; Streeck, 2014a & b), how these depictions have come to dominate the practice of businesses, interest groups, and public authorities. Instead, what I seek to confront head-on are the pervasive, underlying assumptions and priorities which—frequently upon the basis of analyses made and taught within universities—fuel and shore up the limiting viewpoint on the relationship between economics and politics which dominates today's world.

To do so, two major shifts in the framing of this connection will be proposed throughout what follows: first a move from 'economics' to 'governed economic activity', then a definition of politics that emphasizes values and collective choices. Outlined briefly in this introduction, whereas the former builds upon a wealth of institutionalist literature in economics, history, sociology, and political science, the second constitutes a break with most contemporary research. Backed throughout by illustrations taken from twenty-five years of theoretical investment and empirical research, combining these propositions about economics, politics, and their interlocking relationship provides this 'research essay'[1] with robustness but also, hopefully, its freshness.

FROM 'ECONOMICS' TO GOVERNED ECONOMIC ACTIVITY

To begin this quest for rigour and greater analytical bite, just what constitutes 'economics' must be assessed, critiqued, and reformulated in a way conducive to producing and interpreting empirical research data and results. Given the vastness of this issue and of the literatures that have addressed it in the past, chapters 1 and 2 will progressively make the case for the definitional and ontological displacement I consider analytically vital. Put succinctly here, the argument developed embraces a clear rupture with orthodox thinking about the adjective 'economic', the noun 'economies', and 'Economics' as an academic discipline.

What is deemed to be 'economic' has for too long been reduced to 'markets' as mechanisms for exchange and trade. More precisely, this use of the term limits the economic to the relationship between the supply and demand of goods and services, the equilibrium their interaction supposedly spontaneously generates, as well as 'the environment' necessary for enabling the free interplay of 'market forces'. As many scholars have underlined previously

[1] As Gusfield underlines, a research essay is grounded in the results of empirical enquiry but is not constrained by merely presenting such findings. Instead, its aim is to 'create a theoretical perspective' by 'reaching for a general and wider application' (Gusfield, 1981: 2).

(Boyer & Saillard, 2002; Stiglitz, 2006; Blyth, 2013; Boyer, 2015), this vision of social practices that are economic has many failings. The most glaring is its negligence of the sociological thickness of 'market environments', i.e. the social worlds within which markets operate and which firmly orientate the allocation of their outcomes, for example, in terms of price, accessibility, and wealth. Given that these social worlds have experienced distinctive histories, the overall range of market-shaping influences is infinite. Within certain territories or sectors, social science has nevertheless gone a long way towards isolating recurrent key variables such as the structure of capital, class systems, or gender relations. Indeed, since the 1980s and due to intense inter- and intra-disciplinary exchange, these variables which structure markets have themselves come to be widely reconceptualized as 'institutions'. Broadly defined as rules, norms, or conventions (Fligstein, 2001; Hall and Taylor, 2009), institutions are indeed rightly now seen by many academics and commentators as an integral part of social activity in general, and that described as 'economic' in particular (Barma & Vogel, 2008).

As will be shown repeatedly throughout the book, in keeping with most 'new institutionalist' theories, I too consider that it is impossible to analyse what needs to be framed as *economic activity* without addressing the role played therein by institutions. Economic activity is thus defined here as the institutionally-structured financing, production, and commercialization of goods or services. However, along with some 'fellow travellers' (Hay, 2006a & 2015; Abdelal, Blyth & Parsons, 2010), this book departs from the currently dominant new institutionalist research programme for two reasons.

First, it rejects proposals that common ground can or needs to be found between those who see institutions as simply the result of interest-driven calculations (rational choice institutionalism) and those, like us, who envisage institutions as the product of much more complex and richer social and political phenomena. Calls for melding these diametrically opposed definitions have been made for two decades (Hall & Taylor, 1996; Sil & Katzenstein, 2010), but have only generated sterile debates and confused theorizing. Drawing upon a range of literatures is essential, but only logically consistent concepts and theories are of any use to either analysts or practitioners.

My second point of departure from mainstream new institutionalism is to reinvigorate the hypothesis that economic activity is not just structured by institutions, it is *governed* around and through them (Hall, 1986). However, the government at issue cannot be reduced to politicians and public administrations. Defining government instead as the actions through which economic activity is orientated and directed (Lagroye, 1997), the straightforward questions this book seeks to re-open up to enquiry are who governs, how, and, above all, in the name of what?

The second break with dominant thinking about economics made in this book concerns the noun generally used to describe where it takes place: economies. The problem here is not with the term itself—economic activity clearly takes place and is governed within social worlds circumscribed by boundaries. What is problematic is the generalized assumption that the most important frontiers for governed economic activity map neatly onto those of nation-states. The consequence is not only that practitioners and journalists talk and write loosely about 'the French' or 'the German' economy, but also that the vast majority of political economists unthinkingly use this unit of analysis. Of course, the politicians and administrations of many states do indeed possess a certain capacity to impact significantly upon the government of economic activity through their law and public policy. But this certainly does not mean either that analysis should start with the essentialist assumption that the nation-state is *the* primary unit of analysis to be examined, or that one should then only compare research results around it. Unfortunately, however, encouraged by much-cited books such as (national) *Varieties of Capitalism* (Hall & Soskice, 2001), this is precisely what nearly all current research and writings in political economy continue to do. What suffers as a consequence is careful study of the plethora of industry-specific and trans-industry institutions which not only constitute 'national economies', but are also the units of analysis through which important phenomena extending beyond and within the nation-state can be grasped.

Indeed, the antidote proposed here is to posit that research simply must begin by defining what constitutes an economy in each instance. More precisely, starting from the premise that industries are themselves economies that have varying degrees of autonomy from others and from trans-industry pressures, the next step needed is to identify their respective 'institutional order', i.e. the configuration of institutions around which they are governed (Jullien & Smith, 2008a). As will be shown in chapter 2, these orders have recurrent features, meaning that despite their singularities they are analytically comparable. Just as importantly, starting analysis from the institutional orders of specific industries also means that one can then begin to tackle the question of how scales of trans-industry government, i.e. polities or proto-polities, impact upon them. As accepted above, throughout much of the world, national polities still have major influence over the government of industry-specific economic activity. They do so particularly when three key ingredients of a scale (legal and policy density, conventions of commercial calculus, social meaning) combine to orientate the behaviour of producers, consumers, and intermediaries. However, this is not necessarily the case when a state's authority is internally challenged (e.g. many African states or indeed Spain), nor when it experiences external challenges (e.g. from the building of the European Union (EU) or the World Trade Organization (WTO)). Indeed, given the widespread character of such challenges, abandoning formalistic and static definitions of economies in favour of more robust units of analysis provides a vital means of grasping the actual causes and effects of phenomena such as 'globalization' or 'Europeanization' so frequently invoked, but so rarely studied in depth.

The third and final break made here with accepted wisdom around the lexicon of economics concerns its most powerful purveyor: the discipline of Economics. As has been well documented (Lebaron, 2000; Fourcade, 2009), throughout the world and for more than four decades, economists have become the most publicized and listened to experts on the government of not just economic policy, but also many other domains of social activity. For example, a range of social science research has identified the key role played by economists not only in prompting highly visible phenomena such as the privatization of public services (Pollit & Bouckaert, 2004) or the 'instruction sheets' behind the 2007 financial crisis and its treatment by politicians (Blyth, 2013), but also in encouraging reductionist and depoliticizing thinking linked to rational choice theory (Hay, 2007). In a word, Economics as a discipline has changed radically since the 1970s (Piketty, 2014: 32), and this alongside its relationship to the governing of economic activity and politics itself.

However, in critiquing this change and its effects it is important not to treat Economics as a single block, nor to presume that its intellectual output has simply been imposed upon social and political life. Like any science, Economics is in fact deeply divided by competing theories, methods, and factions. The assumptions of neo-classical economics and rational choice, together with methods drawn from mathematics, have indeed come to dominate the discipline in most parts of the world. This said, there are significant divisions internal to that variant of economics, just as within this discipline as a whole there remain other strands which develop and promote quite different ways of being an economist. For this reason, it is insufficient to invoke 'the rise of economics' as a cause of change in the government of economic activity as, regrettably, so many of my colleagues in political science continue to do. Put positively, it is precisely by studying the plurality of theories and doctrines proposed, as well as the usages of 'economist' as a legitimizing label, that research can make progress in better understanding the relationship between economics and politics. Many economists do construct economic 'reality' and make prescriptions which have an impact upon this relationship. But it is distinctly unhelpful for political scientists to continue taking cheap shots against another discipline whilst, on the other, proposing little to encourage shifts in the internal dynamics and relations of economics with other parts of the social sciences. Indeed, a key proposition developed in this book is that academics trained in other disciplines, and political scientists in particular, have the right, and indeed the duty, to analyse and draw conclusions about economic activity and its government. As the economist Thomas Piketty put it within his call for 'a Political and Historical Economics', 'social scientists in other disciplines should not leave the study of economic facts to economists' (2014: 575).

Overall then, for economists, for economies, and for economic activity itself, the proposition made over the course of this book is that phenomena commonly labelled 'economic' become more open to deep analysis by querying their routinized meanings. The preceding paragraphs have begun to present some alternative definitions of 'the economic' that encourage a deeper and pro-active mode of reasoning. To pursue this further, however, we must now address a second problematical lexicon: that of politics.

POLITICS AS MOBILIZING OR SUPPRESSING VALUES

One might have thought that a major sub-field of the social sciences labelled 'Political Economy' would have produced a robust and stimulating definition of politics with which to structure and guide empirical research on economic activity. Astonishingly it has not.[2] Instead politics is either undefined, reduced to formalistic variables or depicted as so all-encompassing that this term is of no use as an investigatory tool. Having first expanded upon this three-pronged critique, the positive point made here is that a major stride forward can nonetheless be made by defining politics more sociologically around the mobilization or suppression of values.

The most common and implicit usage of the term politics to analyse economic activity conflates it with politicians and what they do. Consequently, great attention is paid first to the visible actions of leaders of national executives, be this when conducting international diplomacy (e.g. trade agreements between the US and Taiwan) or making speeches about domestic firms (e.g. discouraging Peugeot from closing factories in the east of France). Actions by other politicians, particularly leaders of the opposition, are of course also covered by such approaches, along with elites from political parties (e.g. their election manifestos: Amable & Palombrini, 2009), as well as legislatures. Less often, the leaders of major interest groups (e.g. the Confederation of British Industry) or trade unions are also granted the status of 'political'. However, in general the term politics is reserved here for the activity of those seen to be 'running the country' (Schäfer & Streeck, 2013). Although such actors must indeed be taken into account by research in political economy, it is deeply misleading to reduce politics to this category of practitioners. Firstly, an unquestioned assumption is made about who acts politically purely upon the basis of their formal status. Large swathes of potential political actors and

[2] Indeed, omitting to define politics and the political is widespread within the very discipline that ostensibly targets this phenomenon full-time: political science. As Colin Hay underlines, this discipline is in fact dominated by 'many implicit and unquestioned conceptions' of politics. He then proceeds to contrast the 'paltry smattering of interest' in defining the latter to the shelves of publications devoted to asserting what 'science' is or should be (2002: 66).

action are thus immediately removed from analysis. Secondly, such a definition of politics is static and therefore constantly at odds with the dynamics of political economy—a dynamics which means, at the very least, that certain actors act politically under certain conditions whilst at other times they do not. In short, driven by normative conceptions of democracy and accountability, this anthropomorphic assimilation of politics with the behaviour of politicians caricatures both political and economic activity, and consequently the relationship between the two.

The second recurrent definition of politics commonly used within political economy enlarges it to encompass all the actions of public authorities. Pushed particularly by scholars trained in public policy analysis, here the label of politics is used to cover all actors who participate in the making and implementation of law and policy. Not surprisingly, a great deal of emphasis is placed upon the civil servants who work within national and local bureaucracies. Particularly in continental Europe, these actors are seen as the architects of public action and even as 'the state in action' (Jobert & Muller, 1987). Since at least the 1970s, however, representatives of interest groups of varying guises are also considered to co-produce public action in sectors ranging from health (Hall & Taylor, 2009) to professional training (Culpepper, 2003). Over the last three decades, the implicit definition of politics most often used here has therefore slid from being rigidly restricted to actors who work for the state or sub-national government to include all those who participate in the 'public space' wherein law and policies are made. This definition clearly has many advantages over one that restricts politics to politicians. Not only does it enlarge the spectrum of potentially political actors, but it encourages detailed examination of how they affect the structuring and evolution of economic activity, and this on sub-national, national, European, and international scales. However, conflating politics with public action comes at a price: starting from the vague and unsubstantiated premise that all public action is political, it prevents research from distinguishing the moments and acts which genuinely belong to this category from those that do not.

Before returning to this point when building our own definition of politics, a third and final unhelpful definition must be dealt with: politics as a synonym for conflict. Omnipresent within the vocabulary of most journalists in search of a hook with which to catch the attention of their editors and readers, this way of thinking about politics is of course also often used by the practitioners studied by political economy. In countless interviews conducted over the years with civil servants and interest group officials, I can recall episodes recounted as 'political' because differences of views were aired polemically. Most often, these events were also labelled as such because the degree of conflict had meant that more senior representatives of the interviewee's organization had become involved. Social science has rightly attempted to theorize such practices and render them open to comparative study (Hall & Thelen, 2009; Buchet de Neuilly, 2013). However, calling them 'political' actually obstructs analysis for at least two reasons. First, it presupposes that conflict is not a more constant part of social and economic life. Focusing upon the most evident cases of polemics runs the risk of overlooking the other more common instances of tension and its mediation. Second, such a definition ends up bringing research back to the conflation of politics with politicians (or at least 'senior actors') critiqued above.

Overall then, existing definitions and usages of the term politics do little to encourage disciplined study of the parts of governing economic activity that are fundamentally political. On the contrary, they blur or obstruct such analysis. In order to make progress over this vital question in the form of a clear and testable proposition, a short-step backwards must first be made in order to clarify the ontology of social life upon which it reposes.

An ontology essentially synthesizes how one considers that the social world operates—what Fligstein and McAdam call 'a foundational social reality' and 'a generic theory of social action' (2012: 4). As chapter 2 will explain and justify in detail, the ontology I strongly believe in and advocate is simultaneously *constructivist* and *institutionalist* (Hay, 2006a; 2015). It is constructivist because it posits that there is no single 'reality', rather each actor defines their own version of what is 'real' and, consequently, their interests, preferences, and strategies. These definitions are built by interpreting the world through *social representations*. These representations are specific to the individual concerned and thus the product of their socialization that is both primary (upbringing, schooling) and secondary (within a profession or sector). However, as socialization studies underline, these representations are also social in the sense that they are built inter-subjectively, i.e. they are reproduced and change within and between social groups, thus through interactions and interdependence. Indeed, as this proviso already underlines, constructions of reality are not random or limitless. Instead, the institutions discussed briefly earlier—i.e. stabilized rules, norms, and conventions—place boundaries upon how reality is generally defined, then upon how these constructions are mobilized during social action. At least for analysis of the governing of economic activity, this ontological position frames the latter as both structured by institutions and fundamentally contingent. Because of this deep tension between quests for stability and the intrinsic uncertainties of economic activity, the institutions concerned need studying as the products of agency, deliberation, decision-making, and, throughout all these processes, power struggles between actors with asymmetric resources. In a word, economic and political activity are inseparable. Both are fundamentally dependent upon each other.

Having declared and explained this ontology, the first move towards a compatible, dynamic and heuristic definition of politics is to zoom in on what Colin Hay calls 'the capacity for agency', 'i.e. actors doing things with consequences' that 'may at any point become strategic' (2007: 66–7). Indeed,

Hay then underlines that this capacity for agency 'counterposes politics and fate' and thus underpins 'a realm of contingency and deliberation' rather than one of 'necessity' (2007: 79). Politics is thus about collective choices that have entailed reflexion, deliberation, and strategic action. Politics is simultaneously argument and alliance-making.

However, from here a step further needs taking to stress that not all of the cognitive and interactive activity alluded to above is necessarily political. For example, the application of patent law to slow down the market entry of generic medicines is certainly an instance of powering but, unless contested, it is not in itself a political act. To distinguish clearly the political from other phenomena, and power in particular, we therefore need a more selective and parsimonious definition of politics that zeroes in upon what lies at the heart of the arguments and alliances made to affect collective decisions and thence institutions. In keeping with Weberian sociology, the claim made here is that values—i.e. representations and points of reference about what is good or bad (Kalberg, 2010: 128–131)—set the explicit and implicit criteria which are constantly used when actors seek to change or reproduce institutions (for example when patent law is challenged as iniquitous or morally wrong). More precisely still, these values determine not only how actors define proposals for change or stasis, they themselves are the product of prioritizing and weighting. As a result, the definition of politics presented here and applied throughout this book, is restricted to *activity to modify or maintain institutions that either mobilizes values explicitly, or seeks to silence them*. The challenge for research is thus to identify the moments in time when the contingency of institutions becomes apparent to the actors concerned and then to study in depth the values that are invoked either to reproduce or change them. Crucially, by centring analytical attention upon the mobilization of values, research produces data on how values structure the normative commitments of the actors involved (e.g. their beliefs in liberty or equality), but also upon how these same values can and frequently are used to build alliances in order to 'win' the negotiations which invariably precede governmental decisions. Moreover, whilst embracing the obvious observation that actors are strategically-minded and mobilize a variety of resources during such negotiations that often include value-laden rhetoric to which they are more or less committed, the focus upon values can and must be maintained for two further reasons:

- Firstly, by condensing and articulating what actors define as good or bad, values intervene heavily upstream of the formulation of interests, objectives, preferences, and thus strategies.
- Secondly, defining politics as when values are mobilized to affect institutions explicitly delineates it from the concept of power, the latter defined as the autonomous capacity of an actor to operate within the set of institutions that structures their domain of economic activity. Clearly

> politics and power are highly interdependent. However, conflating them blurs analysis and blunts action taken to change or reproduce institutions.

More precisely, there are at least three advantages in adopting the definition of politics proposed throughout this book. On a theoretical level, it is sufficiently restrictive to guide research towards certain actor behaviours and away from others, yet extensive enough to encompass the deep uncertainties and dilemmas which constantly affect the government of economic activity. This definition is also heuristic when conducting empirical research because it not only encourages in-depth study of a wide range of actors (as other approaches certainly also do), moreover it ensures that the focus of analysis is retained upon a key dimension of data creation and fieldwork—the relationship between institutions, values, their production, and application—rather than on simply describing every aspect of economic life. Given that the aim of a genuinely political economy is to be sharply analytical rather than encyclopaedic, this definition of politics provides a clear focal point which can be maintained right through to the restitution of research results.

Finally, and perhaps counter-intuitively, the definition of politics proposed here provides a bridge between the academics who practice political economy and potential readers who are practitioners or interested citizens. In a world dominated by discourses of 'complexity' and 'economic imperatives', surely it is the duty of political economists to propose rigorous ways of cutting through such obstructions to analysis in order to identify the value-based decisions that have caused our current economic world and which look likely to structure its future. If, as Hay rightly claims (2007), politics really is about collective choices and a refusal to think and act fatalistically, then political economy simply must more consistently enlighten the processes through which such decisions are shaped and made.

THE STRUCTURE OF THIS BOOK

In order to set out in full the arguments made above, justify them as regards existing scholarship, and back them up with numerous empirical examples, what follows is structured in two stages. The first sets out the theoretical terrain within which the approach to the politics of economic activity advocated has been developed, refined, and tested. To do so, chapter 1 concentrates essentially upon the accounts of this politics presented by others, their strengths but also their weaknesses and blind spots. On the basis of this sustained critique, chapter 2 then describes in detail the analytical framework proposed as a sharper means of studying political economy. Moreover, this chapter will also explain and justify why, within this book, four values in particular—Freedom, Security, Equality, and Tradition—have been concentrated on as structuring the politics of recent economic activity. As will be highlighted at that stage, this selection of key values was chosen deductively upon the basis of existing theorizations of value ranges, but also because an inductive approach that elucidates values from each empirical case study would have made it more difficult to propose the sustained claim about relationships between values that I want to make here. I fully accept that proceeding inductively would generate different findings to those presented. Moreover, this might even be the best option to take were one to launch an entirely new research project on the basis of the politics as values approach. In terms of the claim that I seek to sustain throughout this book, however, it will instead be argued that although a fundamental tension between the values of Freedom and Security lies at the heart of the politics of economic activity, frictions between them are mediated around competing definitions of these values themselves, but also those of two subordinate values: Equality and Tradition.

Centred upon eight case studies of institutional change or stasis, the second stage of this book then conducts a sustained probe into the pay-off of its analytical framework. Accordingly, chapters 3 to 6 focus upon tensions between the maintenance and renewal of economic institutions tied respectively to shifts at the global, European, national, and local scales.

Specifically, chapter 3 challenges the thesis that 'globalization' has inexorably oriented economic activity and its government in a neo-liberal direction by highlighting just two examples of contingency and political choice that clearly remain. Centred upon controls of pesticides and the legal protection of geographical indications for foods, these case studies respectively show how the value of Freedom has trumped Security by sidelining Equality then, in contrast, how Freedom as a primary value can nevertheless be countered by actors who harness an egalitarian acceptation of Equality to a collective definition of Security.

In addressing the question of to what extent the EU makes a difference to economic activity within and without its borders, chapter 4 questions the Freedom–Security relationship firstly over the pricing of pharmaceuticals and secondly around the regulation of inter-firm competition. The first of these case studies highlights how although the Freedom of large medicines manufacturers still tends to dominate EU government of this industry, calls for change in pricing practice are currently gaining more traction thanks to renewed definitions of Security that frequently take support from the value of Equality. Indeed, contrasting definitions of the latter—either as equal access of producers or as an egalitarian principle—also feature strongly in recent conflicts within neo-liberalism that have split the makers and implementers of EU competition policy. On the one hand, ordoliberals maintain that equal access to markets is a principle from which the Freedom of (large) companies must often be curtailed by law and public action. On the other, adherents to the 'Chicago School' of neo-liberalism consider that giving primacy to Freedom is the best means of ensuring efficient outcomes for the widest range of consumers. The chapter as a whole thus shows that, be it over the regulation of competition or the pricing of pharmaceuticals, the EU and its member states currently face a number of unresolved dilemmas about value hierarchization which, moreover, do little to enhance its status and position within debates and tensions regarding the worldwide politics of both issue areas. Indeed, the chapter largely attributes why the EU struggles to affect this global politics to the incapacity of its own elites to critically examine their own value hierarchies.

Whereas chapter 4 also recognizes that the heterogeneous positions often taken up by its member states also partly explain why today's EU does not always 'make a difference' to the governing of economic activity, chapter 5 directly addresses politics at the national scale. More precisely, it tackles the question of the extent to which representatives of the state currently equip themselves with sets of values to significantly affect the course of economic activity as regards a major industry—that of automobiles—and a vital component of all industries: labour markets. Centred upon the failure of European states, and that of France in particular, to institutionalize and expand a market segment for electric cars, the chapter's first case study reveals how proponents of this mode of transport (mobilized around the value of Security and an egalitarian definition of Equality), have been so soundly defeated by advocates of Freedom (who have harnessed the value of Tradition to re-legitimating mobility by car in general, and those powered by hydrocarbons in particular). If the victory of the latter has been fuelled by the vacillation of value-confused state actors, in the case of labour market policies the chapter shows that Freedom can also dominate the government of economic activity even when state actors are driven by a clearer, alternative value hierarchy. Using the contrasting examples of employment policies within Norwegian aquaculture and the French wine industry, the question then becomes how do state actors manage or fail to develop value-anchored alliances with representatives of economic operators in order to safeguard or enhance more collective definitions of industrial problems?

Finally, given the emphasis upon sub-national government that has often been made throughout the world over the last three decades, chapter 6 examines how politics as values also plays-out constantly at this scale. Accordingly, calls to 'act local' are analysed around initiatives which ostensibly favour the production and marketing of local food, then around the very notion of local economic development itself. Drawing upon a case study of how public support for local food markets is affecting farming in Bordeaux and its surrounding area, the chapter first shows that although the values of Security and Tradition have clearly been mobilized to shift the distribution of foods such as fruit and vegetables in favour of local suppliers, thus far proponents of this displacement have failed to significantly challenge either the market share captured by more distant producers, nor the value primacy of Freedom, together with Equality as equal access, which continues to dominate the food industry as a whole. Meanwhile, although actions in favour of local economic development formally aim to give more importance to Tradition and Security, as a study of practices in the Charente highlights, at least in this part of France, Freedom continues to be the principle that dominates both how company managers frame economic growth and how they think public actors should be helping them achieve this goal.

Overall, these four chapters seek to unravel the politics of problem framing, instrument setting and legitimacy to intervene through public policies that so indelibly marks contemporary economic activity throughout the world. More precisely, they demonstrate both how the values of Tradition or Equality mediate the fundamental Freedom-Security tension that lies at the heart of capitalism, but also why the value of Freedom has come to be so dominant over the past three to four decades. A general conclusion compares the results of these empirical studies and, from there, then seeks to make generalizable claims about the causes and consequences of the patterns and hierarchies of values identified. The book's closing pages then restate and reformulate the approach to the politics of the economic that has been advocated and demonstrated throughout. In classical fashion, this passage features an outline of where I personally think research could and should go from now.

In a nutshell, the book's deepest aim is to advocate a mode of research and reflection which challenges orthodox and dominant approaches to economics and its government. It does so by placing a politics that is comprehensible, and therefore both 'studyable' and 'actionable', back at the centre of academic, practitioner, and public debates over economic activity. Since the latest economic crisis of 2007–8, events and trends within economic activity and its government have certainly created more space for the type of heterodox proposals made throughout this book on the basis of the definitions and claims introduced above. Moreover, in seeking to occupy part of this new space, it is important not to lose sight of how the change of analytical angle advocated here could also contribute to the study of, and debate over, previous eras of economic history which, through generating most of the institutions and institutionalized economic thought of today, continue to exert a heavy influence on our current predicament. In a word, seeing politics as values is not only a perspective from which one can clearly see that our world could have been otherwise. This viewpoint also helps reveal how it still can be.

1

What's so Political About the Economic?

The Limits of Existing Responses

INTRODUCTION

Political economy has of course been the subject of debates and publications for hundreds, if not thousands, of years. Formalized as a field of systematic academic enquiry complete with journals and jobs between the end of the nineteenth and the beginning of the twentieth century, it spans at least six major academic disciplines: economics, sociology, history, political science, geography, and business studies. The history and taxonomy of this vast field of study have been extensively presented and discussed elsewhere (Blyth, 2009; Cohen, 2008). What this chapter does instead is focus upon how the most dominant theories within political economy define and problematize the role of politics in economic activity. Astonishingly, this zeroing in upon what existing research on economic activity asserts about politics is not what political economy's dominant textbooks (e.g. Broom, 2014), handbooks, (e.g. Blyth, 2009; Clift, 2014) and literature reviews (e.g. Cohen, 2008) actually do. Instead, they tend strongly to relate and perpetuate standardized accounts of the history of this field as having been structured by political philosophies and general theories of the world economy—e.g. liberalism or Marxism, rather than by analytical frameworks within which conceptualizations of politics itself play a central role. When one unpacks these wide-ranging philosophies and theories, implicit and occasionally explicit definitions of politics can of course be discerned. Where this chapter seeks to innovate is firstly by targeting these definitions directly and, secondly, by separating out the analytical propositions they each have generated from those that are normative and ideological.

As underlined in the introduction to this book, the main aim of this exercise is to move cumulatively towards the purpose-built framework for studying the politics of economic activity presented in chapter 2. In so doing, the next chapter is also where the two approaches to the economic that I draw most heavily upon—Regulationist economics and constructivist political sociology—will be presented and unpacked. Nevertheless, what follows can also be read as a sustained critique of the more standardized and increasingly unhelpful ways of researching, teaching, and discussing political economy. Revealingly, many of these visions are couched in tired binary distinctions—e.g. economics vs. politics, states vs. markets, equilibrium vs. 'crisis'—all of which obstruct research rather than stimulate it. More precisely, the purpose of this chapter is to examine the definitions of politics mobilized by the dominant theorists of political economy by placing them within their respective ontologies, i.e. how each theory envisages and 'investigates reality: the nature, essential relations and relation of being' (Cohen, 2008: 3). From this perspective, four ontologies which currently dominate political economy will successively be presented and discussed:

- material determinism: neo-classical economics, classical international relations theory and rational choice;
- societal structuralism: Marxism, neo-Marxism and neo-Gramscian theory;
- institutions: historical and sociological institutionalism;
- interactionist network theory.

The order of presentation of these theories has some importance because I begin with the most materially deterministic of these theories and end with the least. Specifically, this continuum stretches from accounts of political economy that give most pride of place to assumed 'interests' (neo-classical economics) to those that instead stress the role of 'agency' (interactionist network theory). However, this dimension of my topography of political economy should not be overstated because, as will be shown, each of the four ontologies and concomitant theoretical 'families' combines structure and agency in complex ways. Moreover, it is precisely by examining these combinations that one can reveal each theory's underlying definition of politics.

Consequently, each of the sections that follow sets out what the approach discussed theorizes and assumes about the relationship between politics and economic activity, before refining this question by examining its explanations of change or stasis. Throughout the chapter, illustrations from the world's wine industry will be used in order to distinguish the various postulates, lines of reasoning, and conclusions each approach to the politics of economic activity purveys. This case has been selected as an illustration for two reasons. Firstly, it has been studied to some extent at least by all four of the approaches discussed here. Secondly, as I have had the chance to explain at length elsewhere,[1]

[1] Carried our between 2004 and 2015, this research on wine targeted the question of change or stasis by questioning in particular the role played by 'globalization' (Smith, de Maillard & Costa, 2007) and the European Union (Itçaina, Roger & Smith, 2016a).

although change in the production, distribution, and consumption of wine is frequently treated as a straightforward response to 'economic forces', what has actually occurred over the last twenty years has been highly contingent and therefore deeply political. Critiquing how each of the four approaches to politics presented below have analysed change in the wine industry is thus pertinent to the objective of this chapter. Moreover, it also provides a relatively accessible means of empirically nourishing a part of this book that is necessarily dominated by questions of theory.

1.1. MATERIAL DETERMINISM: POLITICS AS POLITICIANS DEFENDING INTERESTS

Considering that the distribution of material resources determines from the outset who runs any society is of course a highly prevalent and popular ontology. Constant flows of anecdotal information confirm on a daily basis that the rich get richer and that wealthy states dominate international relations. However, simply assuming that stocks of material resources transform themselves into power and influence tells us little about how these stocks emerged in the first place and why they so frequently remain high over time. Within economics and the social sciences, over the course of the eighteenth and nineteenth centuries two large families of theory—liberalism and Marxism—developed largely as a means of providing both analytical answers to these questions and normative proposals about how societies and governments should react to them. The definition of politics proposed by the second of these families will be discussed in the following section. Here, liberalism and its visions of politics will be unpacked by successively examining the guises it has taken within three overlapping theories of political economy: neo-classical economics and Economic Institutionalism, then 'realist' and 'rationalist' approaches to international relations. It will be argued that although over time liberalism's approach to the politics of economic activity has clearly evolved and diversified, at its heart remains a concentration upon decisions made by individuals based upon what are claimed to be 'rational' calculations of their interests. Indeed, as will be highlighted below, precisely because the individual is liberal theory's basic unit of analysis, the defence of interests has then been extrapolated to explain the behaviour of collective action bodies ranging from the firm to the state. Consequently, the predominant meaning of politics deployed by liberal theorists of political economy, but rarely defined clearly, encompasses all activity by politicians or governments to protect and promote the interests of their respective 'clients' and themselves.

1.1.1. Neo-classical Economies: The Root System of Liberal Political Economy

Until the 1970s, the approach to economics that lies at the heart of liberal philosophy and theory was essentially driven by a 'standard theory' which considers that economic activity is structured by the interplay between, on the one hand, 'the supply' of goods and services and, on the other, 'demand' for these commodities. This interplay takes place in 'markets' within which co-ordination between the amounts of supply and demand respond to fluctuations in price. The latter acts as a signal to suppliers of goods such as wine that they should increase production when demand for this product, and therefore its price, is high. Conversely, producers should reduce output when demand and prices fall. Indeed, when this occurs durably, producers are expected to leave that particular market by converting to other types of economic activity—phenomena that occurred throughout the vineyards of Southern Europe in the 1970s and 1980s and has re-occurred consistently since the mid-2000s. Consequently, ever since the writings of Adam Smith in the eighteenth century, liberals have depicted markets as 'the invisible hand' which, by constantly facilitating adjustments between the heterogeneous interests of producers, consumers, and financiers provides national and local economies with 'general equilibria'. Treated as postulates, these assumptions about supply, demand, markets, and price have had massive impact upon how liberals have both analysed the politics of economic activity and sought to act upon it.

Analytically, the standard theory of neo-classical economics posits that all participants in economic activity share not only a rationality of self-interested competition for scarce resources, but also possess the same, or at least highly similar, levels of information concerning trends in supply, demand, and price. Moreover, they assume either that each competing producer possesses sufficiently similar technologies of production (e.g. the levels of mechanization of grape producers), or that producers who are most technologically in tune with the market will force their 'obsolete' competitors (e.g. growers who use old and unfashionable grape varietals) to leave it. Markets themselves are not a subject of uncertainty and therefore of study for this variant of economics. Similarly, the role played by intermediaries during the distribution of goods or services is also put to one side (e.g. the influence of supermarket chains as buyers then sellers of wine). Instead, markets, and more generally the interplay between supply and demand, are theorized as pure, frictionless processes of competition between individual economic operators, be they producers or consumers. For this reason, neo-classical standard theory frequently equates 'politics' with interference in these processes and thus as a nefarious muddying of purity.

As is well known, over the past two to three centuries, these basic analytical premises have frequently fuelled an ideological version of neo-classical economics which has provided a large number of recipes for governmental action over the economy. In the nineteenth century and, in many countries such as the UK or the US well into the twentieth, the central tenet of this ideology was that governments should do as little as possible in order to enable economic activity to operate 'freely' through markets. Although a wealth of research has shown the extensive impact of government intervention during this period in sectors ranging from the railways (Dobbin, 1994) to steel (Herrigel, 2010), this 'laissez-faire' economics was seen as not only efficient for the firms and consumers involved, but also for the peacefulness of international relations. Frequently mobilizing the term 'comparative advantage' (first coined by David Ricardo in the early nineteenth century to capture what nations should strive for through concentrating upon their most efficiently produced goods and trading with others), this approach to the relationship between governmental and economic activity has been used ever since to legitimize the ending of all protectionist measures in the name of 'free trade'. In the wine industry, for example, such arguments have been repeatedly used, most obviously in the mid nineteenth century (e.g. by France's second Empire) and again since the 1990s (by a range of 'New World' producers and states: Australia, Chile, the US, etc.).

Importantly, however, one cannot and should not reduce neo-classical economics and its corresponding ideologies to the assumptions and recipes found within 'the standard theory' résuméd briefly above. This is because since the 1970s, an extended standard theory has emerged which goes much further in formalizing both why markets can become 'inefficient' and what governments should do about it. Developed within 'New Institutionalist Economics' (NIE), this extension of standard neo-classical theory essentially adds three key concepts: transaction costs, institutions, and contracts.

As regards the former, Oliver Williamson (1975) is often credited with placing transactions at the heart of microeconomic theory. Based upon his investment in the very structuring of economic exchanges, Williamson developed an 'organizational failures framework' as a means of explaining why certain arrangements within and between organizations (here essentially firms) tend to generate costs that often become sub-optimal. Specifically, economic actors are depicted as opportunists whose self-interested and short-termist behaviour generates uncertainty that has costs. For example, within the wine industry the concept of transaction costs, and above all the need to reduce them, has been used to explain increases in vertical integration between producers and merchants in many vineyards over the past two decades. What Williamson himself (1985), then Douglass North (1991) and numerous others, have sought to theorize on this basis is how institutions—defined as stabilized rules—reduce the uncertainty surrounding transactions and, thereby, enable markets to operate as efficiently as possible. In their most basic form, these institutions take the form of contracts. Within microeconomics this explains why so much academic attention has been given to contracting, its consequences, and the modelling of both. For example, European wine regions are often criticized from this angle for failing to generate contracts that tightly restrict grower practices such as yield levels (Rousset & Traversac, 2004). More generally, within neo-classical economics as a whole, focusing upon the challenge of transaction costs, then the solutions provided by institutions and contracts, has led scholars to home-in increasingly on ascertaining what level of public intervention in economic activity is efficient. Most often, contemporary Economic Institutionalism considers that 'hybrids' of markets and institutions are what structures, and indeed what *should* structure, economic behaviour (Ostrom & Ostrom, 2014).

More precisely, holders of this theory consider that economic actors 'rationally' put in place explicit or implicit contracts in order to protect and enhance their material interests. The first assumption here is that actors enter into this contractual environment in full knowledge of its constraints and opportunities on the one hand and, on the other, of what is in their own best interests. The second, assumption upon which this theory reposes is that institutions are functional responses to sub-optimal conditions for economic exchange. In the wine industry, for example, economic institutionalists consider that producers from the US or Australia have benefited from transparent contractual arrangements between grape-growers and large wineries based upon strict and verifiable growing and processing norms (Rousset, 2005). In short, these institutions emerged to meet the functional requirements of the national industry as a whole. Although, as Boyer underlines when citing the invention of money, most historians of the economic show that 'dysfunctional' commerce does not spontaneously and neutrally generate institutions—instead dominant actors create them for reasons which suit their value hierarchies and purposes (2015: 34)—it is Economic Institutionalism's form of material determinism, what Boyer calls 'the neo-classical fable', which now dominates the discipline of economics as a whole (Lebaron, 2000; Fourcade, 2009).

The combination of extended standard neo-classical and rational choice theories will be returned to below. For the moment, what is key is that although this major theoretical development reaffirmed the liberal definition of politics as interference by governments in economic activity, it has nevertheless been matched once again by developments within ideologies and the practices of liberal executives throughout the world. Most obviously since the 1980s, neo-liberal thought and the political parties that purvey it have come to focus upon demand, and in particular 'the consumer', as the central principle from which to structure economic sectors. In the case of the wine industry, for example, in the mid-2000s the European Commission strove successfully to replace an EU policy designed to shape the supply of wine with one which, on the contrary, supported only wines that fitted with its perception of contemporary demand. In so doing, their arguments were legitimated in part by the nourishment and support they received from a range of economists wedded to Economic Institutionalism and rational choice theory (e.g. Corsinovi et al., 2013).

Given both the domination of the discipline of Economics since the 1980s by variants of neo-classical extended standard theory, together with the privileged status they have acquired within numerous governments, tensions within neo-liberalism have constantly been playing out during a multitude of crucial decision-making processes throughout the world—not least those that have concerned the 2008 'crisis' and its aftermath (Blyth, 2013). Indeed, as this period has clearly demonstrated, even if some neo-liberals embrace public intervention in the economy more than others, in keeping with the axioms of neo-classical economics, they all see 'politics' as something that is entirely separate from economic activity itself.

1.1.2. Realist and Rationalist International Relations Theory: Two Sides of the Same Coin

An additional reason neo-classical economics has attained such a powerful academic and societal status is because a range of liberal theorists trained and located within other academic disciplines have supported and bolstered their assumptions, claims, and conclusions. This is particularly so in the case of Political Science, a discipline which through its effective delegation of questions of political economy since the 1970s to scholars initially trained in International Relations (IR), has developed two competing schools of liberal economic analysis: 'Realism' and 'Rationalism'.[2] Although generally depicted as quite different (e.g. by Cohen, 2008 or Frieden & Lake, 2010), when examined from the angle of their definitions of politics, I argue that these two schools are in fact similar and even complementary. More importantly still, both have contributed greatly to legitimizing the theorems of neo-classical economics within the discipline—political science—which ostensibly reflects most directly upon the practices of government and the politics that drive them.

As many others have related (Cohen, 2008; Blyth, 2009), the formalization, growth, and stabilization of the Realist and Rationalist approaches is inextricably linked to the emergence in the early 1970s of 'International Political Economy' (IPE) as a category of academic teaching, research, publication, and debate. Until that time, study of economic activity within political science had essentially been carried out by specialists of national public policy (e.g. Shonfield, 1965). Meanwhile, IR specialists had not only avoided this subject area but also the very building of theory and programmes of research. This

[2] It is important to note that scholars belonging to this school most often self-define as 'Liberal' IR theorists. However, as we shall see, this label is deeply misleading in that most IR Realists also adhere to liberal economic theory. In keeping with taxonomies of IR that preceded the spreading of the liberal misnomer (Wight, 1991), I will therefore use the term 'Rationalist' in its stead.

situation changed as a new generation of political scientists, in particular from the US, began to invest heavily in studying the international economy. Driven forward largely by debates over whether US domination of the Western world was coming to an end, two viewpoints rapidly crystallized into the aforementioned Rationalist and Realist schools of thought.

The Rationalist point of view was that US hegemony was indeed under threat firstly from the rise of national economies such as Japan and, secondly, from the consolidation of international organizations conceived to provide a diplomatic and rule-based structure for world trade. From the first of these angles, the US, and indeed Western Europe, were seen as declining in the face of sharp competition from producers in countries better equipped to foster innovation, respond to the needs of the consumer and improve product quality. Here the Japanese car and home electronics industries were depicted as models that deeply challenged the goods and practices of their American and European counterparts. Meanwhile, authors such as Robert Keohane and Joseph Nye (1972) also highlighted how the consolidation of organizations such as the International Monetary Fund, the World Bank, and the General Agreement on Tariffs and Trade (GATT) were all destabilizing established positions of domination within the politics of international economic activity. Significantly, in keeping with their liberal roots in neo-classical economics, such authors saw this politics as essentially being about how governments and public international organizations were intervening in the economy. Frequently associated with the Democratic Party, the take on how politics relates to economics adopted by these authors asserts that governments should, sparingly but assuredly, intervene in the international economy in order to favour a certain structuring of world markets. Indeed, in his book *After Hegemony* (1984), Keohane went as far as to highlight 'the value of institutions'. Nevertheless, his 'thin' conception of institutions as a minimal set of laws and standardized procedures also revealed a proximity to the New Institutional Economics behind neo-classical economics' extended standard theory. More precisely, from a normative point of view, Keohane argued strongly in favour of a strengthening of what he called 'international institutions' in order to reduce uncertainty in global trade and trade diplomacy. Little place, however, was accorded to institutions designed to politically correct imbalances of wealth and economic opportunity.

Meanwhile, despite clear evidence in the early 1970s that the US and Western European economies were in decline, and exacerbation of this trend after the 1973 oil crisis, the conclusions of Rationalists such as Keohane and Nye were deeply contested from the outset by a set of scholars who dismissed as peripheral the influence of international organizations and institutions upon the world economy. Instead, these Realists maintained that the defence of national interests, and those of the US in particular, continued to dominate world politics. Led by scholars such as Robert Gilpin (1975, 1987), arguments were made to highlight the continued wealth of Western economies and the enduring power of their respective governments to act upon what Gilpin called the mutual interactions between states and markets (1987: 9). Seeing 'the state as the embodiment of politics' (1987: 10), Gilpin clearly subscribed to the general liberal perspective on this point. In contrast to Keohane and Nye, however, as a self-declared Republican he championed the market when asserting that 'the elimination of all political and other obstacles to the operation of the price mechanism is imperative' (1987: 11). More generally, Gilpin provided theoretical elements for a 'Realist' programme of research and publications within IPE that has simply rolled on the equation of states with their respective 'economies' that has been so prevalent in journalistic commentary and common parlance (e.g. Gourevitch, 2005).

I have highlighted elsewhere the continuing influence of this ontology of economic activity and its politics upon contemporary IPE,[3] i.e. one that sees it as primarily structured by states and their 'interests'. What needs stressing more here is that despite its espoused emphasis upon choices and the actors who make them, the rational choice theory used by both Realist and Rationalist IR scholars to analyse economic behaviour, and the impact of governments upon it, is actually deeply determinist for at least three reasons (Parsons, 2007).

First, liberal IPE assumes that businessmen and women (e.g. wine producers) define their interests without ambiguity and uniquely as a function of costs and benefits for their particular firm. Issues concerning the objectives and actions of collective entities, such as a wine region or even a producing state, are seen only through this prism of self-interest. Second, this approach to IPE considers these costs and benefits to be so self-evident that not only the actor, but also the researcher, can easily identify them without needing to conduct original empirical research (e.g. it simply assumes that wine producers in the New World are opposed to institutions such as the geographical indications that so heavily affect the economic activity of their European competitors). Third, it assumes that actors who are collective (e.g. local wine guilds) or public (e.g. ministries of agriculture) will also simply calculate the interests of 'their' producers and then defend them on the basis of contracts and by adopting 'efficient' strategies within decision-making arenas such as those of the EU (the existence of which are also taken to be self-evident).

In summary, the very conception of politics purveyed by all these liberal theorists is both highly formal (politics as the actions of governments or states driven by 'interests') and extremely limiting: these actions are studied through the prism of materially determinist rational choice and a thin conception of

[3] For example, amongst the 428 articles published between 1994 and 2011 in one of the leading journals in this field—the *Review of International Political Economy*—no less than 60% were explicitly centred upon the scale of the state (Jullien & Smith, 2014: 15).

institutions. As Mark Granovetter concluded in his much cited critique of early NIE:

> the main thrust of the 'new institutional economists' is to deflect the analysis of institutions from sociological, historical and legal argumentation and show instead that they arise as the efficient solution to economic problems. This mission and the pervasive functionalism it implies discourage the detailed analysis of social structure that I argue...is the key to understanding how existing institutions arrived at their present state (1985: 505).

Other research within the economic sociology inspired by authors such as Granovetter, together with our own on wine and other industries, show instead that the material conditions and inter-individual contracts so dear to liberal political economy never directly determine the way goods and services are produced and sold. For example, in the European wine industry such contracts are often informal, generally avoided, and translated into practice via a logic of negotiation rather than automatic imposition. As we shall see, instead of concentrating excessive analytical attention upon such contracts, the so-called 'interests' they serve and assuming that these accords are *the* institutions which determine economic practice, other approaches to the politics of the economic encourage the studying of a wider and richer range of rules, norms, and tensions.

1.2. SOCIETAL STRUCTURALISM: POLITICS AS POWER

As mentioned above, since the mid-to late nineteenth century and the writings of Karl Marx, a second family of theory which shares an essentially material determinist ontology of the world has developed and evolved within the parts of social science that examine economic activity. Moreover, like liberal theory, this form of structuralism has also frequently crossed over into the world of political philosophy and normative recipes for action. Of course, similarities between post-Marxism and liberalism stop there because, as this section will underline, both make deeply contrasting claims about the causes of the structuration of economics and draw very different analytical and normative conclusions about its consequences. Whereas different variants of liberalism universally embrace capitalism and argue only for adjustments to its institutions in order to produce 'more efficient' outcomes, the societal structuralism proposed by post-Marxists is a self-proclaimed set of 'critical' theories which seek to identify deep problems within capitalist economies, then to propose radically alternative models of production, consumption, and the distribution of wealth. In so doing, theorists from this family have always argued that politics and economics are inextricably interlinked, and this is because the economically powerful within capitalist societies fundamentally orientate what is produced, how, by whom, and for whom. However, as will be highlighted below, whilst such a theory's emphasis upon power as a fundamental cause of economic activity has many merits, it also fails to explicitly define and analyse politics itself.

When beginning to unpack societal structuralism, the obvious place to start is with the writings of Marx himself. Entire libraries of books and articles have been devoted to his life-work which it would be absurd to pretend to summarize in only a few lines. Instead, I will briefly outline just three aspects of Marxist thought which are absolutely key to understanding the implicit definition of politics as power that has invariably been used by his successors right up to the present day. The first of these aspects is the fundamental political philosophy—historical materialism—through which the advent of capitalism has been analysed and critiqued. Contrary to the liberal theory of his time, Marx argued that the form taken by capitalism in each society was not simply the aggregated result of choices made by individuals operating within natural markets. Instead, he maintained, capitalism was a specific mode of structuring economic activity that had emerged through history as a direct consequence of powerful actors working collectively to shape it in their best interests.

This emphasis upon patterns of material forces giving rise to the very shape of capitalist economies spilled over into a second major aspect of Marx's thought: his emphasis upon class in general, and the division between those of capital and of labour in particular. According to this analysis, capitalism emerged from feudalism alongside the building of a new alliance between the aristocracy and the then emerging bourgeoisie (or merchant class). The success of this new alliance was due not only to the competing levels of material resources held by both classes (e.g. ownership of property and the means of production, and more generally the holding of financial capital), nor to a sharing of the ideals of liberal capitalism. Its domination was also caused by the loss of resources inflicted upon much of Europe's peasantry as it became transformed into an industry-employed proletariat.

The third key aspect of a Marxist approach to politics is thus to consider that the political extends way beyond the actions of governments or what takes place within parliaments. For Marx and his followers, politics has instead encompassed all the material and ideological forms of domination which structure societies and their respective economies. Politics is thus the building and imposition of societal power.

Marx's theory of economics and politics clearly had massive influence on leftist thinking in general from the late nineteenth century until the collapse of the Soviet Union in the early 1990s. Normative political philosophers and activists from Lenin to Mao, not to mention others within social democratic movements such as the British Labour Party, clearly bought into both Marx's critique of capitalism and his call to arms in the name of egalitarian societies and international relations. What I will focus upon hereafter, however, are the refinements of the Marxist theory of politics within economic activity that have successively been made over the last century and, consequently, have layered into its contemporary guises.

The first of these adjustments was made by Antonio Gramsci, an Italian journalist writing in the 1920s and 1930s who, having been a founding leader of the Italian Communist Party, was imprisoned by Mussolini from 1926 virtually until his death eleven years later. Gramsci's main innovation as regards Marxist theory was to downplay the impact of material forces upon domination within capitalism in favour of greater accent being placed upon ideology. More precisely, Gramsci argued that this domination was best theorized as forms of 'cultural hegemony' whose causes lay in the constant work carried out by 'organic intellectuals' to legitimize capitalism by making it appear inevitable and even natural. His principal targets were thus not only the fascists that had taken over his country, but the liberal theorists and their fellow travellers who on a daily basis justified, and in many cases glorified, capitalist economies and societies. Significantly, Gramsci's critique of both materialist Marxism (notably that of Lenin), as well as his highlighting of the role played by liberal intellectuals, was above all designed to fight against fatalistic visions of the durability of capitalism. Whereas for Leninists revolution had to await the advent of 'historical material' conditions favourable to the rising up of the proletariat, Gramsci argued strongly that leftist movements could and should mobilize their own intellectuals in order to develop a new culturally hegemonic project that would pave the way for socialism to come to power in every nation.

Gramsci's arguments in favour of a counter-hegemonic project have inspired leftist activists ever since. Indeed, the notion of 'counter-culture' that emerged in the 1960s, before being diluted in a multitude of ways, was indirectly but surely linked to his writings. Meanwhile, Gramsci's influence upon left-leaning theorists of the economy has been even more pervasive. After the Second World War, this influence first became particularly evident within the field of colonial and then post-colonial studies. As actors within a wide range of British, French, Dutch, and Belgian colonies struggled to make their countries independent, intellectuals developed analyses in terms of 'world systems' (e.g. Frantz Fanon, 1963) and 'dependency theory' (e.g. Paul Baran, 1957) to grasp the forms of domination they were up against. As colonialism muted into neo-colonialism in the 1960s and 1970s, increasingly taking the form of domination through multinational corporations such as the United Fruit Company, part of political economy moved with it to develop theories that fitted this shift within capitalism. From this angle, the most cited academic is Robert Cox, a Canadian-born political scientist and ex-official of the International Labour Organization who, from the early 1980s well into the 2000s, gave leadership to what came to be called 'post-structuralism' or 'critical realism'. In particular, Cox (1986) restated and updated a case for historical materialism as a holistic theory of inter- and intra-national patterns of hegemony.

In this enterprise, Cox was supported in particular by a British neo-Marxist economist, Bob Jessop, who in a succession of publications returned to Marx's concept of capital accumulation. Drawing also on the French *Ecole de la regulation* (Boyer & Saillard, 2002), Jessop strove to explain how 'accumulation regimes' that emerge through history explain 'the wage relation', make the state possible and, thus, how hegemony arises and is reproduced over time. Specifically, from this angle each state was therefore envisaged as corresponding to 'a historically specific stage of capital accumulation' (2002: 2). Like Gramsci, Jessop sought to theorize the relationship between material conditions and ideology as sets of self-reproducing and self-reinforcing historical forces (2002: 6). Similarly, Jessop also stressed that although power often transits through each state, its source and pervasive impact lies way beyond governmental bodies in the very structure of society, thus producing a hegemony of 'historical forces' (2002: 40). Using a similar analytical framework, Stephen Gill, strove to explain why US influence throughout the world has remained powerful despite the problems repeatedly experienced by its domestic economy and its major international traders (Gill, 1991).

Where Cox, Jessop, and a set of researchers at the University of Amsterdam[4] in particular have also sought to innovate, however, is to extend Gramscian theory considerably beyond the frontiers of each nation-state. For this reason Cox focused increasingly upon what he called 'transnational historical blocs' (Gill & Law, 1988: 65), and in particular that which purveyed 'globalization' as a political and economic goal. As we shall see in chapter 3, critiques of globalization have emerged from a variety of angles. Tackling it from that of 'post-structuralism' has led the Amsterdam-based team of researchers in particular to focus upon 'a structural change in global capitalism' centred upon transnational capital mobility and worldwide markets which, it is claimed, is 'driven by politics' (Overbeek, van Apeldorn & Nölke, 2007: 19). Empirically, this perspective has been used to analyse, for example, change in the regulation of corporations (Overbeek, van Apeldorn & Nölke, 2007), the 'political project of marketization' in Eastern Europe during the 1990s (Vliegenthart & Overbeek, 2007), 'the growing neo-liberalization' of the EU in general (Van Apeldoorn, Drahooupil & Horn, 2009), and of its competition policy in particular (Wigger & Nölke, 2007). Throughout this research, a focus has been developed upon groups of social actors (e.g. neo-classical

[4] Specifically, those working at the Amsterdam Research Centre for Corporate Governance Regulation.

economists, large shareholder representatives, law firms) who, alongside multinational corporations, have participated strongly in bolstering the pro-globalization historical bloc with policy recipes and legitimizing discourses or symbols. Finally, as for Gramsci, the normative aim of this research and that which preceded it (e.g. Gill & Law, 1988: 64) has been to build a counter-hegemonic project, and this explicitly through teaching and education (Horn, 2009: 125).

As Marx himself would no doubt have applauded, the contemporary form of societal structuralism purveyed by these researchers explicitly sets out 'to take politics seriously' (Overbeek, van Apeldorn & Nölke, 2007: 7). In so doing, they have certainly published a range of stimulating descriptions of the contemporary economy and the clash of asymmetrical forces that have structured it. However, by conflating politics with power and domination, politics is never actually defined for itself. Instead, one is left with the impression that because politics is everywhere, it cannot be traced to precise activities, actions, and actors. Indeed, as Bruno Théret so cogently stresses (2003), 'systemist holism' of this type raises problems precisely because it does not theorize 'the institution–practice' linkage, nor indeed engage at all with analytical approaches to institutions and the politics that generates and reproduces them.

1.3. HISTORICAL AND SOCIOLOGICAL INSTITUTIONALISM: POLITICS AS MEDIATED CONFLICT

Contrary to material and societal structuralism, a third approach to political economy which places institutions and the actual practice of government at its centre has been developed, and this by a large number of self-proclaimed 'historical' or 'sociological' 'institutionalists', as well as by public policy analysts focused upon 'the regulatory state'. Although differences separate these three strands of theory, they are nevertheless united firstly by an overall ontology which considers that economies and societies are structured by institutions defined as stabilized rules, norms, and conventions (rather than as the contracts of New Institutional Economists). Secondly, although recognizing that the hierarchies identified by material and societal structuralists clearly exist, regulation specialists and historical or sociological institutionalists focus their attention upon the sets of actors engaged in the specific activity of building, reproducing, or changing institutions. Above all, these scholars are also highly similar because they consider that this institutional reproduction or change is affected by a politics either reduced to what politicians do or, more frequently, as a synonym for conflict. In order to unpack and critique these enduring features of the institutionalisms which currently dominate European social science and remain highly present elsewhere, its three strands will be set out successively before highlighting their common, and problematic, conception of politics.

1.3.1. Analysis of Governance and the Regulatory State: Back to Politics as Politicians

Since the mid-1990s, specialists of regulation have come to the fore within political science mostly via a background in public policy or 'governance' analysis. Rather than use the term regulation to encapsulate all societal mechanisms of control as the French *Ecole de la Régulation* of Economics has endeavoured to do (Boyer & Saillard, 2002), these political scientists define it either as 'aggregate efforts by state agencies to steer the economy' or, more precisely still, as a specific type of 'governance' wherein socio-economic sectors are structured by detailed rules accompanied by an administrative agency charged with enforcing them (Jordana & Levi-Faur, 2004: 3). As the title of the journal initiated by these specialists suggests—*Regulation and Governance*—at least within political science, enthusiasm for the concept of regulation is therefore linked firstly to what many see as a general shift from state-led government to more pluralistic, multi-actor 'governance'.

Secondly, the take-up of the concept of regulation matches developments within this very governance whereby increasingly, and throughout the world, it has been delegated to agencies, such as the European Medicines Agency or the French Competition Authority. Although still 'public' from the point of view of their mandate and much of their financing, these bodies are ostensibly independent and therefore no longer part of national or international civil services. Moreover, the transnational dimension of the growth of regulation as a governmental practice has been highlighted by numerous authors. Consequently, regulation specialists share some of the conclusions of Rationalist International Relations about the importance of rules, but this time without relying upon neo-classical economics for theoretical support (Büthe & Mattli, 2011).

However, and notwithstanding its undoubted merits, in underlining that the shift to regulation is much more than just the endorsement of neo-liberal ideology, representatives of the regulation perspective have yet to define with precision the 'political forces' they consider have driven this shift (e.g. Jordana & Levi-Faur, 2004: 2; Braithwaite, 2008). This constitutes a serious analytical handicap. Indeed, when examined more closely, the implicit definition of politics used here is centred upon political parties and how they intervene in the economy when in government (Molina & Rhodes, 2006). Such a definition leaves this approach with virtually nothing to say about change in industries such as wine where the variable of party competition has hardly any analytical purchase. More fundamentally, elections and changes in the composition and electoral legitimacy of national executives are invariably posited as key drivers of regulatory, and thus institutional, change. This reduction of politics to politicians therefore ends up mirroring the definition held by neo-classical economists and rational choice theorists.

1.3.2. Historical Institutionalism: Politics as Conflict

Since the late 1980s, and alongside the development of a specialization by many political scientists in regulatory policy, even more widespread growth has occurred within strands of explicitly institutionalist theory known as 'historical' and 'sociological'. Frequently applied to the analysis of economic activity by political scientists, economic sociologists, and 'heterodox' (i.e. non neo-classical) economists, these two similar theories, not surprisingly, have each developed the very concept of an institution as the cornerstone of analytical frameworks. As Hall and Taylor (1996) set out cogently twenty years ago, the origins of both these institutionalisms lay in deep criticisms of two dominant theories at that time. Firstly, there was dissatisfaction with the 'structuro-functionalism' that had come to dominate western social science in the 1960s and 1970s, and the focus of its comparative analysis upon interest groups in particular. Although pioneers in both historical and sociological institutionalism agreed that societies and economies are indeed structured, institutions rather than groups defending interests were identified as being their 'backbone'. Moreover, these institutions, and those of the state in particular (Evans et al., 1985), were no longer seen as simply being functional responses to demands put on political systems by societal groups. Instead, each institution was now conceptualized as having stabilized over time following processes of conflict, co-operation, and compromise involving both state and societal actors.

Indeed, fuelled by comparative analyses of national and sectorial forms of 'neo-corporatism' or 'pluralism' (Lehmbruch & Schmitter, 1982), historical institutionalists in particular have stressed from the outset the variable but comparable trajectories that institutionalization of economic activity tends strongly to take (Thelen & Steinmo, 1992). In a nutshell, these institutionalists sought to re-invent the ontology of the relationship between politics and economics that had prevailed within social science from at least the 1950s until the mid-1980s. In terms of renewing research agendas within political economy, this development had at least three consequences.

Firstly, instead of assuming that for functional (i.e. 'economic') reasons societal groups make demands upon their respective polities and economies,

Historical institutionalists instead theorize political systems and societies themselves as structured by institutions. This point leads into an additional claim made by historical institutionalists concerning the relationship between institutions. Because this relation is envisaged as heavily interdependent, a theorizing of 'institutional complementarity' has been developed. Formalized by Peter Hall and David Soskice in an edited volume on national *Varieties of Capitalism* (2001), institutions concerning finance and labour in particular have been analysed as not only mutually reinforcing, but as contributing to societal-scale, institutionalized models of socio-economic practice. For example, in that book various authors show that institutions within the German banking sector had impacts upon the investment strategies of firms which, in turn, meshed with the institutions of professional training. Applying such a perspective to the wine industry would mean, for example, that analysis focuses upon how national finance institutions fit with those that concern employment practices. In short, conducting research into the causes and reproduction of institutional complementarity has sought to provide a means of comparing relationships between institutions and economics both inter-sectorally and cross-nationally.

The second major contribution of Historical Institutionalism (HI) to political economy not surprisingly concerns its treatment of history. As Paul Pierson (2000 & 2004) in particular has highlighted, within this theory, institutions are considered as emerging then evolving along trajectories during which they embed themselves within societies and economies as part of their very fabric. In so doing, they often generate 'path dependencies' which mean that certain ways of acting and even of thinking become so 'locked in' that actors find them very difficult to deviate from. To return to empirical examples from the wine industry, since the 1970s, the vast majority of producers in Bordeaux came to consider that all their wine should be sold in the prestigious category of *Appellation d'Origine Contrôlée* (A.O.C.). Consequently, even during the difficult market conditions of the 2000s, few operators in this region challenged this institution by selling their wine outside this category. It follows that research on contemporary institutions always needs to go back in time to discover how they initially arose and subsequently became normalized, i.e. which arguments, made by which actors, equipped with what resources, actually consolidated each institution.

There is clearly much to be taken from HI, particularly as regards how one theorizes the government of economic activity around institutions and how it changes or is reproduced over time. However, as I explain more fully below, by conflating politics with conflict, HI theory actually says very little about the former. Indeed, it guides its users instead away from examining politics and towards a set of related but different questions regarding what orientates the Economic once key societal choices have been made.

1.3.3. Sociological Institutionalism: Politics as Powering Again

Much of what has just been said about Historical Institutionalism applies of course to its intellectual 'cousin', Sociological Institutionalism. However, it is important to underline that the latter itself has been fuelled much more directly by economic sociology and by a deep disagreement between this sub-discipline and the approach to institutions so strongly advocated by New Institutional Economists (NIE). As we saw earlier, bringing back the concept of institutions into the discipline of economics enabled economists such as Williamson (1975) and North (1991) to re-theorize how uncertainty is dealt with during economic activity. In so doing, however, according to Sociological Institutionalists (notably Granovetter, 1985; Fligstein, 2001), these authors reduced the very concept of institutions to formalized rules of a contractual type, a theoretical move that has had three important consequences.

Firstly, Sociological Institutionalists have highlighted that many institutions do not take the form of formalized rules and certainly not of contractual engagements. They claim instead that most institutions which structure economies and societies are in fact better qualified as norms which orientate behaviour by defining and communicating what is considered socially 'appropriate' or 'inappropriate' (March & Olsen, 1989). Leaving such institutions out of the analysis of economic activity is thus seen as producing formalistic and erroneous analyses of its structures and causes (François, 2011). For example, Pierre-Marie Chauvin (2010) has convincingly shown how the famous American wine critic, Robert Parker, together with his method of noting the quality of top wines, have become an institutionalized part of the way Bordeaux's *grands crus* are made and sold.

Secondly, sociological institutionalists refute the NIE and rational choice theory claim that social actors only respect and follow institutions on the basis of constant cost–benefit calculus. Without denying that social and economic actors define their own interests and strategies or make calculations, sociological institutionalism argues strongly that actors generally conform to institutions and accept their effects because they have been socialized into believing in their social value (Granovetter, 1985). For this theory, it follows that institutions only break down and fail to continue to guide social and economic behaviour after a lengthy period of deinstitutionalization, a period which entails much more than simply isolated actors, such as grape growers, considering these rules, norms, and conventions to be no longer beneficial to them as individuals. Instead, 'institutional work' entailing collective action (Lawrence & Suddaby, 2006) is theorized as the predominant cause of institutional change or reproduction. For example, from this angle the initial rise of the Napa Valley within the world's wine industry during the 1980s is often attributed to skilful work on local institutions having been conducted around 'the judgement of Paris': the first time a blind-tasting had concluded that wine from California was superior to its European competitors (Anand, 2011).

Sociological institutionalism's third and most recent theoretical proposition to political economy in general has been to import Pierre Bourdieu's concept of a field in order to capture distributions of actor power and interdependence. Here Neil Fligstein and Doug McAdam in particular have defined what they call 'strategic action fields' as 'constructed social orders that define an arena within which a set of consensually defined and mutually attuned actors vie for advantage' (2012: 64). From there, these authors hypothesize that within any field the main dynamic will be between 'incumbents' who seek to reproduce its institutional foundations and patterns of dominance and 'challengers' who, on the contrary, strive to change them. According to this approach, for example, New World wines have acted as an exogenous shock upon wine-growing strategic action fields in Europe, thereby causing many of its actors to doubt previous commercial and policy recipes (Aylward and Zanko, 2008). Moreover, it is claimed, countries such as Australia have provided legitimacy for previously marginalized producers in Europe to bring about change endogenously within their field and respective local areas in particular.

Much more could and should be said about the massive contribution made by the two institutionalisms discussed here to scholarship in general, and to political economy in particular. Nevertheless, the picture becomes much less rosy if one narrows the focus to how these theories guide research upon the relationship between politics and the economic. The most instructive way of presenting this criticism is to examine how these institutionalisms successively formulate and address the question of why and how institutions change.

Initially at least, authors such as Pierson and the *Varieties of Capitalism* literature tended to focus more on institutional continuity. However, over the course of the 2000s, and in particular in the face of accelerating globalization, then the post-2008 'crisis', within Historical Institutionalism the emphasis has switched to discovering when and why certain institutions mutate or are replaced. Indeed, it is here that a new and potentially deep divide has emerged that goes to the heart of how each strand of institutionalism, and indeed each scholar therein, defines politics. On the one hand, a certain number of self-professed historical institutionalists (Streeck & Thelen, 2005; Mahoney & Thelen, 2010) have turned to a soft form of rational choice theory to explain why, at certain points in time, actors seeking to maximize their interests no longer consider institutions to be effective. Moreover, in importing the language of 'transaction costs' and 'efficiency' from NIE, they have also reverted to concentrating on institutions that take the form of formalized, and legally backed, rules. On the other hand, constructivists working within, or attempting to go beyond Historical Institutionalism (Hay, 2006a, 2015), have firmly rejected this rationalist turn. They argue instead that in order to understand institutional change, much more attention needs to be devoted to the arguments and symbols used to legitimize or delegitimize institutions, and thus prepare the very conditions that enable them to be changed or reproduced.

Ultimately this theoretical divide stems from a fault-line over the very definition of politics held by historical, as well as many sociological, institutionalists. For most of the former, the term 'coalition' is now used to describe the 'political' alliances which 'anchor' 'institutionalized arrangements' for governing the economy (Hall and Thelen, 2009). The focus of enquiry has therefore been placed upon 'the political organization of policy-making' defined as both the distribution of authority to participate in this process and the modes of state-led imposition or pluralistic participation this tends to encourage (McDermott, 2007). Moreover, many such institutionalists supplement this definition of politics with another more metaphorical one which equates it with conflict. Authors such as Hall and Thelen also underline that 'coalitions' of actors not only change institutions but, more often, feature heavily in 'a politics of institutional stability' which 'depends on a stream of action that is political in the sense that it entails conflict designed to test the limits of cooperative arrangements and mobilization to bring other actors in line with those arrangements' (Hall and Thelen, 2009: 13). Politics is therefore envisaged as conflictual activity engaged in by actors seeking to reproduce or change institutions.

Similarly, the field theory and focus on 'social skills' advocated by many sociological institutionalists (Fligstein & McAdam, 2012) also ends up avoiding defining politics in a way that distinguishes it from other adjacent terms. In contrast to historical institutionalists, however, they ultimately see politics simply as power that is mobilized within battles between 'incumbents' and 'challengers'. Of course, such battles must be studied with precision and conflicts over institutions are indeed moments where it is vitally important to deploy social science. However, it is analytically counterproductive to conflate conflict or power with politics because the latter simply then becomes a vast, shapeless category that is impossible to study directly and with precision. Turning politics into a 'black box' seen as exogenous to economic activity falls into the classic trap laid by liberal political economy: seeing the economic as separate from the political. Moreover, doing so runs counter to the need to conceive of politics as an activity shaped by contingency within which intersubjective interpretation and collective deliberation, not the mere calculus of isolated individuals, plays a central role (Hay, 2007: 79).

Put bluntly, historical and sociological institutionalists within Economics, Sociology, and Political Science have made important strides towards defining the governing of economies in ways that structure stimulating research. There is indeed wide agreement that economies and markets are structured by institutions (Barma & Vogel, 2008: 3). Nevertheless, the politics of this institution-building invariably remains underspecified and, therefore, understudied.

1.4. INTERACTIONISM: POLITICS AS NETWORKING

As we have seen above, notwithstanding important differences of definition and research design, there is widespread agreement among many specialists of political economy that institutions lie at its centre. Moreover, despite rarely using the concept analytically themselves, many material and societal structuralists would not disagree over the importance of institutions. However, there is a fourth, and here final, approach to political economy which pointedly ignores the concept in favour of a focus upon interactions between a variety of actors engaged in economic activity and the networks through which this occurs. Linked loosely to the political philosophy of pragmatism (e.g. that of John Dewey), this interactionist approach to studying the relationship between economics and politics has gathered momentum since the mid-1990s around two programmes of research which, surprisingly, ignore one another. The first was developed by two French sociologists, Michel Callon and Bruno Latour, subsequently formalized as *Actor Network Theory* (ANT) and then spread throughout the world, whereas the second owes more to an economic geography of international trade centred upon *Global Value Chains* (GVCs). Brief presentations of both these approaches are made below before focusing more specifically upon the similar definitions of politics deployed therein, their causes and analytical consequences.

1.4.1. Actor Network Theory: Politics Denied

ANT's most central claim as regards economic activity is that inter-firm networks enable interactive and collaborative learning.[5] For example, when applied to an industry such as wine, this theory has theorized the 'status' of each firm, i.e. their respective position within a space of producers, as a fundamental cause of industrial structuring. More precisely, status is seen as provoking 'affiliation decisions' which cause economic actors to choose to link up with others (Benjamin and Podolny, 1999). Over this question of choice, Michel Callon and his colleagues have gone a stage further in arguing that networks are above all the product of consciously developed strategies which set the 'principles of co-ordination' in any market. These scholars consider that before engaging in any economic transaction, each actor defines its forseeable consequences by deploying material and cognitive 'market devices', thereby classifying the product or service at issue. In concrete terms, ANT argues that economic operators seek to stabilize judgements about their products or services as a means of building and consolidating their 'affiliation

[5] This section owes a great deal to the work of my colleague Antoine Roger.

networks'. Consequently, knowledge not only gives such actors power, but is itself structured by devices, in particular public and private standards, and other criteria that shape the calculating capacity and anticipations of individual operators. Crucially, those who adapt best to this structuring of knowledge are hypothesized as being in pole position for shaping networks to their own advantage (Callon, 1998 & 2007; Callon, Méadel & Rabeharisoa, 2002).

To date, ANT has been used a great deal to study the financial services sector (MacKenzie, 2006) and 'food networks'. Particularly within studies of the latter, the networks analysed include not only producers, distributors, and consumers, but also public authorities, environmentalist associations, and even technological innovations (conceptualized as 'actants' or 'non-human actors', e.g. Konefal & Hatanaka, 2010: 4). Crucially, and contrary to institutionalist analysis, because 'everything is uncertain and reversible', ANT proposes 'an understanding of governance as the processes and mechanisms of ordering, simplification, and stabilization of the networks, and therefore redistribution of power among network actors/actants' (Tanaka & Juska, 2010: 43–4), wherein the dominant logic is one of 'posturing, manoeuvering, negotiating, bargaining' (Busch, 2007: 259). If networks are freely created, the relations created between them are nevertheless partially constraining (Busch, 2007). Indeed, 'the range of choices open to anyone at any given time is a function of what other networks are available' (Busch & Juska, 1997: 696). Consequently, research from this angle has focused upon the 'interaction and competition between social network segments' and the 'negotiation of boundaries between networks' (Moore, 2011). For example, the global wine economy has been depicted as structured around evolving and re-composing networks which have made up 'an assemblage of social and economic relations, political rationales, expertise discourses, institutions, and related agents, through which diverse social forces, projects, and organizational capacities are mobilized' (Lewis, 2008: 103).

ANT clearly has a number of qualities adapted to the sociological study of economic activity. Firstly, because of its emphasis upon 'market devices', it guides research to focus upon the specific issues over which conflict and cooperation take place, e.g. over categories of product within industries such as wine. As such, it is highly relevant to the 'everyday international political economy' described by authors such as Hobson and Seabrooke (2007) or Langley (2008). Secondly, ANT and the interactionism at its centre provide powerful counter arguments to overly deterministic, and even fatalistic, conceptions of economics which see it as dominated by a small number of large firms (an analytical trap into which societal determinists and sociological institutionalists often fall).

This said, the theory also has two weak points which sap its capacity to directly tackle the relationship between economic activity and politics. The first problem here is that ANT's basic assumption concerning the fluidity of relations within any economic domain systematically overlooks both the asymmetries of power within such spaces and the viscosity of much of its structuration. Consequently, research conducted in this vein neglects the institutions that structure an industry such as wine and the actors that work politically to change or reproduce them. In particular, it accords too little importance to the public policies which provide the grants or bolster the categories for market segments that are so important to so many of its growers and merchants.

This problematical trait has in turn engendered a second concerning ANT's refusal to directly study the role played by public actors within the networks it studies. Without falling into the trap of assuming such actors to be omnipresent or powerful, it is hard to imagine how one can aspire to grasp the politics of the economic without systematically taking such actors, and especially their specific resources, firmly into account. For example, how can one study an industry such as wine without analysing the national and supranational civil servants who, although not part of Actor Networks per se, are nevertheless omnipresent in the industry?

Overall, and as regards the aim of this chapter and book, the fundamental problem once again is that ANT proposes no definition of politics, let alone a theorizing of how it impacts upon the financing, production, distribution, and consumption of goods and services.

1.4.2. Global Value Chains: An Absence of Politics

Much of this critique can unfortunately also be levelled at a second network-centred approach to economic activity centred upon *Global Value Chains* (GVCs) that has also emerged recently and become extremely popular, notably within non-governmental organizations and international public administrations such as the World Bank or the United Nations Conference on Trade and Development (UNCTAD). First developed in the mid-1990s by the economic geographer Gary Gereffi (Gereffi & Korzeniewicz, 1994), then efficiently promoted by him and his colleagues as 'the GVC Initiative' (<http://www.globalvaluechains.org>), the initial and laudable aim of this approach was to systematically map linkages between producers of goods in the global south and their respective processors, distributors, and consumers throughout the world. On this basis, analysis was made about what level of value was retained or captured by each of the first three sets of actors in order to ascertain the asymmetries of power at issue. This was seen as particularly important when world trade was accelerating alongside important, but largely anecdotal, evidence of increasing power for Northern-based multinational corporations. In a nutshell, the concept of GVCs was seen as relaunching a programme of research upon the impact of what in the 1960s and 1970s had previously been conceptualized as neo-colonialism.

Over the last twenty years, mapping value chains has evolved in at least two ways. Firstly, given the increasing power of actors from the 'emerging' BRIC countries (Brazil, Russia, India, and China), analysis has gone beyond North–South asymmetries of value retention to encompass South–South configurations of various types. Indeed, Gereffi himself has recently published an updated typology of GVCs which builds this development into his overall theory (2014). Secondly, some attempt has been made to insert into this approach the role of what it calls 'structures of international governance', such as the World Trade Organization. Consequently, despite sharing its aversion to institutionalist analysis, GVC theory goes beyond ANT by taking into account the uneven distributions of power within the networks that compose economic sectors. However, the roots of such asymmetry are nevertheless often neglected for two reasons. The first concerns the separation between supply and demand inherent in this theory's linear ontology of economic activity. Despite Sociological Institutionalists having shown that 'demand' itself is often largely constructed and created by powerful economic operators (Fligstein, 2001; François, 2011), GVC theory falls into the neo-classical trap of assuming that supply follows spontaneous consumer preferences. For example, in the case of the wine industry it would in all likelihood neglect the work done to reframe demand around the contentious notion of 'the new consumer' and their reputed preference for varietal wines (Roger, 2010).

A second blindspot of GVC theory is that it overlooks how large firms, such as automobile manufacturers, today tend strongly to be present themselves in the global south, and thus throughout 'global production networks' (Coe, Dicken & Hess, 2008). Consequently, GVC theory does not guide research to look for politics within such firms, i.e. where power in a value chain actually resides. In the case of large wine producers in regions such as the Rioja, for example, such a theory runs the risk of overlooking the importance of vertical integration within firms that combine grape growing, wine-making, and marketing (Itçaina, Roger & Smith, 2016a).

More fundamentally, and as regards the focus of this chapter, as with ANT, GVC theory possesses no clear definition of politics, let alone of its relationship to economic activity. Explicitly for ANT scholars and implicitly for partisans of GVCs, if politics is given any consideration at all, this is just as an integral but unidentifiable component of networking.

1.5. CONCLUSION: LESSONS LEARNT AND THE CHALLENGE THAT REMAINS

Were this chapter to be a straightforward literature review of theoretical strengths and weaknesses, much more could and should have been said

Table 1.1. Widely used approaches to the politics of economics

Approach	Most cited authors	Assumptions about economics	Key concepts	Definition of politics
Neo-classical economics and IR	Smith, Williamson, North, Keohane, Gilpin	Supply + demand = equilibrium, national interests	Interests, markets, equilibrium, transactions costs, contracts	Politics as what politicians and governments do
Societal determinism	Marx, Gramsci, Boyer, Jessop, Van Apeldorn	Material resources + ideology = domination; transnational firms and class determine supply and demand	Accumulation regimes, class interests, hegemony, ideology, organic intellectuals	Politics as power
Historical and sociological institutionalism	Hall, Thelen, Fligstein, & McAdam	Institutions structure economics; coalitions build and defend institutions	Institutions, path dependency, Strategic Action Fields, institutional entrepreneurs	Politics as conflict
Network governance	Callon, Gereffi	Networks shape value chains; networked firms predominate; fluidity is high	Actor networks, assemblages, Global Value Chains	Politics as networking

about each of the four families of theories analysed above. However, such comprehensiveness has not been its goal. Instead, and on the basis of the targeted presentations made above, the aim has been to decipher and highlight how each theory defines and guides analysis of the politics of the economic. Viewed from this angle, it is striking how little each theory actually has to say with precision about politics in general, and its relationship to economic activity in particular. Boiled down into Table 1.1., the analysis presented above has shown that politics is either defined too restrictively (as what politicians or governments alone do) or too extensively (as synonyms for power, conflict, or networking). Neither of these extreme positions helps guide research to generate knowledge directly about the role played by politics in economic activity. More fundamentally still, none of the four approaches examined here provides even the basic ingredients for a definition of politics that would fit with achieving that goal.

The role played in the economic by politicians, governments, and public policies is clearly an important object of study that has been tackled with vigour by a wide range of economists and political scientists in particular, and this using variants of political economy theory that range from neo-classical economics to Historical Institutionalism. Similarly, it is highly important to analyse economic activity by addressing the question of the power asymmetries and dynamics that play-out therein. Here neo-Gramscians, sociological institutionalists, and theorists of Global Value Chains have been particularly active in producing vital data and convincing analyses. None of these theories have, however, thus far set out to tackle the political per se. In declining to define politics, or by defining it implicitly and partially during the theorization of other phenomena such as power or conflict, these approaches to political economy therefore do very little to guide analysis towards understandings of economy that are consistently political. Indeed, notwithstanding the considerable contribution of existing research to knowledge about the governing of economies, to date its primary focus has not been upon the forms of argumentation and material, relational, or positional resources which enable certain actors to dominate both commercial activity and its government. As chapter 2 will now propose by defining politics otherwise, more direct attention must and can be paid to how economic activity and its institutions are *politically* built and governed.

2

The Politics of Economic Activity

An Analytical Framework

INTRODUCTION

The approach presented below builds upon, but also departs from, a wealth of literature on the economic and how it is structured by institutions. As we saw in chapter 1, particular emphasis has rightly been placed by many other authors upon the role played by these stabilized rules, norms, and conventions within markets, public policies, and interest representation. However, this literature also features a number of weaknesses, many of which stem from underspecification of 'the politics of institutions'—a term constantly evoked but rarely used as an analytical tool. The challenge is therefore to build an alternative approach to studying the institutions that structure economic activity assembled around a definition of politics that is precise, heuristic, and capable of guiding rigorous empirical research.

Drawing heavily upon constructivist and sociological approaches to political science (Jobert & Muller, 1987; Abdelal, Blyth & Parsons, 2010; Hay, 2015), as well as lengthy collaborations with industrial economists (Jullien & Smith, 2008a, 2011 & 2014), this chapter sets out a generic approach to the governing of economic activities designed to equip research with theory-driven acceptance of both the economic and politics. Above all, the aim is to define a precise line of questioning which coherently and consistently melds these definitions together. Upon this solid base, I then present a central hypothesis concerning what constitutes the politics of this government. Finally, by developing the concept of 'political work', causal claims will progressively be developed. In so doing, the approach to economic activity outlined in the introduction to this book will be fleshed out by presenting more fully the following definition of politics: *the mobilization or suppression of values to change or reproduce institutions.* Throughout, empirical illustrations from research on the politics of the whisky industry will be repeatedly mobilized (Smith, 2009, 2010b). Beyond the necessarily brief empirical data presented here, the first objective of providing concrete examples from a relatively accessible area of economic activity is to begin familiarizing the reader with my analytical framework. The more fundamental aim, however, is to promote the very way of thinking about the politics–economics nexus that my framework advocates in this chapter, before being applied more fully to other empirical cases in those that follow.

2.1. FOUNDATIONS: MELDING CONSTRUCTIVISM TO INSTITUTIONALISM

Before getting to how I define and study politics, I must first set out the building blocks of my analytical framework, and in particular its ontology of economic activity. In line with a range of leading political scientists (Hay, 2006a & 2007; Mangenot & Rowell, 2010; Abdelal, Blyth & Parsons, 2010), economic sociologists (Dobbin, 1994; François, 2011) and the occasional economist (Boyer, 2015), I explicitly and consistently adopt a constructivist epistemology which refutes claims made by material determinists that the government of the economy is simply the result of confrontations between the 'interests' they assume actors to hold (e.g. Gourevitch, 2005; Amable & Palombrini, 2009). Instead, constructivism guides research to closely examine the role of 'social representations' within key components of economic activity: the industries in which goods and services are produced and marketed, together with the 'trans-industry' regulations which constantly criss-cross them. My focus is thus upon representations of reality and how actors seek to 'naturalize' them through social interaction within and between firms, professions, interest groups, and public authorities.

Crucially, however, the perceptions, preferences, and positions developed within and through such a process do not take place in a social or political vacuum where the possible framings of an industry's difficulties and antidotes are limitless. On the contrary, at individual, intra-organisational, and organisational levels, these perceptions, preferences, and positions are all heavily structured by institutions, i.e. by sets of norms, rules, and conventions (Hall and Taylor, 2009). Here, the key contribution of allying constructivist epistemology to compatible institutionalist theory (Hay, 2006a, 2015) is to stress that rules, norms, and conventions not only constrain how actors establish their perceptions, interests, and preferences; they also set parameters on how practitioners think and allow themselves to express their thoughts. More precisely, a constructivist *and* institutionalist approach to governing economies is essential.[1] This ontology postulates:

- that the 'issues' dealt with when governing economic activity are contingent and thus need studying as the products of agency, choice, deliberation, and power struggles;
- such contingency is structured not only by institutions backed by the threat of sanctions (notably the law), but also by institutionalized cognition and symbols (the 'thinkable' and 'unthinkable'); and
- that the actors involved in all the above are also deeply affected by the interactions and webs of interdependencies through which they operate.

In order to systematically study and compare processes of *institutionalization* in specific industries, policy domains, across different polities, and over time, the analytical framework proposed here is structured around four key concepts: Institutionalized Relationships, Institutional Orders, Trans-Industry Regulations, and Scales of Government.

2.1.1. Institutionalized Relationships

The institutions which emerge around the production and sales of goods and services always concern four sets of constraints and opportunities—employment, finance, sourcing, and commercialization—which, through being stabilized, give rise to their corresponding Institutionalized Relationships (IRs).[2] These IRs not only durably connect the actors involved (e.g. for finance: companies, their shareholders, banks, ministries of finance), but also the collective action and public policy instruments through which orientations of business activity are sought (e.g. for the whisky industry's Sourcing IR, a

[1] Authors such as Sil and Katzenstein (2010) are, of course, right to stress that research on politics has much to gain from drawing upon literatures derived from a wide range of disciplines and paradigms. However, when constructing solid analytical frameworks, eclecticism is a distraction political science cannot afford. Instead, all one's energies need to be devoted to combining elements of commensurable epistemologies and ontologies, and this in order to forge robust concepts that guide research towards the generation of new and socially pertinent information. To take the metallurgical metaphor of melding one stage further, a durable and useful alloy cannot be made out of incompatible materials. Combining tin and copper makes bronze, but adding incompatible materials undermines both the mixture and the strengths of its original elements.

[2] This concept has its roots in Regulationist Economics and its emphasis upon the recurrent 'institutional forms' that structure capitalist economies at the macro and meso scale (Boyer & Saillard, 2002). Developed with colleagues who belong to this school (Jullien & Smith, 2008a and 2014), the concept of Institutionalized Relationships extends this approach but also seeks to make it more relevant to the studies of specific industries and their respective modes of regulation.

ban on the distilling, blending, and ageing of the product outside Scotland). IRs are thus sets of institutions in that they simultaneously limit and render possible the action of individual producers or merchants by ostensibly reducing uncertainties, and this via collective or public action (Jullien & Smith, 2008a). For example, the Employment IR typically sets limits upon the hours of work, the training, and often the pay of a company's employees.

The second lesson built into the concept of IRs concerns 'market transactions'. Contrary to the 'New Institutionalist (micro) Economics' inspired by Williamson (1985), the regulation of business-to-business transactions cannot be reduced to contracts and 'rational' calculations of 'transaction costs'. If goods or services are of course transacted and organizations and the law partially depersonalize these processes, commerce is still fundamentally driven by human beings located and socialized within industries, sectors, and societies which bestow rights, duties, and norms upon them. For example, it makes no sense to analyse the Scotch whisky industry without taking into account a number of rules, norms, and expectations—notably concerning collective action within professions—which have predominated within the Scottish economy and polity as a whole. In each IR of each economic activity studied, it is therefore vitally important first to reconstitute the forms of social interaction, be it co-operation, co-ordination, conflict, or coercion, through which its institutions and their inter-connectedness have arisen and continue to exist.

2.1.2. Institutional Orders

Most industries have been institutionalized for decades (e.g. cars), if not centuries (e.g. wine), so it is easy to forget that their very existence depends upon possessing their own durable set of IRs. Indeed, despite the relative independence of each of these relationships, the very categorization of an industry as a distinct entity only stabilizes when it becomes an Institutional Order (IO). As Figure 2.1. depicts graphically, the defining feature of IOs is that they possess a centre wherein certain issues which overlap its four IRs can be debated. In the case of Scotch whisky, for example, intellectual property rights constitute one such issue. Although formally they concern chiefly the commercial IR by protecting 'Scotch' as a collective brand, they also impact upon its Sourcing IR (by defining the product and authorizing production processes), Finance IR by reducing uncertainty for investors over what constitutes the market for this spirit, and the Employment IR by anchoring Scotch's production and ageing in Scotland.

At first sight, IOs thus resemble the metaphoric notion of 'institutional complementarity' much used in contemporary political economy (Hall and Soskice, 2001). However, the IO concept goes beyond this underspecified

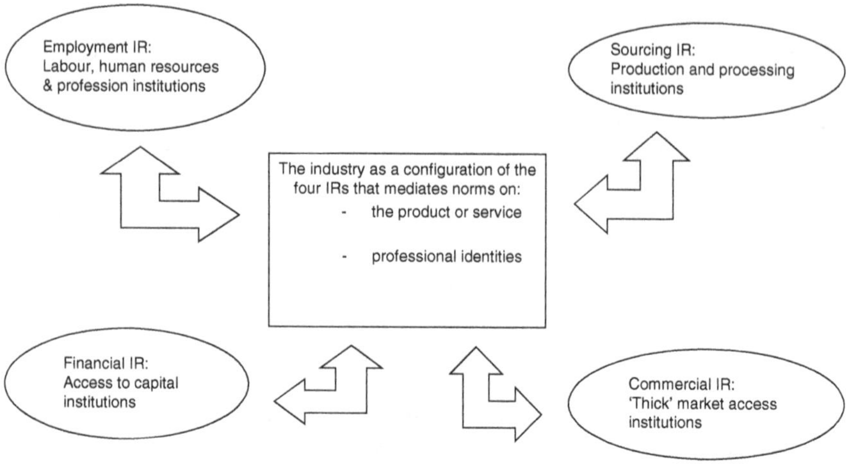

Figure 2.1. An industry as an Institutional Order of four Institutionalized Relationships

The initial version of this diagram was developed by Bernard Jullien. Working together, we subsequently proposed a series of refinements (Jullien & Smith, 2008a & 2014). This however is my own updated version.

notion[3] to guide research towards discovering precisely what sets of institutions are made to fit with which others.

In so doing, an additional aim of the concept of IOs is to rebalance research on the political economy of industries away from analysis of the Employment and Finance IRs and towards the too frequently neglected institutions of sourcing and commercialization. Much existing research into the political economy of industries emerged from the field of 'industrial relations' during the 'crises' of the 1970s. This largely explains why so much attention has since been paid to the question of employment (Lehmbruch and Schmitter, 1982; Hollingsworth et al., 1994; Hall & Soskice, 2001). Subsequent to the waves of privatizations and changes in the organization of capital that have occurred throughout the world since the 1980s, great attention has also rightly been devoted to the Finance IR (Froud et al., 2006; Posner, 2009; Büthe & Mattli, 2011). Nevertheless, many of the key institutions of any economy also reside within the Sourcing (e.g. product specification or environmental standards) and Commercial (e.g. marketing rules) IRs of the industries it encompasses. In the case of Scotch whisky, for example, the Sourcing IR sets strong rules on how this product can be distilled and aged, whereas its Commercial counterpart revolves a great deal around protecting the name 'Scotch' against usurpation or 'passing off' behaviour by spirits producers in other parts of the

[3] A notion which, moreover, has been rightly criticized elsewhere for being 'functionalist' and encouraging 'post-hoc rationalizations' of institutional fit, rather than analysis based upon original empirical research' (Clift, 2014: 112).

world. Although sourcing and commercialization institutions such as these have occasionally been studied by economic sociologists (McKenzie, 2009; François, 2011), or specialists of international trade (Murray et al., 2007), our conceptualization of IRs and IOs brings them centre stage alongside issues of employment and finance. Instead of simply assuming that issues of labour and capital automatically dominate product sourcing and commercialization, the concept of an IO ensures that discovering actual inter-IR hierarchies and mediations is always a goal of empirical research.

2.1.3. Trans-industry Regulations

Governing economic activity is of course not only 'vertical' (industry by industry), it is also 'horizontal' because it features institutions which cross-cut all industries within an economy or indeed a form of capitalism (Boyer, 2015). The most obvious of these regulations concern monetary, fiscal, environmental, and employment issues. In each of these cases, rules, norms, and conventions ostensibly automatically and simultaneously apply to economic activity in all industries. This is also the case for slightly less obvious regulations, such as those that pertain to inter-firm competition or international trade. Often studied and discussed uniquely as 'public policies', from an analytical point of view there are three reasons why each of these domains that traverse a wide range of industries are better conceptualized as 'regulations'.

The first is quite simply that what regulates industries transversally is not necessarily limited to public policies that have been explicitly formalized. Regulation may also encompass social norms—such as the relationship between firms and political parties in a country such as Japan, or state corruption in China—which also orientate economic behaviour. In the case of Scotch whisky, such phenomena are less evident. Nevertheless, the commitment of the UK and Scottish governments to support this industry in a variety of ways also pleads for an analysis in terms of 'thick', societally inscribed, regulations, rather than simply public policies per se.

Secondly, in order to impact upon productive and commercial behaviour, a trans-industry regulation must be 'endogenized' within each industry. Indeed, typically stakeholders within an industry such as whisky will sometimes seek to escape the effects of trans-industry regulation (TR) by obtaining derogations from it. More often, however, they comply by aligning themselves with such regulation. For makers of Scotch, for example, environmental standards are a frequent case of tension. Whilst the industry as a whole considers it is in their interest to present themselves as 'clean' or even 'green', its representatives nevertheless sometimes plead to be treated as special cases, generally in the name of 'the contribution' distillers make to the national economy.

Thirdly, it is heuristic to consider that trans-industry regulations, just like industries, possess recurrent Institutional Orders (IOs) which, once again, need breaking down into their financial, employment, sourcing, and commercial components. Of course, the logic of action of a trans-industry regulation's IO differs from that of a single industry. Nevertheless, by systematically examining these four components, research is better positioned to generate significant data about each articulation between an industry and the regulations that cut across it. Crucially, this data can and should tackle directly the politics that lies at its heart.

2.1.4. Scales of Government

When moving towards empirical applications of the concepts of IRs and IOs, however, one must immediately address the 'reach' of their respective institutions. For example, is the whisky industry's Finance IR 'global' in its setting and scope? This question can only be carefully addressed by defining precisely what is meant by 'scale' for an economy and its government. Rather than simply caricaturing the national scale as 'France' or 'Germany', or reducing this question to the formalistic notion of 'multi-level governance' (Bache & Flinders, 2005), it is necessary to think more deeply about what scales of government are and the effects they have upon economic activity.

The first step in this direction is to consider that despite its legitimizing rhetoric, even national public action in the economy has seldom been effective in achieving complete closure of its frontiers and protection for 'its' economic actors. This reflects the perennially multi-scalar character of economic activity and, consequently, reveals why actors engaged in institutional creation, maintenance, or change have for centuries sought to produce and trade simultaneously within and across several scales of government (Wolfe, 2005). Economic practices associated with 'globalization' (notably the easing of frontiers, increased exports and imports, the fluidity of capital), have certainly increased the multi-scalar character of economies. Indeed, since the 1970s such phenomena have been particularly evident in a Scotch whisky industry where ownership and sales have become dominated by foreign-based firms such as Santory (Japan) or Pernod Ricard (France). However, this development is best conceptualized as an accentuation of pre-existing phenomena (e.g. English ownership of many distilleries in Scotland), not something that is unique or singular.

Having clarified this 'ontology of interdependence' (Hay, 2010), my definition of scales of government consequently has two criteria (Smith, 2011):

- such scales are made up of groupings of institutions, some of which ostensibly apply only to one industry (e.g. categories of whisky), while many others apply 'horizontally' to several or all industries (e.g. employment or banking laws). As such, a scale of government is necessarily a 'jurisdiction' which typically applies to part of an industry's IR;

- these scales are however not exogenous to production and trading activities. On the contrary, because their institutions render possible the durable production and commercialization of goods and services, they are an intrinsic component of both (Wolfe, 2005).

Scales of government thus need studying as spaces for both economic calculus and political legitimation:

- Firms fundamentally hesitate about the jurisdictions in which they should operate and work politically. For example, managers of Scotch whisky manufacturers, such as Diageo, certainly see the EU as a jurisdiction which sets limits upon their liberty to compete and sell their products (e.g. around how EU law on geographical indications affects their industry's Commercial IR). At the same time, such managers constantly make calculations about how to use economically, as well as support politically, the institutions at national scales that relate to finance or employment (e.g. tax rates and national insurance payment levels). In short, and without this necessarily being by design, the co-existence of scales of government generates a certain amount of strategic 'slack' within an industry, the identification and interpretation of which impacts upon how all firms make their respective calculations regarding business strategy;
- The arguments used to make a firm's strategies are nevertheless inseparable from those used to bolster the social and political legitimacy of the jurisdictions under question. Indeed, these arguments are not purely of a cognitive nature. They also frequently mobilize symbols which seek to seduce the target audience concerned by appealing to their emotions (Braud, 1996). For example, politicians and public administrations often couch their propositions in terms sensitive to the regional impacts of their respective policies (e.g. reassuring Scotch whisky producers—and indeed their consumers—that limiting production to Scotland will be preserved). Some of this political communication is pure rhetoric that is empty of social meaning. But other such discourse has considerable effects which need studying as a vital dimension of institution creation, maintenance, or change (Carter & Smith, 2008).

In summary, the analytical perspective developed here seeks to coherently combine the concepts of scale, trans-industry regulations, IOs, and IRs to provide a firm theoretical base and, indeed, a generic dependent variable, i.e. the precise institutions whose change or reproduction is to be explained. As Figure 2.2. seeks to capture visually, both industry-specific institutions within an IO, as well as the TRs that criss-cross them, are typically set at varying scales.

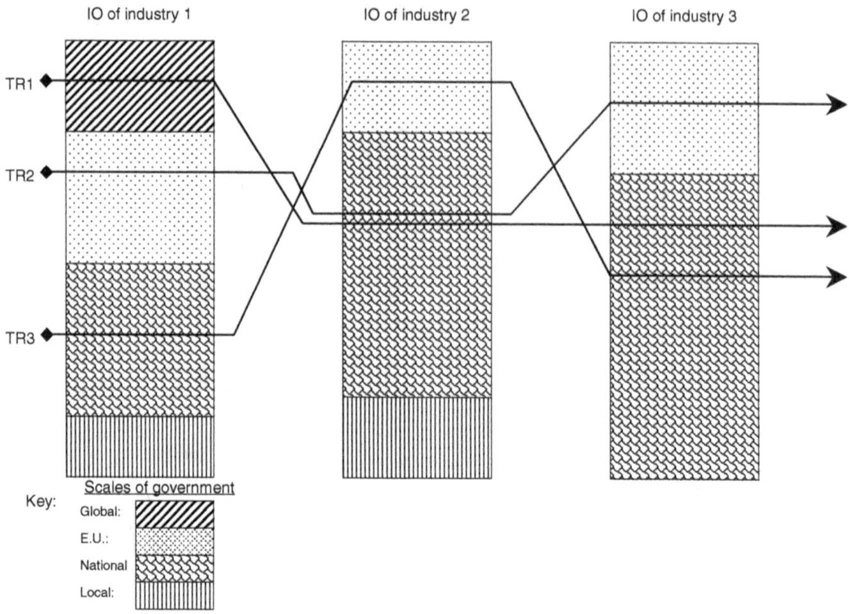

IO = Institutional Order; TR = Trans-industry Regulation

Figure 2.2. A constructivist and institutionalist ontology of economic governing

Moreover, and more fundamentally still, the theoretical foundations used to pin down what needs explaining have also given rise to an equally generic independent variable: my central hypothesis about how politics causes economic change or stasis.

2.2. VALUES AS THE POLITICS OF THE ECONOMIC

If politics causes how economies and their institutions are governed, this independent variable must be defined so as to coherently explain actor power and behaviour, i.e. their *agency*. Capacity for agency 'counterposes politics and fate' and thus underpins a 'realm of contingency and deliberation' rather than one of 'necessity' (Hay, 2007: 79). Consequently, far from being simply 'what politicians and governments do', politics is fundamentally about collective choices around the allocation of resources, choices which have entailed reflexion, strategic action, and deliberation. Crucially, however, these features only define the terrain within which politics takes place. To pin the concept down more precisely, two more analytical steps are required.

The first of these steps is to address the obvious point that the human beings who strive to become participants in politics are armed with asymmetric sets of resources, together with heterogeneous interpretations of their respective interests and of the collective good. This is particularly clear within the governing of economic activity wherein varying stocks of resources are particularly evident. For example, as a company that owns not only many distilleries and brands, but also operates elsewhere in the spirits industry, managers working for Pernod Ricard clearly have more material resources than the owner of a single distillery on the Isle of Skye. Moreover, they are also likely to be positioned more or less centrally within the industry and its institutional order. In a word, the latent power of each of these protagonists is very different.

Nevertheless, both sets of actors can potentially participate in shaping the institutions of Scotch whisky. Starting from the premise that such governing is always contingent is thus a vital methodological step which clarifies the goal of research as being the discovery of what has driven the choices of the actors involved. Rather than reduce this question of choice to the assumed 'interests' of individuals, or addressing it using other terms like power, conflict, or networking (see chapter 1), the constructivist and institutionalist approach mobilized here maintains that such choices are always socially constructed because they concern representations of how life in a society is and should be, representations that are shared to varying degrees between actors within a given territory and over time.

2.2.1. Why Focus upon Values?

The second, more original, step towards a heuristic definition of politics is to consistently consider that the driver of these social choices is always the *values* held by the actors involved, either individually or as members of collective entities (such as firms, interest groups, or administrations). As the social psychologist Shalom Schwartz (2006, 2012: 3–4) has so carefully stated and tested empirically in the case of individuals, values have six recurrent characteristics:

(i) they are beliefs which structure our feelings;
(ii) they enable us to express what we consider to be socially desirable;
(iii) they are transversal in that they transcend specific actions and situations;
(iv) they are benchmarks or criteria that enable us to make judgements and of which we only become aware when our values are in tension;
(v) because of such tensions, values must be prioritized by each individual;
(vi) indeed, such prioritization takes place constantly whenever we adopt an attitude or undertake an action.

I will return to the crucial points about tensions between values and their prioritization shortly. But first the reason for targeting values in research on politics is so important needs to be underlined. This is because if innumerable constructivist social scientists have rightly sought to define and assess the role of 'ideas' within social, economic, and political action (Blyth, 2002; Parsons, 2003), few if any of these valuable theories state clearly that values lie at the heart of any individual or group's cognitive and symbolic 'map'. Consequently, and just as importantly, even such consistently constructivist theories have not guided research to delve as far into the ideational heart of politics as they should, and this by examining directly the values, hierarchies of values, and value tensions that underpin cognition, symbols, and their inter-relations.

Drawing upon the founding work on the concepts of 'axiological rationality'[4] and 'legitimacy' defined by Max Weber,[5] the claim made here on the basis of Schwartz's definition is that, at least within the governing of economies, it is values which express and condense the beliefs and set the explicit and implicit criteria which are constantly used for establishing not only individual and collective actor priorities and the hierarchy between them, but also links in chains of reasoning that add up to arguments for stasis or change. This is why I reserve the adjective 'political' for actions that *in the name of values seek to institutionalize or deinstitutionalize IRs, IOs, and TRs and their component rules, norms and conventions* (Jullien and Smith, 2011). More precisely, I consider that economic activity is affected by politics whenever actors seek to change or reproduce their respective institutions on the basis of what Weber called their 'axiological rationality', i.e. their beliefs and thus points of reference and judgements about what is 'good' or 'bad' (Kalberg, 2010: 128–31; Muller, 1995).

The first analytical pay-off of linking institutional change or stasis to values is to underline that the latter do not simply float freely within the economies and polities in which they occur. In order to be marshalled as part of activity to reproduce or change institutions, instead values are consciously and unconsciously worked into the mobilizations that their holders consider it

[4] As Boudon has highlighted (1999: 114–15, my translation), for Weber the behaviour of actors is best understood through discovering the meaning they themselves attach to it. Rather than simply possessing a consequentialist rationality (one based upon perceptions of their interests), social actors also possess an axiological one that provides them with 'a system of reasons'. The latter structures how they see the world, their feelings of justice and, therefore, their implicit theories of what makes for a good society, administration, or economy. Axiological rationality therefore contains a deeply affective dimension. This in turn explains why so many actors feel so strongly whenever they come across what they perceive to be an injustice (Weber, 1971).

[5] Weber is widely recognized as the first scholar in the social sciences to have theorized legitimacy in secular societies. As he underlined throughout his publications, in such societies competition between values is not only constant; it lies at the very heart of the 'generalized beliefs' which legitimize their political authorities (Duran, 2009: 315, my translation).

appropriate to undertake. Politics thus entails both relatively straightforward confrontations between values X and Y, but also moments in time when actors place the hierarchical position of each value within a line of argumentation or systemized representation of reality that prioritizes values (e.g. placing Y above X but below Z), or uses certain values in combination to defeat others (e.g. Y + X to lower the importance of Z).

The question that then arises is which values need studying and, indeed, how one should proceed analytically in order to make this selection? As regards the latter question, during the preparation of this book two options were given lengthy consideration. Ultimately discarded for reasons I explain later, the first option would have been to proceed inductively by identifying within each case study the most salient values it featured. In this way I could have progressively built up a list of values, then sought to understand the reasons for their importance in each context. This option could have produced rigorous, comparative analysis and, indeed, it may well be one that I will adopt myself in future work. Here, however, I have chosen instead for two reasons to proceed deductively. First, as underlined in this book's introduction, I wanted to test a specific claim regarding certain values that I have repeatedly encountered during my different research projects on questions of political economy. Proceeding deductively thus fitted with a framing of this book as an initial empirical probe regarding my politics as values approach, as well as a sustained attempt to prompt reactions to the approach within and beyond this field of scholarship.

The second reason for selecting certain values before re-analysing and writing up my empirical material was inspired by reading stimulating theorizations of value mobilization conducted within a field that tackles it head-on: psychology. Specifically, I found that the life work of Schwartz enables us to grasp values as crucial social-psychological phenomena, and this through concentrating upon what he has convincingly shown to be the ten basic sets of values present, to varying degrees, within any society: self-direction, stimulation, hedonism, success, power, security, conformity, tradition, benevolence, and universalism (2012: 5–7). Because stimulation and hedonism are values that impact less directly upon the governing of economic activity, here they will be put to one side. For reasons of parsimony, I also collapse Schwartz's category of 'conformity' into that of 'tradition' and his concepts of 'benevolence' and 'universalism' into one of 'equality'. Finally, and more analytically, I accord a specific status to what Schwartz calls the values of 'power' and 'success'. I do so by conceptualizing the former as a means deployed to obtain institutional change or reproduction. Meanwhile, 'success' is redefined as the yardstick individuals and collective actors use to evaluate the effectiveness of their own actions and those of others.

What remains are therefore four broad, but sharply distinct, values—Freedom, Security, Equality, and Tradition—shown in Figure 2.3, within and around

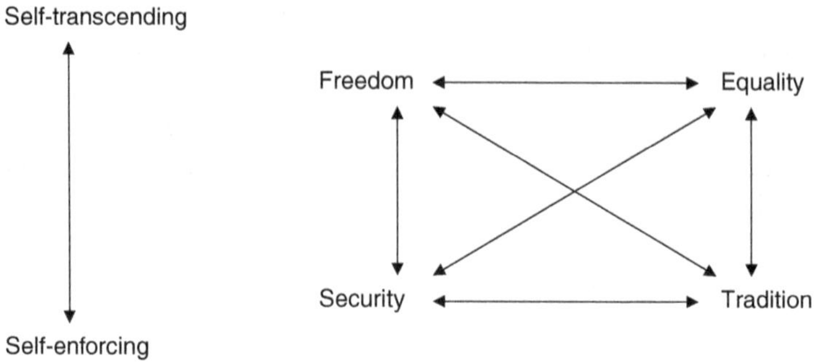

Figure 2.3. Four key values within the government of economic activity

which, I claim, the deepest tensions arise during economic activity and its government through institutions.

Crucially, at least for the government of the eight case studies of economic activity analysed in this book, the set of 'structured dynamic value relations' (Schwartz, 2012: 8) which articulates Freedom and Security have proved to be omnipresent and consistently central. What changes from case to case, however is, on the one hand, the definitions of Freedom and Security mobilized by actors and, on the other, how the values of Equality and Tradition have been made to play varying types of accompanying roles.

Freedom is of course a value espoused by defenders of capitalism in general and of private enterprise in particular. As such, it is no surprise that this value is constantly mobilized during the governing of contemporary economic activity. In particular, in the name of freedom, markets unfettered by public regulations are seen by many actors as the best vehicles for both creating and distributing wealth. Producers of Scotch, for example, frequently proclaim publicly that they could export better were they not hampered by the 'red tape' of 'bureaucracy' concerning advertising in different states. But the value of *Freedom* consistently clashes with that of *Security* not only when international relations are involved, but also when questions of health (e.g. food safety) and food security are at issue. When should a frontier be closed in the name of protecting citizens and consumers at home? When should the production of goods such as foodstuffs be regulated or subsidized to ensure that a population's safety and nutrition is guaranteed? To achieve such security, how can economic activity be made durable or sustainable? Today *Freedom* is often the value that is evoked when the government of economic activity is discussed. However, it is important to recall that historically it has had strong ties with even wider conceptions of liberty and liberal democracy (Berlin, 1990) which often resurface during the governing of contemporary capitalism. Indeed, although this is often forgotten today, the liberty of the individual can also include their right to act collectively to protect their rights (Sen, 2009;

Didry, 2013). This is an important point because it highlights that Freedom does not necessarily equate with the entrepreneur or the firm. In recent years, this value has tended strongly to be defined in this narrow sense. But this has not always been the case even in countries like the UK, is still not the case in others such as Norway, and, conceivably, might not be so tomorrow in any polity.

Although less often advocated publicly because of the 'protectionist' stigma often now attached to it, the value of *Security* is nevertheless omnipresent in debates over the extent to which the freedom to act economically should be curtailed by institutions designed to achieve other socio-economic outcomes (such as keeping a maximum number of operators in business or protecting employees). In different guises (e.g. 'social protection' in France, 'the public interest' in the UK), historically the value of Security has been advocated and defended by many actors ranging from the centre-right to the far left of the standard ideological spectrum. Associated with political philosophers or social theorists as different as Jean-Jacques Rousseau or Anthony Giddens, Security as a value has of course been defined and reformulated in varying guises. Indeed, at least as regards economic activity and its government, today this value is mobilized to defend goals as heterogeneous as enhancing the physical safety of workers, protecting the durability of individual firms or safeguarding the future of more collective entities such as entire industries or industrial districts. Some of these goals and definitions of Security are relatively easily reconcilable with those of Freedom, whereas others are not at all. Indeed, the tensions and contradictions which frequently arise when actors seek to reconcile Freedom with Security are often at the heart of the politics of economic activity. More fundamentally, it is crucial to consider that, at least within capitalist regimes, Freedom and Security are always defined in relation to one another.

This said, the Freedom–Security relationship rarely plays-out on its own. On the contrary, in all the cases of economic activity I have conducted research upon two other values—Equality and Tradition—have often also been 'in the mix'. Before theorizing this point below, a few words need saying about each of these values. As is well known, Equality has traditionally been a value most readily associated with the left, and in particular socialism or Marxism. From this angle, Equality is most often defined as a synonym of egalitarianism, the expectation being that those who hold this value seek above all to promote ways of governing the economic that equalize the substantive rights of all concerned, e.g. their right to a 'decent' standard of living. However, it is important to recall that Equality can also be defined and mobilized to mean something quite different: equal access for all concerned to compete fairly, and this regardless of the social outcomes this produces. As we will see in many of the chapters that follow, this interpretation of Equality is often used hand in hand with the value of Freedom. Small wonder then that it is highly important to study the Freedom–Security–Equality relationship in detail.

If the definition of Equality, along with its links to Freedom and Security, can vary greatly, the same can certainly be said about the fourth and final value examined closely here: Tradition. In general terms, this value encompasses a wide range of phenomena to which individual and collective actors attach social meaning by seeing them as anchored in the past. In certain circumstances, Tradition denotes 'authenticity', for example when actors seek to defend and promote local foods or craft products. In others, this value encompasses social and political practices, such as rights enshrined in employment law (e.g. paid holidays) or social security policies (e.g. unemployment benefits). The effect of allying Tradition to Security or Equality is often to reproduce institutions. For this reason, Tradition is often evoked as a value-driven motive for resisting the liberalizations demanded by proponents of Freedom. Moreover, it is also analytically important to envisage moments where Tradition can be invoked in order to change the government of economic practice in a direction that explicitly limits Freedom (e.g. in polities where religion has regained societal influence).

In summary, these short passages on how the four values selected here can be mobilized to affect economic institutions provide just an outline of the arguments and evidence I present more fully over the coming pages. Indeed, it is already time to move from the general considerations made above to more precise claims and an explanation of how, within a series of case studies, I have sought to generate data with which to back them up.

2.2.2. Hypotheses on Value Content and Prioritization

Indeed, from the point of view of research, this emphasis upon the relationships between values, and that between Freedom and Security in particular, implies firstly that differing definitions of the values themselves need analysing (H1) and, secondly, that links or frictions between values are accorded equal analytical effort (H2).

My first hypothesis stems from the observation that, of course, neither Freedom nor Security are always defined by actors in homogenous ways. On the contrary, within economic activity alone, both have given rise to differing interpretations. Freedom, for example, can be indexed upon the liberty of either the entrepreneur or the consumer. Security meanwhile can in some instances be defined around the safety of workers or, alternatively, around the sustainability of the firms and industries within which they are employed. Put succinctly, the relatively broad character of each value—its intra-value dimension—needs to be embraced by research that is geared to generating knowledge about its value content and its causes.

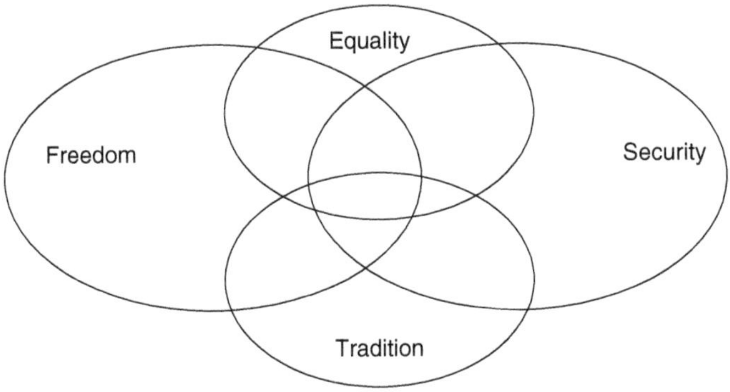

Figure 2.4. Central and mediating values

The second, more original, hypothesis I make on the basis of Schwartz's concept of 'structured dynamic value relations' goes beyond his proposal to analyse inter-value linkages by considering that these relations are not only dyadic but triadic, and sometimes even quadratic. More precisely, drawing upon recent research into the 'principles of justice' (i.e. values) which underpin national higher education regimes (Charles, 2015), the contention made here is that although a tension between the two omnipresent values of Freedom and Security is central to the politics of economic activity, their articulation depends on a third value, and sometimes even a fourth, being interpreted in specific ways which translate each value's meaning and, consequently, produce an institutionalized hierarchy.[6] More precisely, as illustrated in Figure 2.4, I claim that at least within the government of economic activity, Equality and Tradition play mediating roles which range from supporting, to intervening, to silent.

Indeed, distinguishing between the supporting, the intervening, and the silent roles played by Equality or Tradition engenders a line of questioning that needs addressing whenever one examines how an economic activity is governed. For example, as we shall see in in chapter 3 when I examine the politics of 'globalization', recurrent conflicts between Freedom and Security need to be analysed by also taking into account interpretations of Equality and Tradition, which, indirectly but surely, impact heavily upon how the former two are typically articulated on a worldwide scale. A longstanding relationship of course exists between *Freedom* and *Equality*, in particular because the latter is often now defined within liberal democracies as equality of opportunity. Indeed, over the course of the twentieth century, so called 'universalist'

[6] As regards higher education in England, France, and Sweden, according to Charles, each society articulates equality, merit, and autonomy in recurrent ways. Indeed, two of the three principles—which are different in each society—dominate a third which, reinterpreted via the first two, accentuates its own domination (Charles, 2015).

principles regarding this variant of equality came to the fore and became institutionally embedded within organizations such as the United Nations then, much later, the World Trade Organization (WTO). Indeed, at least as regards the governing of economic activity, the WTO now enshrines worldwide commitments to 'free trade' as a universal value. Here Equality has played a supporting role to Freedom by legitimating efforts to achieve 'a level playing field' in markets and industries. However although *Freedom* and *Equality* are sometimes presented as compatible and even self-reinforcing values (notably by aligning capitalism with democracy: McClosky & Zaller, 1984[7]), defending the liberty to produce or trade may also clash with more egalitarian goals such as rights to good health for all, or even to more maximalist forms of income equality. In such cases, equality tends to play an intervening role by attenuating the value of Freedom. For example, this occurs by obliging Freedom's defenders to accept limits upon firm behaviour without, however, making them concede much to partisans of Security.

Moreover, particularly in states other than the US, the mantra of free trade has not automatically translated itself into the elimination of 'traditional' forms of economic activity. As a range of WTO panels over issues such as beef production (hormones) or the presentation of alcoholic beverages and foodstuffs around territorial names (Scotch, Burgundy, Feta, etc.) illustrate clearly, the defenders of values linked to traditions are still highly active. Beyond traditions themselves being social constructions that can be 'invented' to fit a cause that may also have other motivations, defending Traditions remains a value-driven activity which defends particularism against the all-transcending ambitions of Freedom's defenders (supported by Equality as equal opportunities). For example, requiring all whisky sold as Scotch to be made entirely in Scotland may be justified in the name of protecting a Tradition, but it also limits access to this product for producers and consumers alike, and thus the freedom of both these categories of actor. Indeed, this particular tradition has not included any egalitarian content, such as commitments to favour small producers, thereby effectively downgrading the principle of *Equality* within the industry's dominant value hierarchy.

Similarly, antagonisms can also arise between holders of values centred upon *Security* and *Tradition*. Although large swathes of humankind today see both as interdependent—'the more secure we are the better we will be able to safeguard our traditions'—the history of the global economy provides many illustrations of how conceptualizing *Security* as predictable international trade

[7] In their classic book on 'the American ethos', McClosky and Zaller's central claim is that 'capitalism and democracy have always commanded broad support as the authoritative values of the nation's political culture. They determine in large measure what kinds of arguments about public affairs Americans find fair, reasonable, and attractive, what kinds they do not, and hence what kinds of arguments one dares to make (or is better advised not to make)' (1984: 4).

can undermine domestic *traditions*. For example, requiring governments in Taiwan and Chile to abandon high tax rates on Scotch whisky has stopped them defending the makers and consumers of traditional local spirits in their countries against the challenge of foreign, heavily commercially armed, competitors.

Finally, as the well-documented example of the US steel industry testifies (Herrigel, 2010), freedom to produce and trade without constraints is clearly at odds with national and local measures to continue to produce a product in the name of a 'national heritage' (i.e. Tradition) safeguarded using subsidies and import tariffs. Here US actors have reconciled Freedom with Security by using Tradition as a supporting value for both.

In summary, it is clearly insufficient to reduce the relationships sketched above to a few lines which merely suggest how my four sets of values lie at the heart of the politics of economic activity. Indeed, the approach to politics promoted in this book will only be of any analytical interest if the impact of values on economic activity can actually be shown. Frustratingly, such demonstration, will have to await the following four chapters. Nevertheless, these examples have illustrated why and how Schwartz, Weber, and my own development around Figures 2.3 and 2.4 provide a starting point from which to conduct and present empirical research in this area. Before doing so, however, a set of intermediate concepts designed to capture the recurrent processes during which values impact upon economic institutions must now be defined and made compatible with the above.

2.3. BRIDGING THEORY AND EMPIRICS: THE CONCEPT OF 'POLITICAL WORK'

In social science, the role of an 'intermediate concept' has nothing to do with being 'mid-level' or modest. Rather its purpose is to mediate between the abstract definitions and claims made by researchers on the one hand and, on the other, empirical analysis designed to generate data to match them. From this perspective, I have developed the concept of 'political work' to capture the causal role played by the mobilization of values within economies by elites who, as McClosky and Zaller and many other specialists in political behaviour have underlined (1984: 12), are the principal actors in societies who participate the most directly in struggles over conflicting values. Specifically, using the various resources at their disposal, these elite actors constantly seek to influence the constructions of social reality, 'as it is' and 'as it should be', concerning economic activity. To do so, values prompt the expression of attitudes and other actions that either justify the institutions which actors are seeking to establish or reproduce or, on the contrary, wish to replace. In so doing, these same actors are also constantly attempting to build or reinforce their own legitimacy to be involved in institutionalization or reinstitutionalization. Consequently, they seldom can simply impose their views upon other participants in their respective economy. Instead, the values held, and thence the constructions of reality proposed, by one actor are also a means of allying it to others. In short, the building, the change or the reproduction of institutions is the result of argument and alliance-making within which politics as values plays a central role. In order to study this political work, research needs to target three recurrent political processes—*problematisation, instrumentation*, and *legitimation*—and their relationship to economic practice.

Problematization: As a range of research in sociology (Gusfield, 1981) and political science (Rochefort and Cobb, 1994) has convincingly shown, difficulties experienced by private actors as 'situations', do not spontaneously become the 'problems' which collective and public organizations seek to tackle. Instead a major part of political work concerns the social construction of public problems, i.e. not only the hierarchy of values mobilized in order to define and present an issue as demanding intervention by public authorities, but also the way this construction of reality and its hierarchy of values is made social through argument and alliance-making. This is particularly clear when one examines the IRs of an industry and discovers that their respective sets of actors are constantly debating whether tensions over employment, finance, sourcing, and commercialization are 'problems' which demand new, renewed, or perhaps less collective or public intervention. For example, certain actors see the ever-increasing concentration of firm ownership in the whisky industry as a public problem because it constitutes an attack against Freedom, whereas others see the Freedom of all firms to grow as paramount. Within industries, problematization is thus an incessant activity that occurs alongside that of analysing and discussing 'market conditions'. However, this coexistence is more or less harmonious depending upon the range and intensity of values it incorporates. Indeed, as we shall see in detail throughout chapters 3 to 6, within economic activity the construction of problems is deeply political precisely because values are omnipresent throughout this process.

Instrumentation: Defining a problem is one major part of institutional reproduction or change, but it remains largely ineffectual if it does not accompany political work aimed at a second aspect of an industry's IRs: its policy instruments. Be they legal regulations forbidding certain practices (e.g. making whisky from potatoes), subsidies encouraging others (e.g. grants for modernizing distilleries), or finer technologies of government such as statistical indicators or categories, instruments often themselves become institutions and thereby durably impact upon the way an industry's IO and IRs are calibrated (Lascoumes and Le Galès, 2007). Some of these instruments are purely tools of collective action which entail neither the law nor representatives of public authorities (e.g. some food quality labels such as *Fair Trade*). Many other instruments, however, certainly do heavily involve civil servants and politicians, even if they do not necessarily dominate instrument-setting and implementation (e.g. European Geographical Indications which include Scotch). More fundamentally still, all policy instruments are never ideologically neutral. Rather they are always built around value-driven choices. Indeed, as chapter 3 will underline, Geographical Indications provide a case in point because for their defenders they symbolize Tradition and enhance Security, whereas for their critics they are protectionist tools that restrict economic Freedom. More generally, values are again ever-present within the processes that give rise to the instruments of public policy and collective action.

Legitimation: Although public problems and policy instruments are most often specific to a single industry, to obtain sustained public support they must also be legitimized within trans-industry governmental spaces such as inter-ministerial committees, parliaments, or 'social dialogues' (Lagroye, 1997). Within and without industries, practices of legitimation are thus deployed which tend strongly to take one of two forms. In some instances, the proponents of a particular public problem will seek to politicize it by explicitly evoking the value-fuelled judgements upon which it is based and engaging in activities that mediatize the problem and encourage its public debate. For example, representatives of companies in the Scotch whisky industry consistently and publicly call for lower sales tax rates in order that they can make 'just returns' on their investment in 'innovation'. 'Fairness', and a form of Equality, is thus invoked as a means of underlining the political character of the 'problem'. Similarly, as the example of pharmaceutical pricing developed in chapter 4 highlights, 'innovation' is frequently politicized by linking it to the value of Freedom, rather than just as a depoliticized yardstick for measuring economic effectiveness.

By contrast, in other cases actors prefer to depoliticize, or technicize, their problematizations more explicitly by referring to experts' reports on the 'efficiency' of its projected outcomes. This is typically how small distilleries in Scotland argue for subsidies in order to modernize their equipment to meet environmental norms. Here functionalist language dominates and actors seek to restrain discussion within closed and discrete arenas (Radaelli, 1999). At least publicly, the terms of debate are thus restricted to the realm of 'economic efficiency' and open discussion of values becomes less likely.

In short, the legitimation of public problems and instruments can invoke values in sharply contrasting ways. What is vitally important to grasp is that an economy's 'problems' or instruments are never 'technical' or 'political' per se (Hay, 2007: 78), nor are values actually ever removed from problematization or instrumentation. Rather, 'technical' or 'political' labels become attached to them over the course of their construction and legitimation.

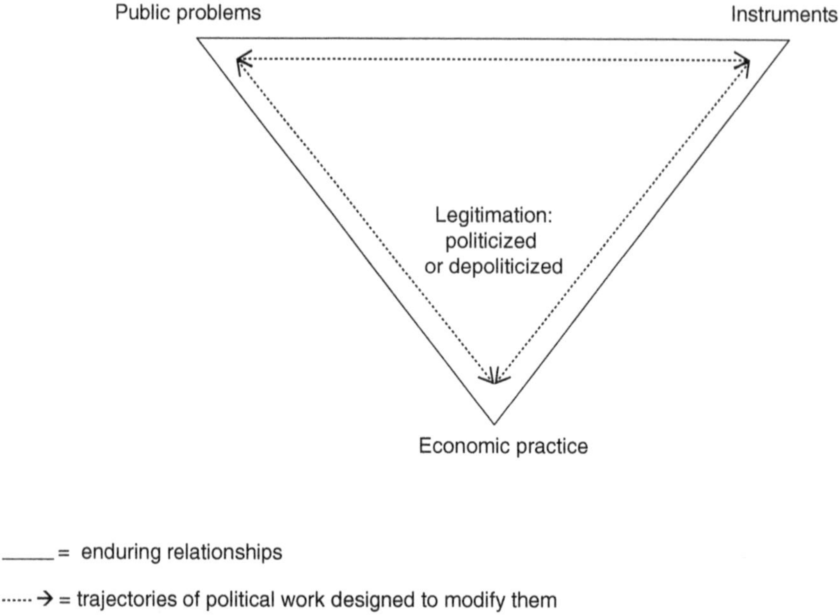

Figure 2.5. Political work on and around economic activity

More generally, it is through combining the concepts of problematization, instrumentation and legitimation as part of a concerted strategy of data generation about institutional change or reproduction that research becomes well equipped for studying the values that drive forward acts of institutional creation, maintenance, or disruption that relate to economic practice (see Figure 2.5.). The intermediate concept of political work facilitates the realization of this goal and will therefore be deployed in a sustained manner throughout the remainder of this book.

CONCLUSION

Based upon extensive engagement with existing research within several disciplines and paradigms, the approach developed in this chapter—and specifically its concepts, hypotheses, and claims—has been proposed as a means of breaking new ground for research on the relationship between politics and economics. In a nutshell, for any form of economic activity, I have argued here that institutionalist concepts—Institutional Orders, Institutionalized Relationships, trans-industry regulation, scale, and indeed institutionalization itself—provide a means of capturing what is to be explained: our dependent variable. For example, when studying the Scotch whisky industry, my initial basic questions were *what are the institutions that structure it and map the terrain within which its commercial and political 'life' takes place? Have these changed or been reproduced since the early 1990s?* In order to go beyond description to conduct actual analysis of what has reproduced or changed these institutions, and thus develop independent causal variables, I then brought in two additional lines of questioning designed to capture the role of agency within this industry. The first concerns the values mobilized or suppressed during institutional reproduction or change: the politics of this industry. The more specific question raised from this angle has thus been *how are four values in particular—freedom, security, equality, and tradition—mobilized or suppressed during the change or reproduction of economic institutions?* Finally, by empirically studying the processes of problematizaton, instrumentation, and legitimation as 'political work', the second line of questioning provides a means of generating data on the hierarchy of these values within an industry or policy domain in a controlled and consistent manner. The chapters that follow now illustrate the analytical purchase of these concepts and questions.

3

Globalization

From Runaway Steamroller to Political Outcome

INTRODUCTION

Over the past three decades a fatalistic discourse about the 'globalization of the economy' has taken hold throughout the world. Purveyed and naturalized as much by academics as by politicians and journalists, this discourse can generally be broken down into three assertions and a normative narrative.

The first and most basic assertion is that economies have become globalized due to increases in trade of goods and services across national borders. Measured in terms of outgoing and incoming 'flows', startling statistics are marshalled in order to demonstrate how economic activity has extended beyond the confines of each country and, in so doing, challenged the very meaning of their respective frontiers.

Building upon this initial analysis in terms of product and service flows, the second common assertion about globalization is that it stems from a deeper shift in economic practice which reflects increased 'interdependence' between key segments of financial, productive, and commercial activity. For example, consumption patterns in the West are said to have become dependent upon production in East Asia, just as flows of investment from the West to the East in the 1990s accelerated the rise in productive capacity of countries such as China. More generally, analysis of 'global value chains' (Gereffi, 2014—see chapter 1) describes in detail the types of dependence that now structure the financing, production, and commercialization of innumerable goods and services. From this angle, globalization has thus been authoritatively defined as a set of processes that embody 'a transformation in the spatial organization of social relations and transactions, generating transcontinental or inter-regional flows and networks of activity, interaction and power' (Held et al. 1999: 16).

A third assertion made around the term globalization concerns how states and international organizations have accelerated its development by removing barriers to trade. The most obvious dimension of this so-called 'political dimension' of globalization encapsulates the lowering or abolition of tariffs at national borders. Here the establishment of the World Trade Organization (WTO) in 1994 is frequently depicted as symbolizing a dramatic, generalized shift away from these classical instruments of 'protectionism' and towards an 'open economy'. Meanwhile, the WTO and contemporary trade agreements in general are characterized as the handmaidens of a 'deep trade agenda' which has globalized economic norms and standards (Büthe & Mattli, 2011). This trend, it is claimed, has prompted states throughout the world to make considerable political and economic changes 'behind the border' (Young & Peterson, 2006), and this in order to bring about a globalized 'level playing field'.

On the basis of these three assertions about the economics of the contemporary world, a dominant normative narrative has also taken hold on how 'economic' and 'political' actors should react to it. According to this view, employers and employees must adjust to a 'new economic reality' by becoming 'more competitive'. In so doing they must abandon their expectations about the economy automatically providing them with security in terms of market share, prices, jobs, wages, and social protection. Instead, steps must continuously be taken to lower costs, fight to attract new customers and struggle to retain existing ones. Meanwhile public actors are urged to lower the costs they impose upon their respective producers and give them a free rein to 'modernize' all their economic practices. The reader will recognize here not only the explicitly ideological doctrine of committed neo-liberals, but also the assumptions and axioms of liberal political economy presented in chapter 1. In short, globalization is frequently said to be spontaneously causing convergence in the way economies are structured and governed. Indeed, even its critics agree that as a set of 'aggregate social consequences' (Bisley, 2007: 30), globalization is driving homogenous and unstoppable swathes of neo-liberal transformations of contemporary economies and polities (Harvey, 2003). Globalization is therefore likened to an ever-accelerating steamroller without a driver which, unless economies get on board, will leave them crushed in its path.

Although many of the points made above do indeed need to be seriously taken into account by researchers, practitioners, and citizens, it is vitally important to frame globalization from the outset *as an outcome, not a cause* (Hay, 2006b). This apparently simple yet profoundly significant step immediately recasts the four points listed above in the following ways:

- Although inter-national trade has certainly increased over the past three decades, there has been nothing natural or inevitable about this trend. Instead, it must be understood as the cumulative result of a myriad of choices made regarding investment, production, distribution, and consumption, as well as the institutions that structure them. These choices themselves stem from the prioritization of certain values over others;

- Consequently, if interdependencies across nations have indeed become thicker, patterns such as those that concern consumption in the West have not spontaneously been driven by high productivity and low prices in 'the East'. Instead, a range of mediations, again involving a plethora of analysable value hierarchies and choices, have been made by both the private and public actors who have participated in the shifting of economic activity within and across states throughout the world.
- Similarly, there has been nothing inevitable either about the removal of 'barriers to trade', nor even the redefinitions of what constitutes an obstacle of this sort.
- Becoming more 'cost competitive' by lowering wages and social protection is also neither 'normal' nor inevitable. Alternative means of maintaining or increasing market share do exist (e.g. upgrading one's product), just as the very importance accorded to many markets and indeed products merits debate (e.g. over their negative externalities and social worth).

In short, the constructivist and institutionalist political economy promoted in this book seeks to contribute to discussions of globalization by building from Hay's observation that although we currently live in a world of 'acknowledged interdependence' (2010), contingency still remains and will always do so. This is because economic activity is continuously structured by politics and thus takes place within social spaces where alternative framings and practices to those favoured by liberals can, and frequently still are, put into place. More fundamentally still, by focusing consistently upon the politics of globalized economic activity as the mobilization or suppression of values to change or reproduce institutions, this chapter challenges head-on the dominant framing of international trade politics as being about unleashing capacity to produce goods and services 'that the consumer wants'. Although promoters of free trade are indeed frequently committed to and driven by the value of Freedom, their belief in the social worth of maximizing the autonomy of employers, traders, and consumers can only be fully understood by examining closely how their varying definitions of Freedom come into conflict with other basic values.

This analysis of value prioritization will first be conducted in this chapter around the deep conflict that has emerged since the 1960s between Freedom and Security over reconciling agricultural production with environmental protection. More precisely, a case study of how pesticide usage within the wine industry has recently been regulated on several scales will illustrate just how the values of Freedom and Security play-out, and this by to the values of Tradition and Equality having supporting but subordinate roles which dilute and confuse their respective meanings.

The second part of this chapter then deepens such analysis around a further case study focused upon the geographical origins of food. In this instance the struggle between Freedom and Security currently takes place more directly between different national and international region representatives. Indeed, the blockage of trade negotiations analysed here has been caused less by the mobilization of Tradition frequently associated with 'geographical indications', than by differing articulations between Freedom and Security which obstruct understanding and agreement across different parts of the world. Here Tradition plays what I call an intervening role, whilst Equality has been reduced to that of silence.

Throughout both sections, globalization will often be encountered as a powerful vector for legitimizing regulatory change within specific industries. However, by reconceptualizing this phenomenon as a historically contingent outcome not a cause, this chapter does not simply repeat the banal finding that globalization provokes 'divergent responses' (Braithwaite and Drahos, 2000, Levi-Faur, 2006; Bisley, 2007; Held and McGrew, 2007). By retaining throughout a focus upon the politics of economic activity, my argument instead is that the very term globalization should be shelved. In its place what analysis and public debate needs to be focusing upon are the values that drive the governing of cross-border economic activity in certain directions rather than in others. In this way, the politics of transnational business can be better understood and discussed in terms which embrace the contingent formulation of individual, collective, and public choices.

3.1. THE SUBORDINATION OF EQUALITY AND TRADITION: PESTICIDES AND WINE

There are two reasons why the wine industry provides a particularly revealing illustration of this book's thesis about the politics of economic activity at a worldwide scale. The first is that over the past twenty years, change in the making and selling of wine has invariably been ascribed to the steamrolling image of 'globalization'. According to this narrative, sharp rises in supply from 'the New World' (Australia, Argentina, Chile, California, South Africa, New Zealand), as well as in demand in new markets (China, the UK, Japan, Taiwan, Scandinavia), have encouraged increased sales of standardized, branded wines to the detriment of 'traditional' products made on a smaller scale in countries like France, Italy, and Spain. Identifying the many holes in this simplistic and apolitical explanation of economic change thus provides a heuristic means of showcasing my alternative analysis in terms of the worldwide value confrontations that have lain at the heart of the wine industry's politics.

The second reason for choosing the wine industry here is that its history also contains a much less discussed controversy concerning the protection of the environment and human health. At least in the Western world, agriculture and wine production in particular have been seen for centuries as taking place in areas and landscapes within which the 'natural' environment has been preserved by healthy farmers and farmworkers against the polluting effects of industry and urbanization. Indeed, constant reproduction of this rural idyll has taken innumerable forms ranging from the veneration of American farmers by rock singers like Neil Young, to its omnipresence on the lids of British chocolate boxes (Williams, 1973). However, the countryside is of course by no means free of pollution. Indeed, since the 1960s, and notably the publication of Rachel Carson's evocatively entitled *Silent Spring* (1962), a sustained critique of agriculture's impact upon rural environments has developed and mobilized a range of non-governmental organizations. Prompted by the latter and their mediatization of the numerous threats to human and environmental health attributed to intensive agriculture, public authorities throughout much of the world have introduced legislation to curb the usage of pesticides, herbicides, and fungicides.[1]

Defenders of intensive agriculture today argue that levels of pollution in rural areas are no longer at the heights reached in the 1970s and 1980s. Indeed, at least in the global North, usage of these products has often decreased overall, whilst a number of particularly dangerous pesticides have been taken off the market altogether. Notwithstanding this overall trend, reduction in pesticide usage has nevertheless been slow and uneven from sector to sector. Moreover, for some crops such as the grapes used to make wine, change in farming practices has been distinctly small. France is still the third largest consumer of pesticides in the world and its famous vineyards account for a fifth of this consumption. 'The need to compete on price', in particular with New World wines, is regularly invoked as justifying this continued high usage of pesticides. 'Controlling plant health' is therefore seen as an inevitable means of safeguarding or improving 'productivity'. As a representative of Bordeaux's wine producers put it in an interview, 'nobody takes any pleasure in applying pesticides, but the object of the exercise is to produce healthy grapes in order to make good wine' (official of the *Conseil interprofessionnel des vins de Bordeaux*, November, 2011). However, this seemingly depoliticized argument has largely obscured the fundamental value conflicts which underlie the institutionalized usage of pesticides. In seeking to reveal such conflicts, our research on the wine industry has therefore proved particularly relevant for analysing not only the politics of environmental and human 'protection', but also the 'globalization' this sector is said to have experienced.[2]

[1] The official term that groups these three types of products together is 'phytosanitary'. In keeping with common speech and a great deal of other research, however, I will use the term 'pesticides' because it is more readily understandable.

[2] This section draws indirectly upon more than a decade of research on the wine industry as a whole (Smith, de Maillard & Costa, 2007; Itçaina, Roger & Smith, 2016a). It also takes direct

As I will show first, pesticide usage has long been reproduced within the wine industry's institutional order. Justified in the name of 'economic necessity' and the 'Freedom' for farmers this requires, quite how massive use of pesticides has permeated the Institutionalized Relationships (IRs) that make up this order will be carefully unpacked. Indeed, recounting history using these concepts goes some way to explaining the lack of change in both the government of this aspect of the industry and the daily practices of most grape growers. However, to fully grasp this example of political reproduction one must then delve deeper by scrutinizing a hierarchy between Freedom and Security that consolidated in the 1950s and 1960s by subordinating issues of Equality related to human safety, thereby producing the value hierarchy which has prevailed until the present day.

3.1.1. Institutionalizing 'Crop Protection' in the Wine Industry

At least for the wine industry, pesticides have been considered dangerous for the farmers and farmworkers who apply them, for neighbours of the fields sprayed, and for consumers. Revealingly, however, very little action has been taken to restrict or reduce pesticide usage within the industry's Employment or Commercial IRs. In the case of the former, in recent years, and particularly within the European Union (EU), codes of good practice and obligatory training requirements have been introduced and intensified. However, if anything these rules and norms have only transferred responsibility to individual growers, and above all their workers, to spray and protect themselves 'better'. Actually reducing or stopping pesticide usage has not been problematized within the Employment IR (Ansaloni & Smith, 2014). Meanwhile, because research on pesticide residues in wines sold to the consumer has yet to be institutionalized as a consumption problem,[3] at least at the global and EU scales, virtually no direct action has been taken within the Commercial IR. Instead, progressive institutionalization of rules, norms, and expectations designed to control pesticide usage has taken place almost entirely within the wine industry's Sourcing IR. From a purely functionalist point of view, this finding is not surprising given that the Sourcing IR contains most of the institutions that shape how grapes can be grown and wine can be made. However, the deeper cause of the confinement of the politics of pesticide

inspiration from a targeted study of the regulation of pesticide usage in the Bordeaux wine region. The latter has been conducted with Matthieu Ansaloni.

[3] And this despite new scientific research which show that residues in wine are far from insignificant. See on this point articles published by the French consumer organization *UFC—Que choisir?* in 2013, together with the controversial summary of this data made by the journalist Isabelle Saporta (2014, chap. 8).

control within issues of Sourcing goes considerably beyond a function-driven division of political labour. It resides instead in the work undertaken by a range of actors to orientate and control the values potentially at issue by problematizing pesticides in narrowly defined ways. This confinement has in turn deeply restricted the range of policy instruments developed to regulate their usage. Moreover, as the following succinct history of the political work involved underlines, this sanctuarization of the Sourcing IR has been consistently buttressed by powerful institutions located in the industry's Finance IR. These institutions, as well as the actors who supported them such as bankers, not only wholeheartedly supported the expansion of pesticide usage in the mid to late twentieth century. Ever since, the values which drive these institutions and actors have bolstered this practice by remaining silent but omnipresent forces for continuity.

As a great deal of research has shown, the production and the usage of pesticides has a long history which accelerated in the nineteenth century before taking off in the twentieth (Wright, 1990; Jas, 2007). As with other parts of agriculture, grape-growing has of course been the subject of technical innovations for hundreds if not thousands of years, many of these concerning plant health. However, in Southern Europe this subject became a collective and public problem from the 1850s onwards because of the spread of the plant diseases phylloxera, mildew, and odium. Indeed, the former was experienced as particularly traumatic because it not only attacked and killed particular harvests, but vine plants themselves. Local wine guilds and public authorities raised funds for sustained scientific research (Garrier, 2002) which eventually met with considerable success, thereby legitimating the role of science within Europe's major vineyards. Indeed, from this moment onwards, a significant part of this science became a consistent supporter of the intensification of viticulture not only through reparatory actions on plant health, but also through providing indirect support in the form of fertilization and mechanized techniques (Roger, 2010). Accelerated by innovations in synthetic chemical production sparked by World War I, during the 1920s the application of pesticides thus participated strongly in the post-war rebuilding of French, Italian, and German vineyards, thereby becoming an institutionalized part of their respective Sourcing IRs. Not surprisingly, some of these chemicals were highly toxic, particularly because many contained arsenic. Indeed, following outbreaks of illnesses amongst farmworkers, in 1916 the French state introduced its first legislation that not only removed certain products from the market, but also made users of legitimate products responsible for the health of workers and consumers. However, no sustained collective mobilization accompanied this event, let alone used it as a springboard for more restrictive legislation and norms (Jas, 2010). Indeed, although a movement we call today 'Organic farming' emerged on a small scale as early as the 1920s, and this largely as a counter-project to the synthetic chemical-based modes of production outlined above (Besson, 2011), within the wine industry, its philosophy, principles, and practices were marginalized to the point of silence for the next five to six decades.

Explanations of the rise of intensive farming in general are abundant. Because farmers throughout much of the world were encouraged by public subsidies from the 1920s to the 1990s to increase production and productivity levels using scientific innovations and new techniques, many Regulationist economists conclude that the causes of this trend were exogenous to the sector itself (Allaire & Boyer, 1995). Focused upon the interactions and interdependencies that developed between farmers and their 'partners' in external professions, sociological research has instead identified more precisely how and why during the 1950s and 1960s so many farmers invested in, and wholeheartedly identified with, the political project of 'modernization' that accompanied technical modes of intensification (Muller, 1984). In particular, the latter approach has guided my own analysis of intensification of the wine industry to fully take into account how, in the name of reconciling farmer Freedom and Security, a range of scientists, pesticide manufacturers, bureaucrats, and bankers worked alongside leaders within the wine industry itself to reproduce the legality and legitimacy of high pesticide usage within the making of wine.

As noted above, the role played by scientists in general within the intensification of viticulture has been consistently high since the mid-1900s. From the 1920s to the 1990s, a particular type of science rose to prominence, then institutionalized within universities and research institutes chiefly dependent upon public funding. Dedicated to tackling plant health and performance through the eradication of insects, fungi, and undesired 'weeds', this strand of science first enabled many vineyards to increase levels of production by extending the area within which red wines in particular could be produced. The most startling example of this science-abetted transformation occurred in Bordeaux, a vineyard which, until the 1970s, produced more (low-priced) white wine than red. Indeed, by encouraging expansion of monocultural grape-growing in parts of the region that had previously been polycultural, the application of this science vastly increased production levels of red wine in the Bordelais as a whole.

Secondly, since the 1980s in particular, this science has increasingly turned itself to the question of producing 'higher quality' grapes and wine. Extremely elusive, the very term quality has consistently provoked disagreement within vineyards throughout the world. Indeed, science itself has not provided an objective answer to defining wine quality. However, what it has done is enable the production of wines that are more consistent in taste. To this end, pesticides have been deployed to standardize as much as possible the grapes produced, while other synthetic products have become increasingly used to reduce uncertainties that occur during the other end of wine production: vinification. As one French state official put it in an interview, 'the objective became to produce the most beautiful grapes possible, never mind the environmental consequences' (Bordeaux, April 2012). Indeed, as Antoine Roger has so convincingly shown (2010), this generalized aim reflects a shift within the scientific field towards a new, more applied group of sciences focused less upon production issues for their own sake, than upon producing wines that are seen as easier to make and sell. To cite a different state official, 'a lot of pesticide usage is just repeat behaviour without it being technically necessary. Growers prefer not to take risks, so they apply pesticides systematically and then they feel they don't have to worry any more' (Bordeaux, April, 2012). In so doing, the value Security has become synonymous with the commercial predictability of each wine and thus increasingly divorced from previously dominant conceptions of objectives for the collective sustainability of a wine region as a whole, i.e. producing a distinctive area-anchored wine and promoting it via the symbols and language of territory (*terroir*). Meanwhile, and crucially, by reducing Security to the profitability of each wine, this value has increasingly been conflated with the reinforced importance given to the Freedom of each individual grower to produce and sell as he or she best sees fit.

Moreover, evoking the role of science and universities in the intensification of viticulture through promoting pesticides must not, of course, distract analysis from analysing the overlap between research and the actual manufacturing of these products. Except within communist regimes, pesticide manufacturers have rarely been state-owned. Nevertheless, because of their close ties with state-funded research centres, direct support received in the guise of research or industrial policies and, more generally, state backing for intensive agriculture, these firms have long been present within the Sourcing IR alongside producers and bureaucrats. Their legitimacy to do so resides not only upon their linkages to science but also in the steadily increasing role these firms have come to play in giving advice to growers on viticultural practices. Indeed, since the 1980s, as state advisory and training services have been withdrawn or privatized, many pesticide manufacturers have been quick to fill the void by deepening their presence within individual vine farms or co-operatives and alongside the bodies that ostensibly aggregate and defend their interests (e.g. French Chambers of Agriculture).

Consequently, analysing the contribution of public administrations to the intensification of viticulture is essential from at least two angles. Firstly, and most obviously, EU, state, and local civil servants have participated strongly in the problematization and instrumentation of wine's Institutional Order. Indeed, from the 1950s to the early 2000s, their involvement in this industry was focused upon developing and updating an Order within which the Sourcing IR was central (Smith, de Maillard & Costa, 2007). Restrictions on the freedom to produce were introduced in the form of plantation rights, permissible oenological practices, and product specifications. However, within this framework the freedom to use pesticides was never discouraged.

Examining the involvement of bureaucrats in the intensification of agriculture in general, and wine production in particular, is also important from a second, less often examined, angle. As sociologies of the state have underlined (Genieys & Hassenteufel, 2015), it is vital to emphasize that bureaucrats are not selected, trained, and allowed to develop their careers in a social vacuum. On the contrary, in preparing for, then working within, their country's administrative elite, they develop a range of networks and value-based ideological homologies with actors who participate strongly in other dimensions of agricultural affairs. The management of pesticide manufacturers is one such dimension whilst, at least in France, that of the banks who lend money to growers is another. Indeed, banks and bankers constitute the fourth and final set of actors who participated strongly in the intensification of viticulture. Although massively understudied, organizations such as *Crédit agricole* in France have constituted silent but omnipresent partners in this enterprise as a whole (Allaire, 1988), in particular by normalizing the unquestioned conflation of Freedom and Security upon which it is based and, therefore, institutionalizing pesticides as a legitimate economic practice.

In summary, from the mid nineteenth century until at least the early 2000s, pesticides as a standardized artefact of economic practice heavily backed by institutions, lay at the heart of the wine industry's IO. During this period, its Sourcing and Financial IRs dominated and had numerous 'contagious' effects upon its Commercial and Employment IRs. Throughout, a particular conception of Freedom became the dominant value, a conception according to which wine farms should have the fewest restrictions on how they use pesticides. Indeed, since the early 1990s as the selling of wine has become represented as more competitive than in the past, and the narrative of globalization used to explain this phenomenon has become more prominent, institutionalized references to Freedom have intensified. Omnipresent in the discourse of actors and states from the New World as of the 1980s, this emphasis upon the Freedom of individual growers and merchants, together with the individualization of Security, began to permeate European and International decision-making arenas over the period 1995–2005.[4] In order to counter this trend, critics of pesticide usage have attempted instead to prioritize the value of Security with reference to both human health (safety) and the environment (its sustainability). However, this conception of Security has been delegitimated by actors defining it instead in terms of commercial predictability, and thus as totally in sync with the value of Freedom. Moreover, as will be shown

[4] For evidence of this trend, see Itçaina, Roger & Smith (2016a). In this book we show in particular how previous commitments to *Appellations d'origine contrôlées* based on a collective conception of Security have been challenged by the notion that each producer and merchant should be as free as possible to target the demands of the so-called 'new consumer'. In so doing, the value of Equality has also had its egalitarian connotations replaced with a recurrent discourse about producers needing to have equal access to markets.

in more detail below, this institutionalized conflation of Freedom and Security has been achieved largely through giving Equality a new meaning and translating Tradition as simply ensuring the continuity of pesticide usage—and this despite the latter being of course a relevantly recent productive practice.

3.1.2. Reproducing Pollution in the Name of Individualized Security

Despite the stability of the wine industry's IO and the key role played by pesticides therein, since the 1970s this immovability has been repeatedly contested from two angles. The first concerns intensive agriculture as a whole and how it has been pressurized to change by a range of environmentalist movements, public policies, and even supermarket chains. The former have sought to put the 'extensification' of agriculture, and thus the reduction of pesticide usage, firmly on the agendas of executives and legislatures. Meanwhile, public policy analysts have shown how this agenda has been translated into governmental actions at EU, national, and local scales which notably includes the EU's 2009 'Pesticides package' (Ansaloni & Smith, 2014). Finally, recent research into the setting of standards within a variety of industries involving both public and private actors all in the name of 'sustainability' (Carter, 2015), has increasingly encompassed the introduction of limits upon all freedoms to produce. In short, the very idea that agriculture can be as intensive as possible because this fits with both the Freedom of the entrepreneur and (food) Security has been challenged by a variety of actors who, for differing reasons, consider instead that the key security issue concerns the safety of workers, consumers, citizens, and the environment. For this reason, they have consistently argued that absolute freedom to produce must be curtailed.

As regards the more limited domain of viticulture, a second source of contestation has arisen in the shape of alternative modes of production. Most frequently labelled 'Organic', these practices specifically outlaw pesticide usage in the name of protecting the soil and air in which vines grow, and thence the environment as a whole. Relatively frequently used in other parts of agriculture since the 1970s, and even inscribed in French law as long ago as 1980, organic farming practices have become increasingly codified and monitored, in particular around labels such as *Agriculture biologique* (AB). However, and crucially, it is only in the 2000s that a significant proportion of wine in countries such as France has been made from 'organically farmed' grapes. In this country, between 2001 and 2013 the number of wine farms adopting such practices rose by nearly 400 per cent, a trend that has entailed 8.2 per cent of the French national vineyard becoming 'organic'.

Notwithstanding these two considerable sources of challenge to intensive viticulture, the overall story told below is nonetheless one of only incremental change and fundamental continuity. Not only do more than ninety per cent of growers in virtually all the vineyards of the world still apply pesticides intensely, resistance to further reductions in their usage has become highly organized. This has been particularly so in France where the defenders of pesticide usage have even invented a term, *agriculture raisonnée* (reason-based farming), in order to problematize, instrument, and symbolize their willingness to accept the progressive introduction of certain restrictions upon their freedom as entrepreneurs. In terms of problematization, the step taken by the *agriculture raisonnée* movement has been to accept that when pesticides are badly used they do represent a socially unacceptable level of danger for human health and the environment. The challenge, they argue, is not to ban pesticides but instead to encourage individual users to be more restrained and precise when deploying these products. From this definition of the problem, partisans of *agriculture raisonnée* have argued that public authorities should intervene less to punish wrongdoing and more to encourage the 'reasonable' and justified use of pesticides. Even if this movement has not attracted large numbers of active members (Teil et al., 2011), it has nevertheless succeeded in reproducing the balance of power within the wine industry's IO. Indeed, in countries like France, *agriculture raisonnée*'s mode of instrumentation has been largely adopted by public authorities in the form of communication campaigns and pedagogical actions within agricultural colleges, or via obligatory professional training courses (Ansaloni & Smith, 2014). Overall, this movement has sought to re-legitimize farmers in general as responsible actors who, through their deep, daily, immersion in the countryside, know best how to preserve the environment, protect their health, and that of their workers—and all this while remaining competitive despite the challenges of globalization. In so doing, intensive farming practices have become associated with protecting a Tradition, a value that has thus come to support individualized conceptions of Freedom over more collective goals and practices. In short, in this way the claim that farmers themselves remain the best guarantors of Security has been naturalized, whilst Security as a value is claimed to be best upheld when the Freedom of farmers to manage their respective businesses is not heavily restricted. To give just one example, here is how the National Farmers' Union of England and Wales argue in favour of the right of farmers to use pesticides as they see fit: 'Farmers and growers need access to all modern farming methods to enable them to respond to the food production challenge that lies ahead; to produce enough, safe, affordable food to feed a growing population both at home and abroad'.[5]

This victory for advocates of the status quo is often reduced to the 'power' of vested interests within and without wine production. Research in this vein has

[5] NFU briefing, <https://www.nfuonline.com/assets/20829>, accessed the 24 November 2015.

frequently shown how defenders of intensive viticulture continue to dominate the representation of their profession and the bodies which ostensibly 'co-govern' this industry alongside the state. In France, the *Institut National des Appellations Origines* (INAO) and *France Agrimer* provide prime examples. In short, the analysis which predominates is that neo-corporatist arrangements between the state, incumbent interest groups and large firms continue to dictate both public policy and the practices of individual entrepreneurs (Teil et al., 2011; Jas, 2007 & 2010). The existence and effects of these arrangements have indeed had considerable impact upon this example of successful resistance to change. However, if this analysis in terms of unequal power is often empirically accurate and highly informative, it is not equipped to discover the political roots and cause of such asymmetries.

Instead, and more fundamentally, deep explanation of the reproduction of pesticide usage within the wine industry and beyond must be found in terms of the politics which orientates and legitimizes this economic practice. This politics is located in the values present in the very framing of the question as to whether and how pesticides should be used to produce what is, after all, only a drink. During this framing, the issue of equal rights to safety in terms of environmental protection and respect for the health of those actually working and living on the land, and thus an egalitarian reading of Equality, continues to be suppressed. Instead those of Freedom, individualized commercial Security and a reduction of Equality to equivalent opportunities are constantly invoked to represent pesticide usage not even as a 'necessary evil', but rather as a normal, and even desirable, part of wine production. Indeed, this reconstruction of the normal has been accompanied by political work to make the non-usage of pesticides a synonym for poor quality wine, harvest failures, and economic 'inefficiency' that is out of step with 'globalized markets'.

Seen from this angle, explanation of inertia in economic practice in terms of the power of dominant actors is clearly insufficient and even misleading. As the politics as values approach has just indicated, the cause of continued pesticide usage must also be attributed to the failure of those who promote more extensive wine production to reframe Security as a collective goal synonymous with improving wine quality, traditions, authenticity, and local economic development. Moreover, they have not ensured that their critique of the very notion that pesticide users are 'free' is shared more widely. Indeed, such actors have not managed to gain traction for the claim that the Freedom of pesticide users is highly relative given their dependence upon these products. For example, a case could be made that the pesticide dependency of individual growers is 'locked in' by the conditional support of bankers armed with the value of Freedom and an individualized take on Security for whom intensive production rhymes with guaranteed levels of production, productivity, and turnover, regardless of how this translates into profitability, sustainability, and, therefore, long-term viability. Such a case is rarely made and has clearly had little impact. Instead, most growers in regions such as the Bordelais continue to fear any environmental issue as negative because it is seen as depreciating the image of their products (Saint-Gès & Belis-Bergouignan, 2009), or even threatening their professional identities (Nicourt & Girault, 2011).

In order to further substantiate these claims, and thereby my thesis on politics as values, two episodes of recent history will now be presented, both concerning the wine industry's relationship to 'globalization'. As will be underlined, during both periods the issue of pesticide usage was well and truly sidelined.

The first of these episodes concerns the most obvious 'suspect': the WTO. Nothing in the GATT treaty it replaced had directly mentioned either limits on the usage of products such as pesticides, or how national legislation on this matter might be used as a barrier to international trade. During the Uruguay Round, negotiators of the WTO treaty considered that the latter point needed specifying in a new, multilateral normative framework. Consequently, an Agreement on Sanitary and Phyto-sanitary Measures (SPS) was drafted, negotiated then came into effect as part of WTO law in 1998. As Wolfe has clearly explained (2005), the first aim of the SPS agreement was to 'recognize and validate' 'sites of normative authority' on these matters throughout the world. Whilst accepting that these authorities might well set differing standards, a more constraining rule was also introduced which obliged any deviation from the most common standards to be based upon 'scientific risk assessment'. As is reasonably well known, this part of the SPS agreement has sparked considerable controversy in the case of foods sourced from Genetically Modified Organisms (GMOs). Without going into the detail of this conflict,[6] nor the value confrontations that are its cause, the least one can say is that the politics of this global scale episode has been publicized and made fairly plain for all to see. However, the same can certainly not be said for pesticide usage in general and within viticulture in particular. Despite the fact that within numerous states the spraying of pesticides has been widely criticized, it has thus far not been problematized either multilaterally or bilaterally. What national restrictions there are on pesticide usage have instead been accommodated through technical adjustments to commercial practices. For example, since 1986 the US Food and Drug Organization has required all products that may have come into contact with sulphites to include this information on their labelling. As no such requirement exists in the EU, its

[6] To summarize a conflict which, in particular, has opposed representatives of the US and the EU, those from the latter consider that they have legitimately banned the import of GMO sourced foods into Europe on the basis of science-based risk assessments. In contrast, actors from the US contest not only the findings of these studies, but the science used to research them (Epps, 2008).

wine producers looking to sell in the US have had to modify their labels accordingly. By contrast, any suggestion that the use of certain pesticides, or their modes of application (e.g. by helicopter),[7] should be invoked to prevent the import of wines from 'offending' countries, has yet to have any impact on trade law and agreements, let alone upon the rationales that accompany them.

Liberal political economy would explain away this absence by assuming it was in the interests of all wine traders, no matter their national origin, to avoid the introduction of additional institutions that 'interfere' in the marketplace. Meanwhile, neo-Marxists or neo-Gramscians would point instead to the large multinational companies who, in dominating both the international trading of wine and pesticide production, 'have an interest' in avoiding new restrictive institutions. However, in order to go beyond these interpretations in terms of assumed interests and visible power asymmetries, once again it is indispensable to focus upon the values that have been mobilized or suppressed, by whom and with what resources.

From this angle a means of discovering the politics that lies at the root of the non-construction of pesticide usage as a global problem is to examine closely the international organization that for more than eighty years has ostensibly provided neutral scientific expertise on the wine industry: *l'Organisation internationale de la vigne et du vin* (the OIV). Formally linked into a range of other international organizations which include the United Nation's Food and Agriculture Organization and committees of the *Codex Alimentarius*, the OIV is a venue for exchanges of views between national representatives with a view to producing global standards and norms. As its own website highlights, part of the subjects treated from this angle have concerned 'health and safety'. However, a close look at this aspect of the OIV's work reveals that this heading is solely problematized around the question of wine's impact upon the health of its drinkers. No mention of the health of farmworkers or neighbours, and thus of an egalitarian take on Equality, is made. Another aspect of the wine trade examined by the OIV is legal requirements about labelling. Given that some critics of pesticide usage consider that the most efficient way to restrict this practice is to require sellers of wine to clearly state on their labels whether or not they have used chemicals (Saporta, 2014: 250), one might have expected the OIV's formal recommendations to contain at least some reference to this issue. However, again they most evidently do not. Finally, in recent years the question of wine production's impact upon the environment and the growth of organic wines has made it onto the agenda of the OIV. Nevertheless, although the OIV has formally decided to sit on the fence and not favour organic wines over those from 'precision agriculture', its total refusal to challenge the latter in any way clearly reveals the institutionalized hierarchy

[7] This example is far from trivial or absurd given that in 2010 the French government banned the spreading of pesticides by helicopter (within its *loi Grenelle II*).

of values which continues to structure the work and the norms produced by this organization: Freedom trumps all. Indeed, this bias has been bolstered since 1998 by the creation of a World Wine Trading Group (WWTG) composed of representatives of New World governments. Far from being merely a neutral discussion forum, this group has since become an arena for aggregating interests before meetings of the OIV in order to push the latter towards positions more favourable to New World producers (Roger, 2010). Not surprisingly, these include avoiding any multilateral commitments to restrictions on pesticide usage and recourse instead to the SPS agreement as the way to achieve the WWTG's own goals: 'A successful, competitive and growing global wine industry, characterized by social responsibility, sustainability and focus on consumer interests, operating in a climate free of trade-distorting factors'.[8] In a nutshell, by reiterating the primacy of Freedom to produce and to trade, the wagons have been drawn up into a tightly closed circle of WWTG and OIV members, a circle from which alternative value hierarchies have been fundamentally excluded.

A second episode of recent history which reveals the deep linkages in the wine industry between evocations of globalization and pesticide usage, and thus its institutionalized hierarchy between Freedom and Security, concerns the radical reform of the EU's wine policy adopted in 2008. Set out in detail elsewhere (Itçaina, Roger & Smith, 2016a), this reform transformed the underlying logic of EU intervention from:

(1) controlling supply within the industry's Sourcing IR (through planting rights and subsidies for distillation of surpluses and grubbing out 'excess' vines), to

(2) liberalizing all the above controls on production while supporting instead the international promotion of EU wines (within the Commercial IR).

Beyond the evident change in instrumentation made by this reform, however, lay even deeper shifts in problematization and legitimation. Until this reform, the problem of EU wines had essentially been seen since the 1980s as one of steadily improving their quality while intervening when necessary to correct fluctuations in the quantities entering the market (as for other agricultural products). In short, the value of Equality (between vineyards) and their Traditions predominated over the Freedom of the individual grower or trader. Indeed, these values, together with a collective interpretation of Security, were consistently mobilized to legitimize EU policy through references to history and the symbolism of *terroir* (Smith, de Maillard & Costa, 2007). However, since the mid-1990s a sustained challenge to this problematization and legitimization had been developed by a range of academics, traders, dissident growers, and

[8] Source: <wwtg-gmcv.com> (accessed 28 October 2014).

bureaucrats, all driven by the values of Freedom and Security as commercial predictability for individual wine farms or merchants. According to these actors, by removing 'obsolete handouts' and excessive restrictions, EU producers would spontaneously produce wine 'for the market' rather than making the product they preferred and simply hoping it would sell. Inspired by neo-classical economics, this problematization was legitimized not only in the name of the entrepreneur, but also by invoking a mythical 'new consumer' supposedly only interested in the types of standardized and branded wines supplied by New World producers. Indeed, the model of economic activity and public support prevalent in countries such as Australia was clearly seen as an ideal that needed transposing to Europe.

This is not the place for explaining in full how and why the latter set of values, problems, instruments, and symbols came to be victorious in the EU. Rather I focus here specifically upon a short period during this process when an entirely different political project, based upon drastic reductions in pesticides, might have reached the EU agenda but clearly did not. Between 2002 and 2006 proposals for reform of EU policy began to be discussed in increasingly detailed and intense ways by three sets of actors. Firstly, the proponents of radical change introduced above began to meet, write, and communicate their views. During this process the confederation of European wine traders (the *Comité Vin*) became a consistent venue for this exchange but also modified its own internal values, priorities, and structures. Secondly, defenders of a supply-centred policy grouped within the corresponding confederation of growers (the *Comité des organisations professionnels agricoles*: COPA) experienced great difficulty in agreeing amongst themselves to accept any changes in EU instruments, let alone contemplate a shift in problematizations or value hierarchies. Thirdly, a final group of producers and merchants within the wine industry committed to organic production, and therefore to strong restrictions on pesticide usage, also began to discuss the possibility of change in EU policy. Although their position was never clearly formalized, like that of the COPA, it was inspired by the values of Equality and Tradition, together with a collective interpretation of Security. However, in this instance Equality was framed in egalitarian environmental and human health terms, principles from which it was argued that the durability of production and the respect of wine traditions could best be achieved. Moreover, the position of organic growers and their supporters included the argument that restricting pesticide usage would automatically reduce levels of supply, thus freeing up EU monies to assist in the conversion of wine farms to organic logics.

Needless to say, actors working in or around the COPA or the *Comité Vin* took great pains to silence the position of organic growers by refusing to even discuss their propositions. Facilitated by the weak organizational resources of organic growers at the EU level, to paraphrase Fligstein (2001), debate polarized instead between the 'incumbents' (COPA) and a set of much better resourced and organized 'challengers' (the *Comité Vin*). At this point, key actors within the European Commission came out in favour of the latter as being in sync with their own values and policy goals. From then on, a combination of Commission representatives, traders, and dissident growers consolidated their new framing of how the wine industry should be governed at the EU level and, in the space of two years, convinced the Council of Ministers to accept it (Itçaina, Roger & Smith, 2016a). Rather than fully explain here this paradigmatic change in value hierarchies, symbols, problems, and instruments, the key point to focus upon is how early and quickly an alternative hierarchy of values was delegitimized and discarded, in particular by public authorities such as the Commission. A partial explanation lies in the ways traders and prominent growers manipulated the language of sustainability to argue that they too knew how to protect the environment in the name of Security. But deeper analysis must focus upon how the very issue of human health, and thus egalitarian equality, was silenced from the outset by a wide range of actors, for whom the health of farmworkers and the residents of wine regions must always be traded off either against the value of Freedom, or versus an individualized principle of Security driven by abstract notions of viability, rather than being anchored to concrete and collective concerns over human safety.

In conclusion, the global scale has clearly had an influence upon the continued usage of pesticides in the wine industry by spawning fora which have promoted the free trade mantra, and this while singularly failing to generate regulatory arenas or organizations where open debate about values and their prioritization can readily take place. This absence encourages the idea that producers in the EU, for example, cannot unilaterally restrict pesticide usage if competitors elsewhere do not do the same. However, as this section has repeatedly shown, it is not 'the global' that has prevented actors on a European, national, or local scale from taking action in this area. Rather its cause has been a much more pervasive politics overwhelmingly dominated by the value of Freedom and a narrow definition of Security—a blend of values which has systematically subordinated those of Equality and Tradition to a supporting role. This combination of Freedom and Security clearly influences the behaviour of the majority of individual growers who continue to choose pesticides over investing in alternative viticultural practices, and this even in wine regions where they could act otherwise relatively easily.[9] What is more surprising is that this value combination predominates even within the public

[9] See for example Saporta's interview with an organic producer in one of the most prestigious vineyards in the world: Pomerol in the French Bordelais. During this encounter, the interviewee castigated his neighbours by exclaiming 'how in a *terroir* where bottles sell between 30 and 300 euros can this behaviour go on? They just need to renew their 4 wheel drives a bit less often and work upon their soil!' (Saporta, 2014: 103, my translation).

bodies charged with regulating this industry. Although representatives of these organizations are ostensibly trained and paid to look after 'the general interest', the latter continues to be reduced to short-term financial calculus. Moreover, this line of reasoning singularly fails to re-examine what constitutes a Tradition by factoring in environmental and human health costs as deep challenges to the value of Equality and the collective dimension of Security and, indeed, Freedom.

3.2. DEFENDING TRADITIONS? THE INTELLECTUAL PROPERTY OF FOODS

The previous section concerned the politics of *how* a foodstuff is made, but examining *where* this takes place is equally heuristic for understanding how the things humans drink and eat are structured. Indeed, over the past quarter century the provenance or origins of foods has become a global controversy which sharply divides supporters of their legal protection through 'geographical indications' (GIs) from those who, on the contrary, consider these intellectual property rights to be 'protectionist interference' in markets. In geopolitical terms this division has most visibly taken the form of a conflict between representatives of the EU, who by and large defend the former point of view, and those of the New World who virtually unanimously support the latter. More fundamentally, however, this division separates actors with varying statuses (notably company managers, officials of interest groups and administrations, politicians) who come at this issue area armed with a value hierarchy that either:

- prioritizes Tradition and Security, the latter envisaged as legitimizing a durable, collective right to produce; or
- reasons instead from principles of Freedom and Equality as equal opportunities, a value combination which reduces Security to being just an issue of food safety.

Over the past century, these contrasting value definitions and hierarchies have given rise to two trans-industry Institutional Orders, each with their respective interwoven sets of problems, instruments, and legitimizing narratives and symbols. In what follows, I first set out these Orders before then proceeding to analyse how, over the last two decades, friction between the two has intensified. As with the case of pesticides, the WTO treaty was initially seen as a means of settling conflict over this issue once and for all. However, once again implementing that legislation has instead remapped the battleground of a politics which, precisely because of its deep, value-laden roots, remains inflammatory and regularly explodes into flame.

3.2.1. Two Contrasting Value Hierarchies and Institutional Orders

3.2.1.1. The New World's Order: Universal Freedom Through Markets, Trademarks, and the Courts

Formalized in the nineteenth century essentially in the US, the UK and several of its colonies, the value hierarchy which today is defended most ardently by 'New World' food and drink producers, along with their respective governments, has three major components.

The first is an overarching, Freedom-driven belief in the efficiency of providing and allocating goods and services through unfettered markets. This belief clearly stems from the liberal, neo-classical economics and political economy set out in chapter 1 which is defended today most visibly by political parties located on the right of polities throughout the world. However, during key historical periods when intellectual property rights were first codified into national laws, in particular between 1879 and the 1930s, in certain countries this belief in the primacy of markets was held by an even wider swathe of their respective elites. This largely explains why in the US, the UK, and then states such as Canada and Australia built upon British law, public administrations were distanced from the outset from the instrumentation and upholding of intellectual property rights (Dobbin, 1994).

The prevalence of Common law in these countries also largely explains why the second key component of this institutional ordering, trademarks, has been accredited with so much legal backing and social meaning. As the US example shows particularly clearly (Strasser, 1989), trademarks as instruments of legal and public action take their legitimacy from protecting the brands of private companies (Boy, 2003), themselves seen as the building blocks of markets and thus of the economy. More precisely, trademarks protect brands which are seen as the best way of transmitting information to the consumer. From this angle, detailed information about the provenance of a food can also be given on its labelling. But it is the brand that always takes prominence. Trademarks are also defended because, like a brand, they must actually be continuously built and rebuilt in order to transmit effective information to the consumer. As such they reflect the value of Freedom and the equal opportunities of all commercial operators to compete for consumer preferences. For this reason, defenders of trademarks are opposed to other forms of property rights, and in particular GIs, because without even being activated the latter can lock out newcomers from certain product markets (e.g. for types of cheese). Indeed, such actors fear the capturing of generic names (e.g. cheddar) by certain producers who will then monopolize the information given to the consumer and thereby lock-in an illegitimate rent. Finally, although this is not codified in law, proponents of trademarks also often argue that Europe's cultural heritage extends way beyond Europe itself to include the New World. Consequently, attempts by European states to prevent actors in say Canada from using a geographical name that has existed in that country for centuries are seen as a form of 'neo-colonialism' (see here a paper given by the then Australian ambassador to the WTO: Hellwig, 2003).

Finally, the third component which structures the value hierarchy and Institutional Order of the New World concerns the important role given to the courts whenever a conflict arises over intellectual property. Advocating the primacy of the courts here rests upon the belief that they are more objective and more consistent than public administrations. But this choice of judicatory body also stems from the belief that jurisprudence built up in New World countries heavily favours trademarks over other forms of intellectual property rights (Strasser, 1989).

'Markets', trademarks, and recourse to the courts thus make up an interwoven order of institutions which, over decades, have been continuously developed, maintained, and promoted as a universal and egalitarian ideal precisely because they are claimed to favour competition and the consumer throughout the world. Here Equality may well have been reduced to 'equal chances to compete', but as a value this narrowing of its content has nevertheless had numerous structuring effects because actors have used it to strongly support the value of Freedom. In so doing, evocation of the entrepreneur as a societal hero, and the stigmatization of public actors as 'unreliable' and 'interfering' 'bureaucrats', have been very much part and parcel of a process that has produced a remarkably stable set of problems, instruments, narratives, and symbols. To give just one example, in a text presented in 2003 to the conference of the World Intellectual Property Organization by a representative of the US Patent and Trademark Office, Eleanor Meltzer (2003: 10 & 15), proclaimed: (in the EU system) 'there are many possibilities for bureaucratic mischief'...'It is difficult to avoid thinking that the arguments of the European Union against trademarks and for a system of protection based upon geographical indications are not, in reality, simply trade arguments'.

3.2.1.2. The European Order: Protecting Tradition Through Territorial Collective and Public Action

Just as the deepening of the state occurred in the US and the UK at a time when elites who believed in liberal political economy were hegemonic, corresponding developments in Southern Europe came about when its respective elites were more inclined to preserve a role for public intervention in the economy. Over the last three decades, neo-liberalism has of course since taken a strong hold in all these states and elites, but in France, Italy, Spain, Portugal, and Greece, the legitimacy of public action to structure and correct markets remains firmly institutionalized. Indeed, this belief in the capacity and duty of public authorities to engage with economic activity also extends to a range of local collective action bodies, such as cured ham guilds or cheese 'interprofessions'. All these authorities and bodies claim to protect GIs in the name of preserving territorial Traditions and, thereby, both the collective Security of producers and 'the public interest'.

The initial problematization of GIs as intellectual property rights to be protected for these reasons emerged at the beginning of the twentieth century at a time when the usurpation of prominent wine names had become commonplace and a source of considerable commercial conflict. This was particularly so in areas such as Pomerol in the Bordeaux vineyard. Having built up reputation for their wines, producers from this area not only felt cheated that competitors from elsewhere could simply use the name Pomerol on their bottles, they also feared that the poor quality wine sold in this way would end up both depreciating Pomerol as a collective brand and eroding the identity of its producers. A host of court cases were brought to end such practices. However, the inconclusiveness and unpredictability of their results throughout France led to a nation-wide movement in favour of legislation and intervention by the state. It took until the mid-1930s for these goals to be achieved through the instrumentation of *Appellations d'origine controlées* (AOCs). However, along the way not only did the initial problematization change and thicken; during the 1930s, this French system was also emulated in virtually all the other major European wine-producing states.

In terms of problem definition, the key development concerned the addition of legally-backed product specifications for each AOC designed to define its specificity and authenticity. From having been solely a means of protecting against usurpation, GIs thus took on the form of standards and certification processes which differentiated products and segmented markets. To govern this certification of an extended conception of Security, guilds were formed for each *terroir*-defined AOC (e.g. St Emilion) and a national norm-setting and arbitration body—today's *Institut National des AOC* (INAO)—was created, a body staffed by growers, merchants, and public officials (Warner, 1960).

Between the 1930s and 1990s, this system of AOCs and its equivalents in Spain, Italy, Portugal, and Greece firmly embedded itself within each national food and agriculture policy and extended themselves to cover other alcoholic drinks and cheeses. The creation of the European Community (EC) in the late 1950s, and of its Common Agricultural Policy (CAP) in particular, could potentially have destabilized the development of these national systems and the approach to Security upon which it was founded. After all, West Germany had no equivalent to GIs and the Netherlands had long been a bastion of liberal values as regards the economic. However, any threat to GIs at this stage was headed off by French and Italian actors who went a stage further by placing this policy instrument at the very heart of the EC's wine policy launched in 1970. Subsequent potential threats due to the EC's first enlargement that brought into the fold three non-GI states (the UK, Ireland, and Denmark) were thwarted in similar fashion. Indeed, it is not until the early 1990s following an expansion of GI applications to other products, such as duck-meat and cured ham, that sustained intra-European conflict arose. Without going into the detail of this episode (Smith, 2010a), what is important to remember is that around the adoption of a Regulation in 1992, four arguments in favour of GIs and their linkage to Security were more explicitly articulated:

- they provide important information to the consumer about the origins of certified foodstuffs and beverages;
- they encourage improvements of product quality and guarantee its traceability;
- they enable producers, and in particular smallholders, to defend their intellectual property rights without incurring the costs or the uncertainty of court cases;
- they provide levers for encouraging local economic development by anchoring productive systems in remote localities and generating spin-offs such as tourism.

In short, GIs came to be explicitly legitimated as protecting Traditions through enhancing the Security of the producers concerned by structuring their markets as regards the medium to long term.

Backed by the 1992 EU Regulation, together with its updating revisions, today the EU's policy on GIs is presented by its supporters as having been particularly successful. Internally, the policy has generated a register of more than 600 products which, through possessing a GI, are said to benefit in the above-mentioned ways. Externally, this system, legislation, and policy have enabled public, collective, and private representatives of the EU to not only defend themselves on a global scale, but to have significantly shaped worldwide institutions for the protection of this form of intellectual property.

Overall then, spokespersons for the EU approach to GIs have institutionalized a set of instruments, problem definitions, and symbols which above all promote the values of Tradition and Security, the latter framed as durability and as a collective good. In so doing, they have relegated to secondary importance the Freedom of individual producers and Equality (seen essentially as equal rights of areas to obtain GIs should they meet the established criteria). In this way, public and collective intervention in the name of the Security and Traditions of territories has consistently and confidently been legitimized.

3.2.2. When Institutional Orders Collide: The TRIPS Agreement in action

Not surprisingly, the two value hierarchies and corresponding Institutional Orders presented above have repeatedly clashed, and this primarily because traders based in each jurisdiction have sought to operate in that of the other. So long as such conflicts were only sporadic, governments and interest groups left them to be dealt with by the courts. In this way, for example, in the 1980s Australian wine producers were forced to stop labelling many of their products 'Burgundy-style'. However, as the EU system of GIs expanded and a WTO treaty loomed, attempts intensified to create a worldwide order that would reduce or even remove intellectual property rights as a source of controversy within the food and drinks industries. Formally, this was achieved through the Trade Related Intellectual Property (TRIPS) agreement signed, then ratified, by all WTO members in 1994–95. More precisely, articles 22 and 23 of this agreement codified geographical indications as legitimate instruments of public policy that fell within the WTO's free trade mandate and rules. Indeed, this part of TRIPS was seen as a victory for EU negotiators since it largely enshrined in international law the principles of the 1992 regulation on GIs. However, twenty years on, TRIPS has clearly not given rise to a global International Order for intellectual property rights for foods. Indeed, by following closely how EU representatives have repeatedly attempted, but so far failed, to transpose their value hierarchy and set of institutions to the global scale, one understands better both the politics of this and many other quests for worldwide government of economic activity.

Like any law or international agreement, TRIPS's articles on GIs only came to life through the political work undertaken to implement them and thereby affect trade, production, and investment. Since the agreement itself said virtually nothing on this point, in the late 1990s actors from the EU decided to take the lead by proposing that an 'international register' of GIs from throughout the world be established. Similar to the EU's own list of accredited GIs, this register, it was argued, would efficiently meet one of the main objectives of TRIPS's articles 22 and 23: avoid producers who considered their GI had been usurped from having to go to the national courts of their opponents to seek justice for their cause. An international register was claimed to be an instrument of public policy that would drastically reduce such court cases because, firstly, each registered GI would automatically have precedence and, secondly, WTO law obliges national administrations to take action to discipline producers in their respective jurisdictions. In short, a register at this scale was seen as a vital means of instrumenting both the safeguarding of local Traditions and providing producers with greater collective Security as regards their intellectual property rights.

Although the problematization behind an international register seemed straightforward and 'normal' to many actors from the EU, it was not perceived as such at all in New World states. On the contrary, given that these countries had no equivalent of a register (because territory-linked certification of foods rarely existed), and in keeping with their preference for common law, the very concept of worldwide registration was treated with suspicion and hostility. These sentiments were also so strong because, according to many actors from the New World, the EU's own registration process was far from perfect. First, they claimed, the criteria for becoming a GI in Europe were not as transparent and specific as the 1992 Regulation had intended them to be. In particular, definitions of eligible territory and justifications for it having a GI on the basis of the specificity of local production conditions were seen as vague and often specious. Secondly, New World actors criticized heavily the decision-making processes at local, national, and EU scales which led to a product being authorized as a GI. Considered too open to 'political' influences, and at worst corruption, opponents of an international register thus saw it as a recipe for unpredictable and arbitrary government. Thirdly, they argued that the EU's register was biased against GIs from third countries, a complaint moreover upheld by a WTO dispute settlement panel in 2006. Finally, and more generally, the New World critique of this mode of implementing the TRIPS agreement contained frequent stigmatizations of any administrative involvement in markets as 'bureaucracy' and excessive 'red tape' that only served to fetter the Freedom of the entrepreneur and the Equality of their opportunities.

As actors on both sides have continued to talk past each other, it comes as no surprise that as yet no international register of GIs has come about. Partly for this reason, representatives of the EU opened up a second front in their struggle to implement this part of the TRIPS agreement. Known as 'extension', political work undertaken in this direction has taken two forms. In its narrowest sense, 'extension' was first used to describe an attempt to transpose the higher level of protection of intellectual property given to wines and spirits by TRIPS's article 23 to the remainder of the world's GIs. Specifically, this article forbade any mention of a protected GI even if no attempt to mislead the consumer had been made, e.g. by labelling a wine *Australian Burgundy*. Arguing that this higher level of protection for a limited range of products was a one-off conceded to EU wine producers in the context of the 1994–95 negotiation, New World actors have adamantly refused to even consider it being extended to foods with GIs. Faced with this resistance, EU representatives have since worked to give an even wider meaning to 'extension' by opening the door to local craft-based products, such as textiles and ceramics, as potential candidates for globally protected GIs.[10] If part

[10] EU support for this mode of extension was re-legitimized by a lengthy study it funded, published in February 2013: Insight Consulting, 'Study on geographical indications for non-agricultural products in the internal market'.

of the reason for so doing stems from a belief that the values of Tradition and Security should be extended to the government of such products, this political work has also been inspired by the knowledge that doing so could generate new allies for the EU's value hierarchy and policy instruments amongst developing countries such as India or Thailand.

Indeed, this alliance-making and consolidating dimension of the global divide over GIs in itself merits careful analysis because, once again, it provides a window upon the politics of this issue area. Over the last fifteen years, the EU in general, and the French administration in particular, have actively sought to promote their approach to GIs in developing countries throughout the world. This has been done through networks, research funding, conferences, and seminars, on the one hand and, on the other, through aid to local projects in the form of 'technical assistance'. In the case of the former, the EU has given strong discursive and even financial backing to two networks which, according to an Australian diplomat, are 'the Ayatollahs of GIs'.[11] The first, the *Organisation for an International GI Network* (OriGIn) claims to represent more than 350 products from over forty countries. Representing twenty-seven regions and 400 GI products from the EU itself, the second is *l'Association des regions européennes avec produits d'origine* (AREPO). Often working in harness, these networks act as unofficial ambassadors for the EU over GIs. Meanwhile, national administrations themselves operate more discreetly through funding the training of local actors as part of EU or national development policies. For example, the French INAO spends more than 1 million euros a year on this policy.

Although much less visible than their counterparts from the EU, actors from the New World have not neglected the alliance-making dimension of political work. According to such actors themselves, across the New World there has been little need to continue meeting-up to bolster the ties initially made in the 1980s and early 1990s. In their view, their sharing of goals and values is so high that mutual understanding is spontaneous. From this strong base, certain New World actors have not surprisingly also sought to convince producers and governments in the developing world that their approach to intellectual property rights for foods is the most efficient and legitimate. This has taken the form not only of consultations between trade missions in Geneva, but also clauses within a myriad of bilateral free trade agreements signed by the United States or Australia with states in the developing world.

In summary, no middle ground has been found in the issue area of GIs. Indeed, there is little evidence of even a softening of positions. On the contrary, the discourse and practices of protagonists from both sides have hardened over the years with many witnesses to exchanges across this great

[11] Interview, Australian Trade Mission, Brussels, 2005.

divide highlighting their 'violence'.[12] Examining the values that lie at the heart of this politics clearly provides its deepest explanation. When Freedom, supported by Equality as equal opportunities, clashes so explicitly with Tradition and Security, sparks fly. More precisely, the New World position on GIs has been caused and consolidated by problematizations, instruments, and modes of legitimation which consistently champion the Freedom of individual producers, merchants, and consumers in the name of Equality of Opportunity. Crucially, Security is seen as an outcome of applying Freedom and Equality in the combination sketched out above, not as a value in itself. By contrast, the European position stems from a commitment to governing the industries concerned in the name of a vision of Security as a collective good that, in this domain at least, is best achieved by continuing to give some importance and legitimacy to the protection of Traditions. Power asymmetries abound within the industries concerned and obviously impact upon the way each value hierarchy is defined and defended. However, the interests of the firms and states concerned are frequently ambiguous and thus do not in themselves explain the depths and intensity of New World–EU disagreement. Ultimately, and precisely because of the strong coherence within each of the value hierarchies and Institutional Orders highlighted above, very profound political work would have to be accomplished in order to put out this particular global fire. Indeed, this work would have to be centred upon the values that shape the public problems of the food and drinks industry, its instruments, and how both are legitimated.

CONCLUSION: NO SUCH THING AS FREE TRADE

More generally, in this chapter we have seen that increased trade across national borders has neither led to an absence of regulation, nor to the end of politics. Over both pesticide usage and GIs, public and private actors throughout the world have undertaken problematization, instrumentation, and legitimization to introduce rules, norms, and conventions. Trade is therefore never 'free' because there are always institutions that structure and limit it. Moreover, because it produces externalities that have to be dealt with somehow by someone, trade is most definitely not free in an even wider sense. These institutions and policies are often justifiably seen as weakly constraining economic activity. But one can only assess, then explain the extent of their strength or weakness by fully grasping the deep political struggles that have been their cause. As neo-Gramscians in particular have highlighted, asymmetries of

[12] Interview, DG Trade official, Brussels, 2005.

power certainly abound at the global scale and must be fully taken into account. Nevertheless, uneven stocks of material resources do not speak for themselves. Instead, what has divided or brought together the actors mentioned in the foregoing pages has always been values and how they impact upon the very definition of interests, public problems, and policy instruments.

In the case of pesticides, a thus far dominant coalition of actors have worked politically to reconcile Freedom and Security by redefining the latter as the commercial viability of individual firms, whilst consistently downplaying the safety aspects of this value. In so doing, Equality in the guise of equal opportunities has played a supporting role for this Freedom–Security relationship, while more egalitarian concerns, such as the rights of farmworkers to have their health protected, have been silenced. Meanwhile, in recent years Tradition has come to be frequently evoked as a value which legitimizes the conservation of intensive agricultural practices, and this despite their relatively recent invention.

A similar relationship between Freedom, Security, Equality, and Tradition marks the New World's value-driven approach to geographical indications for food and drinks. Freedom and Security are reduced to being goals for individual producers, whilst Equality is only one of opportunity to participate in markets and Tradition is stigmatized as an argument for 'protectionism'. By contrast, the EU's framing of this issue area places a more collective definition of Security of both producers and their territories above Freedom, and this in the name of what are presented as longstanding Traditions of authenticity which, European representatives claim, can only be preserved through collective and public action. In turn this approach to Tradition has supported a more egalitarian conception of Equality that, in the name of the smaller farmer and time-honoured production methods, legitimizes collective and public intervention in industries and their markets.

More generally, as both these case studies highlight, struggles over the institutions that regulate economic activity at the global scale are not only about the raw power so frequently invoked as an explanation by liberal and neo-Marxist political economists alike. Of course, actors seek to defend their interests at this scale and some possess many more resources to do so than others. Similarly, as historical and sociological institutionalists rightly underline, institutions structure these unbalanced struggles. However, these institutions, as well as how each actor defines and defends their interests as regarding them, are nevertheless ultimately caused by the value hierarchies through which each protagonist interprets their respective industries and their place within them as a function of their value hierarchies. In the cases of controls on pesticides and the protection of geographical indications, some change has occurred over the last two decades, as well as a great deal of institutional reproduction. But all of these outcomes cannot be fully understood without tackling how actors have defined, prioritized, and synchronized their key values over time.

The analytical proposition that stems from these findings is that by conceptualizing globalization not as a cause in itself, but as an outcome generated by a plethora of private, collective, and public value-driven decisions, both research and practitioners can equip themselves much better to understand or participate in the types of worldwide politics this chapter has sought to reveal. In so doing, however, it is just as important to simultaneously take into account other scales of politics. As Robert Wolfe has so cogently argued (2005), international economic activity is not regulated solely 'in Geneva'. For this reason, the next three chapters on the European, national, and local scales supplement, rather than provide alternatives to, the analysis of the politics of global economic activity presented above.

4

Does the EU Make a Difference?

INTRODUCTION

Those of us old enough to remember the period between 1985 and 1995 when Jacques Delors was president of the European Commission, will probably recall his discourse that the EU is different to the rest of the world and, moreover, that being part of the EU makes a significant difference to its member states, public and private organizations, and citizens. Research which documents not only Delors' speeches, but also his acts within and without the Commission (Ross, 1995), highlights that representing the EU as different from the rest of the world entailed emphasizing its quest to combine a single market with the retention of high levels of social protection. Using the terms deployed in this book, the declared aim was to reconcile the values of Freedom with Equality, and this as a means of enhancing both the Security of European citizens and protecting their Traditions. According to those who have supported Delors' project for the EU, this ordering of values is not only logically and practicably reconcilable, it is precisely what makes the EU a well-defended rampart against 'globalization' by legitimizing a range of interventionist policies, in particular the 'economic policy' promised by many of the initial advocates of monetary union. Accompanying this view, has also been the claim that the actions of the EU make a difference to the global political economy because, by taking the moral high ground, it has become 'a normative power' (Manners, 2002), well equipped for leading global debates on issues ranging from the death penalty to climate change.

Not surprisingly, the first part of the Delorist narrative has been consistently attacked by neo-liberals who see Freedom as the only plausible primary value. Given the deepening of neo-liberalization at the scale of the EU that has taken place since the mid-1990s, however, critics from the left have been even more vociferous in dismissing as empty rhetoric the EU's commitments to a different, 'more social' Europe made during the Delors era (Salais, 2013). Meanwhile, the supporting argument that the EU is a normative power has been criticized by those who, instead, consider that at the European scale 'a retreat from liberal internationalism' has taken place (Youngs, 2010).

Rather than take sides in the normative debate outlined above, the aim of this chapter is to test the heuristic value of a value-centred approach to the EU's actual involvement in economic activity using research recently conducted on the pharmaceutical industry and competition policy.[1] For each of these case studies, this book's analytical framework is first applied to set out the extent to which the EU's government of an industry or a trans-industry regulation has changed as the dependent variable of our empirical studies, i.e. what is to be explained. From this base, my conceptualization of politics as values is then mobilized as the independent variable which explains how and why both these examples of EU government of economic activity have recently been challenged. Comparing pharmaceuticals to competition policy has also been chosen because despite such challenges, the government and politics of the former has essentially been reproduced whilst that of competition has undergone considerable change.

As will be highlighted throughout, focusing upon the role played by values during these examples of EU government, and thus their politics, provides a means of revealing key choices, stifled alternatives, and patterns of domination. In so doing, a further goal will be to go considerably beyond visions of the EU as inextricably and inevitably 'neo-liberal' and depoliticized. Although many actors at the centre of this scale of government clearly are neo-liberals, and just as many do indeed constantly seek to take the politics out of EU policies, blanket claims about these trends tell us nothing about the value confrontations that nevertheless occur at this scale. More fundamentally, such contentions overlook the contingency for thought and action that still remains at the EU scale. For both analytical and normative reasons, this politics simply must be researched then debated more directly and openly than social science, and European Studies in particular, has thus far been able to do.

4.1. EQUALITY FOR WHOM? GOVERNING PHARMACEUTICALS

Pharmaceuticals is often described in the media as a quintessentially 'global' industry because it features huge multinational firms (e.g. Pfizer, GlaxoSmithKline, Sanofi-Aventis: often known collectively as 'Big Pharma'), products marketed throughout the world and rules set multilaterally via the WTO, or within bilateral

[1] Much of the data presented here is drawn from a programme of research I co-led with Bernard Jullien from 2009 to 2012 which examined four industries (wine, pharmaceuticals, cars, and aquaculture) and four trans-industry regulations (competition, trade, sustainable development, and employment). Entitled '*le Gouvernement européen des industries*' (GEDI), this programme was funded by the French *Agence Nationale de la Recherche* and its results have been published in book form (Jullien & Smith, 2014). My thanks go to the fifteen members of the GEDI team for their respective input. However, the analysis presented here, and thus responsibility for it, are mine alone.

trade agreements. However, a closer look reveals that despite the Institutional Order of this industry becoming deeply multi-scalar, within which the EU takes on greater importance, many of its key practices continue to be structured nationally. This is particularly so around the issue of pricing, a political activity within which the values of Freedom (of Big Pharma) and Equality (of patients) are constantly in tension and frequently in conflict. How then, and in the name of what hierarchies of values, have EU-scale actors sought to regulate medicines differently from their opposite numbers either at national scales or in less regulated markets, notably that of the US (Carpenter, 2010)?[2]

4.1.1. An Institutional Order under Threat

Over the course of the twentieth century, the pharmaceutical industry both grew in size and became governed around a set of institutionalized practices. By the mid-1970s, these were stabilized throughout most OECD countries by legislation and policy instruments, but also by norms and expectations deeply rooted in societal, value-based constructions of problems and legitimacy.

Beginning with US Federal legislation in 1902, a *Sourcing IR* emerged as a means of defining legitimate medicines, encouraging constant improvement in their safety and, consequently, providing a durable, Security legitimized, structure for markets around which firms developed long-term investment, production, and commercial strategies. Specifically, the principal regulatory instrument of this IR entails the according (or not) of a 'Market Authorization' ostensibly upon the basis of each drug's safety. Indeed, in the name of security, an application procedure involving clinical trials, then therapeutic assessment by panels of medical experts, can take ten years or more. In European countries this instrument was only formalized and tightened in the 1960s and 1970s along lines first developed in the US and after a series of 'scandals' (notably concerning the drug Thalidomide). During the 1980s and early 1990s, most West European states then proceeded to distance the assessment and approval of medicines from ministers and ministries of health through the creation of agencies akin to the US's Food and Drug Agency. Moreover, in 1995 control at a national scale was partly replaced by the introduction of a European Medicines Agency (EMA) based in London (Permanaud, 2006; Hauray, 2006). Notwithstanding this 'agencization' and partial EU governmentalization, nor further sporadic therapeutic scandals (e.g. the French 'Mediator crisis' of 2010/11), over the last four decades the industry's Sourcing IR has

[2] This research has been carried out with Matthieu Montalban, Philippe Gorry, Marie-Claude Bélis-Bergouignan, and Mustafa Erdem Sakinç from the GREThA economics research centre in Bordeaux University, as well as with Cyril Benoit from the same university's Centre Émile Durkheim (see Bélis Bergouignan et al., 2014 for an overview of this work).

nevertheless remained remarkably stable. This is largely because the value of Security has been uncontested as the provider of value-based support for the Freedom of pharmaceutical companies to 'innovate' in order to provide cures and alleviate human suffering. Security has thus been defined in terms of both the safety of medicines and the durability of the firms that make them. However, the Freedom of pharmaceutical firms has not been heavily curtailed, in particular their capacity to make extremely high profits in the name of their 'returns on investment'.

Indeed, in this way pharmaceutical markets have also been politically shaped by this industry's *Commercial IR* and its two principal sets of regulatory instruments concerning patents and pricing. Since the late nineteenth century, firms have sought to protect and enhance their investment in research and development through an industry-specific system of Intellectual Property Rights (IPR). By formally reconciling Freedom and Security for 'innovative firms', the registering of a patent for a medicine forbids competitor firms from copying it for up to twenty years (including ten years after its initial marketing). Since 1995, the World Trade Organization (WTO) has consolidated a global scale of government for this IPR though its TRIPS agreement (on Trade related Intellectual Property and Services) (Abbott & Dukes, 2009). Over the last two decades, moreover, repeated attempts have been made to create a European patent. Nevertheless, in Europe the actual registering, policing, and judicial review of patents still occurs essentially on a national scale.

The continued significance of the national scale of control also predominates in the setting of medicine prices, and this chiefly because the pricing of prescription medicines is actually an administered process within which ministries of health and social insurance organizations play major roles. Crucially, it is here that two variants of the value of Equality are mobilized or opposed to defend contrasting approaches to the price of medicines:

i) equal opportunities discourse has supported the Freedom of pharmaceutical producers to produce while enjoying public support for their Security (seen as a synonym for commercial viability);
ii) meanwhile, egalitarianism in the name of patients seeking Security through equal access to medicines has also been mobilized in order to regulate pharmaceutical markets. Specifically, because the fixing of such prices overlaps with the setting of rates of reimbursement by insurance that is either public or private, and thus impacts directly upon national health costs and budgets, in each European state representatives of the civil service and insurance bodies intervene heavily in pricing.

More generally, in the name of Security—defined here in terms of durable supply rather than safety—many states have used pricing as a means of encouraging the development of indigenous production, and thus engaging in industrial policy. As will be shown below, over the 2000s both pharmaceutical patents and pricing have been increasingly challenged. Nevertheless, it is important to underline that the Commercial IR itself has remained particularly stable.

Of course, the development of pharmaceutical firms and their invention of medicines could not have occurred without capital. At least in Europe, initially a myriad of small, family-owned firms emerged, often alongside chemical producers in search of diversification (Chauveau, 1999). After World War II, many of these firms progressively merged or were taken over, frequently benefiting from financial injections by national governments (e.g. Rhône Poulenc in France, the precursor of today's Sanofi-Aventis). Since the 1990s, however, the *Financial IR* of this industry has been considerably affected by the liberalization of financial markets, a trans-industry regulation founded upon the value of Freedom and its handmaiden, liberal political economy (Froud et al., 2006). The most obvious impact of this regulation has been to encourage a rise in mergers or takeovers which cross national borders (e.g. GlaxoSmithKline in 2000). Another major effect of this 'financialization' (Montalban, 2008) has been to increase the power of large shareholders within the governance of these large corporations. Two highly evident consequences have been a change in the profile of their managers (with priority now given to senior personnel trained in finance) and an acceleration of quests for shorter-term investment to secure more rapid returns on investment. As with the increased prominence given to the value of Freedom, the liberalization of financial markets has certainly been encouraged by EU scale discourse, initiatives, and legislation (Posner, 2009). However, government at the European scale of this trans-industry government of capital is less evident. Indeed, as the case of pharmaceuticals testifies, the generation and mobilization of capital now depends upon a plethora of policy instruments set at varying scales and without consistent hierarchy between them.

By contrast, this industry's *Employment IR* continues to be governed essentially at the national scale. Most, if not all, producer state governments claim to be committed to retaining qualified personnel, particularly scientists, in order to maintain medical invention and clinical trials within their borders. Various instruments are used to address this 'problem' which include education and training policies, tax credits, subsidies for bio-tech start-ups, and hospital research grants. Meanwhile each country's general employment laws and social protection systems are also invoked either to attract trained personnel from abroad, or as an argument for more government interventions in order to compensate for the supposed comparative advantage enjoyed by lower-wage countries, particularly for clinical trials (e.g. Poland or the Ukraine). The value of Security is thus regularly invoked in the discourse of both firms and public authorities. However, and in contrast to other industries such as automobiles where massive 'relocation' has objectively occurred, and been fiercely but largely ineffectually resisted by trade unions, within the pharmaceutical industry the Employment IR is not where most political work has taken place. Instead, the prevalence of an essentially stable, national scale of governing employment issues in this industry is viewed as a given.

Table 4.1. The Institutional Order of the pharmaceutical industry in 2014

	'Problems'	Instruments	Legitimacy	Key values	Scale of govt.
Sourcing IR	Safety, therapeutic quality	Market Authorizations	'Evidence-based medicine'	Security	National & EU
Commercial IR	Effectiveness	Patents, prices, and rates of reimbursement	'Rewarding innovation'	Freedom & Security vs Equality	National (pricing) & global (IPR)
Financial IR	'Free' capitalization	Stock exchanges, R&D or 'innovation' policies	'Free movement of capital'	Freedom & Security	Global, partly EU, & national
Employment IR	Qualified labour	Labour law, social insurance, training policies	'Maintaining industrial capacity'	Freedom & Security	National

In summary, the Institutional Order (IO) of the pharmaceutical industry at the EU scale currently fits relatively seamlessly with its global and national ones (see Table 4.1). Its Sourcing and Employment IRs have remained remarkably stable and unchallenged since the 1970s, and this despite the addition of EU-scale government during this period. The industry's Finance IR experienced considerable upheaval in the 1990s, but again this did not challenge either the setting of problems and instruments, or the modes of legitimization typically deployed. Finally if, as will be highlighted below, this industry's Commercial IR has recently experienced deeper threats to its institutions, since the late 1990s the IO as a whole has been largely reproduced.

4.1.2. The Politics of Reproduction: Pricing, Evaluation, and 'National Sovereignty'

Since Market Authorizations based upon systematized clinical trials in the early 1970s were adopted in Europe and elsewhere, this industry has been dominated by large firms capable of:

- protecting each 'innovation' with a patent;
- developing a continuous 'pipeline' of new products undergoing trials then applying for Market Authorizations;

- marketing the product throughout the world so as to make the most of its protection from imitations;
- financing all these processes through recourse to stock markets;
- concentrating research on the production of 'blockbuster medicines' that generate sales of more than $1 billion per year;
- attracting the support of public health authorities (through high prices) and financiers (through investment).

As Pignarre (2003) recounts in fascinating detail, although this model took much of its legitimacy and support from its supposed dependence upon rigorous 'science' and 'original' medicinal discoveries, very quickly it routinized and came to actively discourage a great deal of fundamental research and radical innovation. However, given the institutionalized character of the IRs underlined above, and the resources developed by the organizations who by then had been built to defend this state of affairs (e.g. the ABPI in the UK, the LEEM in France, and the EFPIA in Brussels[3]), the domination of this 'blockbuster model' rolled on virtually unchallenged into the 2000s. Indeed, despite a noticeable slowdown in the development of new medicines, it is only over the past two decades that the blockbuster model has begun to be challenged from two angles: patents and pricing. The former has been researched thoroughly by others, particularly over challenges to the TRIPS agreement sparked by the availability of treatments for AIDS in Africa (e.g. Muzaka, 2011). Here the case of pricing will be concentrated upon instead firstly because it has suffered from relative scholarly neglect, but also because the pricing of medicines highlights particularly clearly the institutional reproduction of the pharmaceutical industry as a whole and the value conflicts that lie at its heart.

Far from being the direct consequence of the 'play of market forces' so dear to liberal political economy, since World War II the setting of pharmaceutical prices in Europe, as well as much of the rest of the world, has essentially been an administered process. More precisely, firms have requested prices for their products which differing configurations of civil servants and representatives of insurance organizations have analysed, debated, and reached compromises over. In France, for example, this process takes place in and around meetings of the *Comité économique des produits de santé* (CEPS) within which representatives of the ministries of health and industry, together with those of social and *'mutuelle'* insurance, possess institutionalized roles (Benoît & Nouguez, 2016). Since the late 1990s, most such actors have sought to reduce pharmaceutical prices in order to lower the cost of medicines in the name of Equality of service for patients. Specifically, the argument is that because drugs account

[3] ABPI = Association of the British Pharmaceutical Industry; LEEM = *Les Entreprises du Médicament*; EFPIA = European Federation of Pharmaceutical Industry Associations.

for at least a fifth of health care expenditure, savings made here could be transferred to other parts of the sector where inequalities are increasing (e.g. the availability of hospital beds). If the exception to this trend includes 'innovative' firms and representatives of ministries of industry (both sets of actors arguing instead for higher prices in the name of 'innovation', Freedom and Security as industrial durability), a general consensus has nevertheless been built across Europe that medicines should not only cost less, but that their cost-effectiveness should be examined more closely. However, despite this consensus and the emergence of a field of expertise (Health Technology Assessment: HTA) explicitly wedded to achieving its goals, national pricing systems in Europe remain inflationist and in line with the wish list of Big Pharma. Material determinist analyses in terms of 'the interests' of these firms abound (e.g. Permanaud, 2006; Mossialos et al., 2010). However, the story of institutional reproduction can only be fully told by highlighting the conflicts between values that lie at its centre.

The problematization that has dominated Europe's pharmaceutical industry since the early 1970s defines the goal of pricing as follows: prices of medicines must be set high enough to encourage 'innovation' by guaranteeing a sufficient return on investment, and thus the Security of pharmaceutical producers. When unpacked, this theory legitimizes nothing less than a form of active industrial policy which, far from being restricted to 'the usual suspects' like France, is present within all European states where pharmaceuticals continue to be produced. For example, a civil servant from the British Department of Health stressed in an interview that British policy in this industry is highly interventionist: 'we have an approach that is surprisingly Colbertist!' (Interview, London, December 2010). This problematization of pricing has nevertheless recently been challenged from two angles.

The first features representatives of health ministries and insurance organizations who have all sought to lower prices and, in general, to achieve this by introducing processes of evaluation between the moment a Market Authorization is awarded to a medicine and before its price is set. In some national cases (e.g. the UK), the problematization promoted here is one of only rewarding medicines that can prove their added value in terms of both therapeutic advances and 'value for money'. In others, notably that of France, problematization in this area is less formalized and, in any case, focused upon identifying therapeutic added-value rather than cost-effectiveness.

Alongside this first potential source of reproblematizing prices in the pharmaceutical industry, a second has emerged in the shape of a community of experts in HTA. Containing physicians, epidemiologists, health service managers, and economists, the HTA community first emerged as a consistent advocate of pricing reform as early as the mid-1970s (Benoît & Gorry, 2013). However, their coalition only institutionalized over the 1990s, notably around projects financed from the unlikely source of the EU, and encouraged by the

European Commission's DG SANCO (Health and consumers). HTA problematizations always strive towards the 'evidence-based decision-making' that has so frequently been sought in other sectors over the past two decades. Although differences of opinion and approach exist within the HTA movement, the reproblematization of medicines pricing proposed from this angle consists of beginning each pricing decision-making process with both an assessment of societal needs and a questioning of the supposed novelty of the medicine in question. In short, the values of Freedom and Security that Big Pharma and its supporters so frequently invoke as their inextricably linked sources of inspiration and legitimacy, have both been questioned from three angles.

Firstly critics, such as representatives of French '*mutuelle*' health insurance organizations, argue that the much-vaunted Freedom of large pharmaceutical companies is a myth given the support they have been given by public authorities since the 1950s. To cite a representative of *La Mutualité Française*:

> We also want a competitive industry, but one that makes real medicines. Frankly, their business model is in freefall...When you look at their expenditure and see they spend 23% on marketing and only 17% on research, public support for this is clearly unjustified (interview, Paris, November 2010).

Secondly, a range of actors now maintain that Security in this industry, i.e. both the safety of its products and its durability, could be achieved without recourse to policy instruments that lock in the rents of its biggest operators. For example, representatives of the European Generic Medicines Association consider their companies suffer from:

> an increasing regulatory burden in the name of safety. More specifically, we are concerned that when the Commission introduces more regulations, its impact assessments always underestimate the burden this places on companies, e.g. fees for pharmacovigilance controls (interview, Brussels, December 2012).

Finally, certain actors have sought to instate Equality as an egalitarian inspired value from which the health sector, and thence the pharmaceutical industry, should be reinstitutionalized. For example, a representative of the Consumers Association of the EU (BEUC) declared in interview:

> we think that one should strike a better balance between the protection of intellectual property rights and the right of patients to access affordable medicine...it is obvious that the patent system is not working to the benefit of consumers (Brussels, April 2010).

Despite the increasingly cohesive character of HTA alliances and their deepening linkages with ministerial and insurance representatives, a fundamental reframing of prices in this industry has yet to take place. As alluded to earlier, an initial explanation of this reproduced problematization lies in the support given to previous framings by ministries of industry and other allies of Big Pharma (patient associations, centrist and right wing MPs or MEPs, local politicians, etc.). Deeper explanation, however, lies in the institutionalized character of the 'high prices as reward for innovation' value hierarchy and theory of action that has dominated public problem-setting, together with the policy instruments and registers of legitimation they have fed into and upon. Throughout, the hierarchical role accorded to a particular relationship between Freedom and Security has protected institutionalized problems, instruments, and modes of legitimation.

Although decision-making arenas such as the French CEPS possess sets of criteria for grading the social worth of new medicines, even omnipresent actors within such bodies recognize that they do not know how to evaluate the cost-effectiveness of medicines with precision. Moreover, even if they did, such evaluations would not be supported by their own minister. For example, the director of the medicines 'bureau' within the French Ministry of Health declared in an interview that the legitimacy of cost-effectiveness is seen quite differently in his country than it is across the English Channel:

> What the English no longer put up with are experts who just say, 'well, we won't accept that price for that medicine because it's too expensive'. By contrast, what the French will not put up with is a ministry of health that says 'no, it's too expensive'. If we had good quality data and a minister who was capable of using it within a lively public debate, perhaps we could embed cost-effectiveness within the French public space (Paris, January 2012).

Instead, civil servants within this administration depend upon statistics on the existing usage of competing medicines and their costs, an opinion on the therapeutic value of the medicine provided by the agency *La Haute Autorité de la Santé* (HAS), data provided by the manufacturer during the Market Authorization procedure, and any statistics the Ministry of Industry cares to mobilize (often provided by pharmaceutical firms and/or the LEEM). In contrast, the UK possesses a price-setting procedure which has systematically used wider economic data and methods from economics in order to calculate the cost-effectiveness of many new medicines. Run within the National Institute for Clinical Excellence (NICE), these calculations have been formalized as a policy instrument, known as 'Quality life years' (QALYs), which has since become a central part of the British pricing system (Drummond, 2007; Drummond and Sorenson, 2009). Indeed, this instrument, NICE's involvement in pricing and, more generally mobilizations of Equality, have clearly modified the problematization of pricing in that country.

Moreover, the HTA movement in general, and the parts of it financed and encouraged by the European Commission in particular, has largely taken on board the instruments developed by NICE. However, their success rate in terms of encouraging other national decision-making systems to shift their policy instruments towards the British model has thus far been limited. As the French case testifies particularly clearly, the pricing of pharmaceuticals was initially institutionalized at a time when cost savings were not a priority and when doctors dominated decision-making. Since then, the medical profession may have lost its aura in some countries, but in order for its expertise to be replaced, competing sources of knowledge need to emerge. In the British case, this has largely been provided by the growing (sub) discipline of health economics, itself a by-product of changes to the UK's higher education system initiated in the 1980s. The latter encouraged 'applied' economics and systematic grant-seeking by its academics in particular. Indeed, divided internally between those whose primary values are Freedom, Security, and Equality as equal opportunities for producers (e.g. experts closest to the Conservative Party) and those who instead hierarchize a more egalitarian Equality (e.g. many of the academics who have worked as experts for NICE), British health economics itself can be seen as a policy instrument which has contributed significantly to reshaping how the problem of health care is now defined in the UK.

At least in countries like France, however, this phenomenon has not emerged to anything like the same extent. Indeed, 'a lack of expertise in health economics' is often cited by actors in ministries and insurance organizations as one of the reasons why, over the last twenty years, the instruments of French medicine pricing have been reproduced. A study is currently being undertaken on the groups of actors involved in this process in order to deepen and bolster this assertion with more evidence (Benoît, 2016). From this research, it is already clear that in France a network of HTA experts who give primacy to egalitarianism has not emerged. Instead, the field has been left open to domination by liberal economists for whom hierarchizing the value of Freedom, while subordinating to it that of Security and Equality (of opportunities), has been used to argue that only incremental change to existing policy instruments is necessary.

Representatives of certain professions in France have therefore not only supported the instrumentation of decision-making over issues like drug prices, more fundamentally still, they have also participated in legitimizing or delegitimizing both policy instruments and public problems. Meanwhile, the actors who, at least in the health sector, continue to hold the most resources for legitimizing policy reproduction or change nonetheless continue to be either national civil servants or politicians. Both these sets of actors readily brandish 'the general interest' and 'national sovereignty' as justifications for not changing pricing practices in line with what either the HTA movement or representatives of the European Commission advocate. What such terms cover up, however, are potent hierarchies between the values of Freedom, Security, and Equality which systematically favour the first two while emptying the latter of practical content.

Indeed, 'the general interest' is repeatedly used by such actors alongside arguments of the type 'our population would not accept X', and this in order to present each national case as singular and incomparable. Here, some national civil servants are aware that this discourse often puts them in a schizophrenic position: on the one hand they claim to be open to ideas from the rest of Europe about how to better regulate medicines whilst, on the other, they consider they alone know what their national public will accept. Indeed, this claim to monopolize knowledge over what constitutes 'the general interest' provides powerful support to politicians and civil servants who would rather not take what they perceive as the risk of institutional change. In so doing, it is public actors who have been particularly prominent in the harnessing of Security to the primacy of Freedom and equal opportunities for producers. Meanwhile, egalitarian Equality has been quietly ushered out of policy-making equations with their blessing.

Such positioning takes even more strength from modes of legitimation based upon 'national sovereignty' which, notably by invoking clauses on health in the EU's Lisbon Treaty adopted in 2009, consistently minimize the importance of exchanges over HTA at the scale of the EU while reiterating that only national administrations are authorized to structure and spend health budgets. Notwithstanding the effects that prices in one member state have upon those in others, nor the increased interest of the European Commission's DG ECFIN in this subject area because of the scope it holds for cutting public expenditure, pharmaceutical pricing continues to be legitimized as a '*régalien*' (regal) national competence and, thus, as belonging in the same category as defence and fiscal matters. Faced with this discourse, opponents of the status quo currently consider that they have little option than to refocus HTA development on the therapeutic (i.e. quality and safety) dimension of the evaluation of medicines. Having built legitimacy using the register of universal science, some forecast they will subsequently be in a better position to ensure that issues of cost and efficiency become part of what can be debated around the pricing of medicines. However, in doing so, these critics of the pharmaceutical industry's Institutional Order have unwittingly assisted in side-lining debate over the value of Equality. This in turn has enhanced the legitimacy of continuing to proclaim that combining Freedom, Security, and equal opportunities produces the most effective and just public policies and socio-economic outcomes.

In summary, the case of pharmaceutical pricing, and the modest role played at the EU-scale therein, illustrates once again the heuristic value of analysing the value-driven processes of problematization, instrumentation, and legitimization that constitute the politics which has caused the institutions and substantive outcomes outlined above. Rather than vaguely concluding that in today's Europe, regulation of this industry is 'a patchwork' of EU and national measures (Mossialos et al., 2010), my analysis has indicated not only how and why this industry's Commercial IR has been reproduced over the last fifteen to twenty years, it has also revealed why this IR has been so central to the enduring patterns of domination within the Institutional Order of pharmaceuticals as a whole. Although some shifts of scale have certainly occurred, to date the representatives of Big Pharma have successfully 'tamed' such displacements and, in most cases, bent them to their own ends. Far from the fatalism of material determinism, these case studies have underlined that in each instance contingency has existed. However, thus far Big Pharma have consistently won out during these moments of contingency, and this largely because public authorities at both national and European scales have not built themselves the capacity to contest, or even seriously question, institutionalized prisms, arguments, and symbolic action. From this respect, growing European integration has thus far only served to reinforce an Institutional Order within which the relationship between Security and Freedom has been further stabilized at the EU scale around the notion of equal opportunities for manufacturers. The consequence is that deep change in the name of more egalitarian takes on Equality has not even been seriously considered by most stakeholders. From this perspective, the EU has very clearly not made a difference. Instead, it has simply acted as a catalyst for the alignment of practice at the European scale with that which, since the 1970s, has dominated its national and global counterparts.

4.2. WHEN EQUALITY INTERVENES: GOVERNING COMPETITION

Today competition policy often makes the headlines when a high profile corporate merger has been blocked for creating an oligopoly (e.g. the proposed merger between Deutsche Börse and NYSE Euronext in 2012 rejected by both the European Commission and the US Department of Justice) or when the Commission prevents an EU member state from subsidizing one of its companies (e.g. Poland and the Gdynia airport in February 2014). But this has not always been the case by any means. In fact, given the prior strength of neo-mercantilist thinking, at least in Europe and in many other countries other than the US, competition policy has only really had significant and consistent effects upon economic activity since the late 1980s. Many 'power' and 'interest' theorists attribute this development to competition policy being a key tool in constructing the EU's single market and, more generally, to it becoming an instrument central to the 'neo-liberalization' of both politics and economic policy (Wigger and Nolke, 2007; Van Apeldoorn, Drahokoupil & Horn, 2008). However, these interpretations are misleading and fail to capture the full relationship between politics and economic activity. The first confuses a consequence with a cause by overlooking that the original single market programme actually contained no competition policy element (Armstrong & Bulmer, 1998). More significantly, conflating competition policy with neo-liberalism greatly underestimates the depth of political divisions within this ideological family, particularly between 'ordoliberals' and the 'Chicago School of law and economics'. These competing schools of neo-liberalism have developed precisely over their competing hierarchies of values used to evaluate legitimate economic activity in general, and inter-firm competition in particular. Specifically, the priority given by each to Freedom, Security, and Equality differs considerably.

Indeed, as I shall show, the full story of the changing fortunes of competition policy is both more complex and more revealing of the politics–economics nexus. It is more complex because it has entailed many more actors within and outside public authorities than are generally admitted, several scales of government, and intense debate over doctrine and policy instruments. It is also more revealing because the story of how competition policy has been applied in different polities, and above all in the name of differing value hierarchies, illuminates profound fault lines within the contemporary politics of the economic. Indeed, this is particularly so when competition policy is conceptualized as a trans-industry regulation which ostensibly applies to all industries and, at least in Europe, across three scales of government (EU, national, regional).

Building upon a vast literature in law, history, economics, and political science, together with my own research,[4] this section's analysis of competition policy will be structured in two parts. Having first set out the Institutional Order that has developed around this policy, hypotheses will then be presented regarding the value conflicts, and thus the politics, that has institutionalized this highly significant, yet not all-encompassing, trans-industry regulation.

4.2.1. The Institutional Order of Inter-firm Competition

Considerable public debate remains over how competition policy should be problematized, instrumented, and legitimized, debate soaked in value conflicts frequently criss-crossed by inter-scale tensions. From an analytical point of view, it is salutary to begin examining such debates and conflict via the

[4] Three sets of work have been undertaken on this issue area. The first concerned Leon Brittan's role as European commissioner for competition, then for trade from 1989 to 1998 (Joana & Smith, 2002). Secondly, research was conducted on the role of competition policy in the EU's government of industries in general, and that of pharmaceuticals and cars in particular (Montalban, Ramirez Perez & Smith, 2014). Finally, analysis of policy transfer between DG COMP and the French and British competition authorities has been tackled (Smith, 2013).

concept of an Institutional Order and the four Institutionalized Relationships (IRs) it helps unpack and compare.

Competition policy's *Finance IR*, has had a major impact upon the politics of governing economic activity through two channels. The first concerns the outlawing of aid to businesses from the public purse. In an age when public finances are framed as particularly tight and multinational corporations tend to dominate most industries, it is easy to forget that until the 1980s national governments throughout the world frequently gave large sums of money directly to certain companies either simply to keep them in business or, more strategically and in the name of Security, to bolster their 'national champion' in its efforts to compete both intra- and inter-nationally. Here analysis of the rise of neo-liberalism has considerable analytical purchase because it highlights the manner through which this ideology was used to reproblematize how governments ought to support 'their' industries by introducing new policy instruments (e.g. the encouragement of inward investment). Moreover, neo-liberalism has legitimized the 'independent' private firm whilst stigmatizing all public ones and, in particular, those that had taken the government's shilling but continued to fail ('lame ducks'). From steel, to coal, and the car industry, since the 1970s most governments throughout the world have progressively reduced their systematic granting of subsidies. Usages of competition policy have certainly driven forward this trend and institutionalized it to the extent that government intervention is now seen as 'abnormal' and 'unnatural'. Of course, as repeated examples entailing European car manufacturers illustrate, this does not mean that many attempts are not still made to derogate from state aid policy, nor that many such attempts are temporarily successful. Similarly, there is little doubt that states such as China continue to pump money into their largest firms despite having established a competition agency. Nonetheless, because the value of Equality (of opportunity between firms) has become uncontested in this issue area, how competition policy impacts upon the Finance IR of all industries is rarely as controversial as it was thirty years ago.

More controversy, however, still frequently surrounds the second aspect of regulating competition that concerns company finances: the control of monopolies and mergers. Whereas virtually all the experts and actors engaged in this issue area accept that large companies should never be allowed by government to 'abuse their dominant position' in particular markets or industries (for example by raising prices to the consumer or dropping them to eliminate competitors), much disagreement persists about what constitutes 'dominance' and 'abuse'. Indeed, far from being just technical terms with legally codified definitions and criteria, both 'dominance' and 'abuse' frequently split the neo-liberal camp around the hierarchies of values their application entails. For ordoliberals, Equality (of firms) is a value to which Freedom must remain subservient, thus any dominant position within a market is negative, whether it has actually been taken advantage of or not. Consequently, mergers or take-overs that create such positions of dominance should be prohibited outright by competition agencies. By contrast, for supporters of 'the Chicago School' to whom Freedom can and should frequently trump Equality, a dominant position does not in itself represent a threat to consumers. Indeed, they argue, the efficiency gained through this position is actually beneficial because it will lead to lower prices. In short, 'efficiency' trumps legal rectitude and equality of opportunity. The political fault line here is thus within the equal opportunities wing of Equality. The latter is thus an 'intervening value' because rather than support either Freedom or Security, Equality (of opportunities) generates a space of debate within which the Freedom–Security relationship is frequently mediated.

If, as we have just seen, competition policy impacts heavily upon the way businesses are financed, throughout much of the world its *Sourcing IR* has come to have similar effects upon the way such entities purchase their raw materials and transform them into products. Often called 'anti-trust' law, the official aim here is to outlaw 'restrictive practices' in general and those that produce cartels (i.e. collusions between firms) in particular, both seen as interrupting and biasing the 'free flow' of inter-firm competition. In many industries, sourcing takes place through a relatively straightforward relationship between suppliers and purchasers. For example, farmers who rear ducks sign and generally honour private contracts with the hatcheries that provide them with ducklings. In this instance, a practice judged to be restrictive would only occur if such contracting was seen as imposed or unfair. However, in many other industries, rules and norms exist regarding how and where a raw material has been produced which clearly infringe general competition law but have been authorized in the name of other values. Here a case in point concerns Parma Ham. As we saw through similar cases in chapter 3, producers of ham in this region in the mid-1990s decided that for a product to bear its name, its curing had to take place within a locality defined as 'Parma'. Codified in a product specification, this restriction was contested by certain operators on the grounds that it infringed competition law. However, the European Court of Justice upheld the right of Parma Ham producers to impose this restriction in the name of both 'enhancing regional development' (Security in the sense of sustainability) and 'protecting a Tradition'. Far from being exceptional, such arguments and restrictions are relatively commonplace. For example, just as all Rioja wine has to be bottled in that region, as we saw in chapter 2, so does all Scotch have to be matured and bottled in Scotland. What all these cases highlight once again is that the actual implementation of competition policy is never value-free and thus a-political. Rather its application within specific industries and markets always entails hierarchizing values through the political work of argument and alliance-making.

In so doing, many of the arguments made over product sourcing spill over into competition policy's *Commercial IR* which concerns how goods and services are distributed and sold. Once again, in many industries the relationship between sellers and consumers can be relatively straightforward. So long as all sellers have access to the market, consumers simply choose between competing products, thereby entering into a more or less implicit contract with the respective producer. A first contentious issue may, however, arise whenever the distribution of a good or service is dominated by large operators such as supermarket chains. As is testified in the case of basic farm produce such as milk, intermediaries may make huge profits by significantly reducing prices to farmers whilst increasing them to consumers. More fundamentally still, inter-firm competition may be affected by a range of norms that restrict the access of goods and products to markets in the name of a variety of values. Here one of the classic examples concerns patents for medicines. As we saw earlier, since at least the 1970s patents have been consistently used by pharmaceutical firms not only to protect their respective inventions, but also to ensure that during each period of legal protection they can achieve high returns on the investments which, they argue, were made in order to generate such 'scientific progress'. In short, for such actors, patents are instruments that respond to the problem of 'rewarding innovation' in the name of Security, whilst 'innovation' itself is seen as their primary legitimizing resource because it concretizes a relationship between this conception of Security and Freedom. If, for many years, patents were indeed seen by competition authorities as an acceptable restrictive practice, in 2009 this representation of the just was put to the test when the European Commission's DG COMP launched a 'sector inquiry' into how market entry was actually occurring within this industry. As explained fully elsewhere (Montalban, Ramirez Perez & Smith, 2014), officials in DG COMP suspected large pharmaceutical companies of abusing patent law in order to prevent generic products entering the market and effectively lowering prices (thus locking-in a hierarchy of Security over Freedom). Although patents as a property right were ultimately relegitimized as acceptable restrictive practices by this sector inquiry, the importance that had once automatically been accorded to scientific innovation has nevertheless been destabilized and increasingly questioned. Specifically, the hierarchy between Security and Freedom has been opened up to debate. In so doing, this case illustrates once again how markets never regulate themselves. On the contrary, their regulation is constantly dependent upon the value-based choices made by those able to participate in their institutional ordering.

Finally, although the *Employment IR* is not directly affected by competition policy, it certainly has been, indirectly. On the one hand, as the case of Parma Ham again illustrates, saving or creating jobs in specific regions (collective Security) is often used as an argument to obtain derogations from competition policy. On the other hand, and more generally, the underlying problematization

Table 4.2. Competition policy doctrines and economic activity

	Neo-mercantilism	Ordoliberalism	Chicago School
Finance IR	Monopolies	No monopolies	Efficient monopolies
Sourcing IR	Cartels	No cartels	Efficient cartels
Commercial IR	Price fixing	Free pricing	Free pricing
Employment IR	Interventionist	*Laissez faire*	*Laissez faire*
Dominant value	Security	Security	Freedom

of economic activity that pervades competition policy is one of businesses only being durably viable when they are 'competitive', i.e. not dependent upon government subsidies, an illicit dominant position or set of restrictive practices. Implicitly, as the case of coal in the United Kingdom in the 1980s illustrates, the view taken here is that it is preferable that 'uncompetitive' businesses go to the wall so that their ex-employees seek out viable employers and industries. Because 'viability' is often a heatedly contested concept, however, this then begs further questions. In the case of British coal, for example, trade unions accused employers and the UK government of deliberately exaggerating costs of production and reducing forecasts of the amount of coal that could still be viably mined.

More fundamentally still, the controversies that frequently still break out over competition policy highlight just how disarmed proponents of problems and instruments designed explicitly to save employment currently are compared to their neo-liberal opponents. Indeed, as stated earlier and as Table 4.2 highlights, if, arguing from the value of Freedom, the latter are regularly divided over interpreting competition policy, meanwhile social democratic thought has singularly failed to produce a sustained alternative viewpoint which, through mobilizing a collective connotation of Security backed with an egalitarian take on Equality, does not fall back upon the easily discreditable principles of neo-mercantilism.

This situation has emerged largely because social democrats in Europe have not unpacked and reproblematized the value of Equality within this issue area. Instead, neo-liberals have been allowed to kidnap Equality and reduce its meaning to the equal opportunity of firms to compete within markets. More fundamentally, the very notion of equal opportunities has rarely been examined in ways that would make its content a subject of open public debate. There is little doubt that some particularities of the EU as a polity have contributed to this situation. For example, the European Parliament has been set up in such a way that debate is skewed towards the detailed scrutiny of legislative proposals rather than explicitly ideological debate (and indeed this assembly has very little legal competence in the issue area of competition). Moreover, the media continues to view the EU as a whole through the lens of national interest rather than one of value-driven conflict (Picard, 2015). In this sense then, the EU has made a difference to the politics of inter-firm competition. More fundamentally still, however, this politics is more deeply structured by shifts within social democratic thought and action that extend way beyond what gets decided 'in Brussels'.

4.2.2. A Politics where Values Are Masked by Expertise and Sovereignty

Indeed, this section begins to explore more fully two major reasons why Table 4.2 does not feature a column on left wing or even social democratic competition policy doctrine and why, consequently, the range of politics around competition policy is essentially limited to debates within neo-liberalism. The first is that a set of policy recipes for regulating inter-firm competition based on left of centre values has rarely been brought together and given a voice. This is partly because left-leaning economists and other social scientists have neglected this policy area. More deeply, however, the non-translation of socio-democratic principles into problematizations of competition policy, instruments, and legitimating discourse has been obstructed by a narrowing of what constitutes 'expertise' in this issue area, together with the primary values of its dominant experts. The second explanation of the absence of pluralism in this domain concerns the relationship between national and EU scales of government. More specifically, the hypothesis examined here is that by conflating the value of Tradition with national sovereignty, a range of actors have implicitly removed contingency from debates over *which* competition policy economic activity needs within contemporary capitalism.

4.2.2.1. The Autonomization of Experts and the Silencing of Values

Political science and sociology have consistently shown the extent to which 'experts' with specialized knowledge have come to play powerful roles in policy-making throughout the world and across virtually all issue areas. Indeed, the most interesting work on this question traces this influence back to at least the end of the nineteenth century when Western state bureaucracies began to become multifaceted organizations (Saint-Martin, 2000). Ever since, just who constitutes an 'expert' has become a deeply political question because far from stemming simply from formal qualifications or 'the complexity' of an issue and its instrumentation, the legitimization of their knowledge is the product of work to build the reputations of, and thus attach status to, both individuals and their professions (Robert, 2010; Roger 2010). Indeed, the vague nature of the very term 'expertise' in fact highlights the fluctuating and contingent nature of just who is qualified as an 'expert' and by whom. In some instances, the term is restricted to bureaucrats employed by public authorities (e.g. the civil servants in DG COMP). In others, it is instead reserved for external advisers who work within academia, for consultancy firms or even for interest groups. From the point of view of research, therefore, identifying who has been legitimized as an expert in a given policy field, as well as the resources they hold or that are attributed to them, and above all their hierarchies of values, constitutes an essential first step. The second is to discover to what extent these experts have developed autonomy for themselves and, in particular, a freedom from oversight by actors charged with protecting the public interest (notably parliamentarians).

In the field of competition policy, the overwhelming majority of experts have been trained in, and take much of their legitimacy from, the academic disciplines of law and economics. Moreover, the dominance of both is also reflected in the career trajectories of officials who work within competition regulatory agencies. Indeed, many of the latter have moved seamlessly between such bodies and these parts of academia, thereby consolidating cognitive links with relational ones. Meanwhile, law and economics dominate the wide range of journals (e.g. *World Competition*) which both facilitate communication across an international 'community' of competition policy experts, while encouraging a standardized problematization of its thought and action. Indeed, research has strongly suggested that competition policy is considerably affected by transnational networks and an 'epistemic community' of scholars, bureaucrats, and even judges (Van Waarden & Drahos, 2002; Wigger, 2008). Moreover, administrations such as the European Commission have further encouraged this trend through and around the establishment of a European Competition Network which, since 2004, has imposed highly structured 'co-operation' upon competition policy agencies and their experts across the EU.

Notwithstanding these pressures to transnationalize the doctrines and practices of competition policy, important differences remain regarding how experts trained in law or economics are mobilized within each polity. In France, for example, law continues to be the dominant source of expertise drawn upon by the *Autorité de la Concurrence* and its predecessor the *Conseil de la Concurrence*. In the field of anti-trust, this organization made 335 decisions between 1999 and 2011, but economic analysis was evoked in only 24 of them (Smith, 2013: 428). Moreover, if it has possessed a Chief Economist complete with dedicated staff since 2007, these actors are in a tiny minority when compared to the legally-trained officials which surround them. By contrast, in England both the Office of Fair Trading and the Competition Commission regularly use economic analysis to problematize, instrument, and legitimize their decisions (e.g. over restrictive practices the former did so to the tune of 19 out of 67 decisions between 2001 and 2011, whilst the latter did in 23 out of 25 of its reports: Smith, 2013: 434–5). In short, the tension between law and economics plays out differently in each polity.

This said, it is important not to see this law–economics tension as simply an opposition between users of legal texts or statistics. Firstly, skilful representatives of either discipline repeatedly deploy both. Secondly, as we saw earlier in this chapter, the key division which orientates doctrine and practice lies in a value-driven cleavage between ordoliberals and proponents of 'the Chicago School of law and economics'. For the former, law is certainly the field of expertise its supporters have traditionally and most spontaneously drawn upon. But ordoliberalism also has its economists who, in the name of placing Equality of opportunity above Freedom, use arguments from their own discipline to problematize, instrument, and legitimize its policy recipes. Conversely if, as its full name underlines, the Chicago School has always sought to combine arguments from both disciplines, it is vital to grasp the key role played by lawyers, and even supreme court judges (e.g. Richard Posner or Robert Bork), within its development. It is certainly true that just as today economics has a higher public profile than law in most polities, economists are the most well-known promoters of Chicago School interpretations of competition policy. Ultimately, however, it is the combination of law and economics, mobilized around a hierarchy of values wherein Freedom trumps Security in the name of equal opportunities, that deserves the most analytical and public attention.

Indeed, what research could usefully be doing, but to my knowledge rarely does, is to examine the activity of key competition regulators, such as DG COMP, in order to identify precisely how doctrinal debates are influenced by broader discussions within and between law and economics. However, such research should not only focus upon the highly detailed and technical arguments made. In so doing, attention also needs to be devoted to the values that reside in the assumptions and judgements that drive and derive from these arguments. This politics of competition policy has yet to get the academic attention it deserves, and this because the disciplines best equipped to do so—political science and sociology—have largely ignored it. Small wonder then that when public authorities such as parliamentary committees turn their hand to examining competition policy, they too overlook the value-based choices that are constantly being made in its name and which merit much more public and political deliberation. Indeed, it is only through opening competition policy up to discussion of the politics of competition that there is any chance that the ordoliberal vs. Chicago School opposition might one day be destabilized by the emergence of another set of doctrines.

4.2.2.2. When Tradition is Reduced to National Sovereignty

Opening up the sources of expertise on competition policy, and therefore the plurality of policy options under consideration, could also help to unblock a second important aspect of competition policy which concerns its possible introduction at a global scale. An EU-led initiative to move in this direction emerged in the early 1990s but has since run into virulent opposition which essentially uses the card of 'national sovereignty'. There are of course many legitimate concerns about the internationalization of competition policy, particularly within the developing world. However, opposition in the name of national sovereignty has tended to polarize debates around a pro- vs. anti-competition policy axis, whilst ignoring the range of institutions which currently indirectly structure transnational inter-firm competition. The alternative viewpoint presented here is that be they explicit or implicit, competition policies exist throughout the world and therefore have a deep impact upon the relationships between firms, nations, and societies. Invoking national sovereignty as the sole expression of the value of Tradition obstructs thinking about what is in practice the overlapping regulation of finance, production, trade, and competition. In doing so, this failure to problematize competition transnationally facilitates nefarious economic practices, misleads public decision-makers and perpetuates the inequities generated by the status quo.

Academics first began to problematize international competition law in the early 1990s. Specifically, a professor of law at the Max Planck Institute at Munich University, Wolfgang Fikentscher, headed a 'Munich Group' that worked up its proposal into a draft international antitrust code presented to the director of the GATT in 1993. In parallel to this intellectual enterprise the European Commissioner for competition (1989–92) then for trade (1993–99), Sir Leon Brittan, spearheaded an initiative, eventually backed by the Commission, then the EU as a whole, to transpose many of the instruments developed to regulate competition within the EU into propositions for an extension of the WTO's mandate. More precisely, Brittan, a lawyer and renowned neo-liberal attracted to Chicago School thinking, considered that the problematization and instrumentation of competition policy that had proved so successful in relaunching DG COMP's authority, could and should be used to tackle the 'beyond the border' issues he considered were continuing to obstruct and harm free trade (Joana & Smith, 2002). Within the Commission a working group on the issue was created which published its report in December 1995. A year later, Brittan himself then presented formal EU proposals for adding competition policy to the mandate of the WTO at the latter's ministerial meeting in Singapore. In a word, at that stage the EU clearly sought to make a major difference to world trade policy.

The immediate upshot of the proposals made in Singapore was the creation of a WTO working group on the interaction between trade and competition policy which, from 1998 to 2001, then published a series of reports. These, together with work conducted in parallel by staff of the United Nations Conference on Trade and Development (UNCTAD), essentially sided with the EU proposal and saw it as positive for developing states in particular. The reports then fed into draft proposals for a Multilateral Agreement on

Competition Policy (MAC) that began to circulate amongst WTO member countries. The EU delegation immediately backed this proposal and were supported by the representatives of Japan, South Korea, and Canada. More generally, widespread consensus then existed that a MAC would be particularly useful in improving transparency over contentious competition cases, outlawing non-discrimination between firms on the basis of nationality and prohibiting cartels. However, these consensual elements were quickly drowned out by two series of opponents.

The first were dominant actors within competition regulation in the US. Not only did they see the MAC as unworkable in practice and liable to just create 'bureaucracy' (a common charge made against international institutions by US representatives, see chapter 3). More deeply still, the very logic of competition policy being proposed was denounced as being at odds with competition regulation in their own country. As Fox underlines, US antitrust policy itself is essentially 'defensive' since its aim is 'to prevent obstructive acts that harm consumers but not to create environments or duties that might help them' (2009: 153). In other words, as theorized by the Chicago School of law and economics, US competition policy is clearly dominated by the value of Freedom whereas that of the EU and many of its member states tempers this commitment with another to Security and Equality (of opportunities to compete). Given that the main aim of the MAC was to create an 'environment' within which the value of Security would have a role, US representatives were at best sceptical as to the prospect of achieving global competition regulation (Fox, 2009).

However, US ambivalence about the MAC quickly paled into insignificance when compared to a second and more fundamental type of opposition led by developing countries. From this angle, three criticisms of the EU-backed proposal were made.

Firstly, representatives of developing states criticized the draft proposal as being excessively focused upon the WTO's traditional mandate of guaranteeing market access. Rather than problematizing the MAC as a means of protecting international competition in trans-border markets, and thus legitimizing competition as an international public good (Drexl, 2004), the draft was seen as favouring the large companies of the global North. More fundamentally, as Bhattacharjea reveals (2006: 29), Freedom as a value was specifically downplayed: 'Several developing countries claimed that development required giving greater priority to policy objectives other than promotion of competition'.

Secondly, many representatives of developing states were concerned that during its implementation the MAC would give even greater powers to the WTO's dispute settlement procedure, thereby undermining national competition regulators and courts. In so doing, they were particularly concerned that an overly rigid codification of the very principles of competition policy would be enshrined at a global scale, thus preventing developing states from engaging in any form of industrial policy. To quote Bhattacharjea again, 'some of them did not want to surrender the "policy space" for implementing industrial policies discriminating in favour of domestic firms and promoting "national champions"' (2006: 29). In a nutshell, competition policy was delegitimized as a profound threat to national sovereignty.

Led by delegations such as India's, but also fuelled by many NGOs based in the global north, opposition to the MAC came to a head in September 2003, just before the WTO's Ministerial meeting in Cancun. Given that WTO decision-making is rarely single issue focused, opponents of the MAC were able to take further strength from other politicized North–South conflicts of that period, in particular over the trading of cotton. Ultimately, such actors insisted that, 'competition policy is different from any other trade topic. It relates to the very philosophy of world trade law and, therefore, is of a quasi-constitutional character' (Drexl, 2004: 456).

It therefore came as little surprise when, in July 2004, the MAC proposal was formally dropped by the WTO's General Council. Ever since, official emphasis has instead been placed upon 'improving' national competition regulators and the signature of bilateral agreements (e.g. within trade agreements signed by the EU and individual developing states). More fundamentally, however, the global politics of competition regulation has been relaunched as a domain for experts in general and the International Competition Network (ICN) in particular. Founded in 2001, largely at the initiative of the International Bar Association backed by the US government, the ICN brings together national competition regulatory agencies. Structured around working groups, an annual conference and a range of publications, this network now constitutes the main forum within which 'best practice' is defined and from which 'technical assistance' is given to developing countries (Fox, 2009). In this way, and most obviously, the urgency and politicization that marked the period 1996–2003 has been taken out of this issue area.

Crucially, this depoliticization has been facilitated and legitimized by evoking sovereignty as a value which, despite appearances to the contrary, actually stifles debate about how it should be hierarchized as regards genuine values such as Freedom, Security, and Equality. Indeed, by naturalizing existing nation-states through discourses and practices of 'banal nationalism' (Billig, 1995), and thus reducing the value of Tradition to national sovereignty, debate about the very principles behind competing visions of competition policy has become virtually impossible.

On this deep level, what has also almost disappeared is debate about the values, principles, and application of competition policy within arenas whose legitimization is not as experts, but as guardians of 'the general interest'. Of course, scrutiny of regulators who are ostensibly independent is not without its own problems. As Kovacic's work (1982) on the impact of the US Congress on the Federal Trade Commission underlines, legislatures and legislative committees can also be deeply biased over competition policy. But such scrutiny is not even attempted in the EU where the European Parliament has virtually no say over the orientation and application of competition policy. Indeed, as with other areas of European economic life such as central banking, in the name of 'independence' competition policy has repeatedly been distanced from value-driven debate. As Vauchez underlines, however, this absolutely does not signify that 'independent' agencies are not political. As we have seen above, value-driven debates and conflicts abound in and around the issue areas invested in by such organizations. What this means is that researchers and actors alike all need to realize that having been brought up under the ideals of parliamentary democracy, we are 'intellectually under-equipped' to grasp and engage with a politics within which such agencies are now centrally important (2014: 10).

CONCLUSION

As Vauchez also underlines more generally in his analysis of how the EU has evolved over the last two decades (2014: 35), the social sciences, practitioners, and indeed the general public all need to *retrain* our way of looking at politics, and its role in economic activity in particular. The constructivist and institutionalist approach explored once again in this chapter provides a means of doing so by rejecting images and implicit ontologies of the economic as 'messy', 'anarchic', and outside politics. On the contrary, as this chapter's examples from the worlds of medicines and inter-firm competition have sought to highlight, this approach firstly guides research to discovering the institutions and other socio-political constructions which structure and shape economic activity. Secondly, it encourages identification of the political work, itself rooted in frictions over values which have been their cause.

To underline just one of the lessons that comparing the governing of pharmaceuticals and competition from this angle reveals, national sovereignty has clearly been conflated with the value of Traditions in both cases. For pharmaceuticals, this association has been used to legitimize the reproduction of this industry's domination by large multinational companies, whereas for competition policy sovereignty has repeatedly been wheeled out to justify an absence of international regulation which, paradoxically, could become a means of reining-in the power of large corporations. Crucially, rather than either of these developments having been inevitable or 'natural', this chapter has shown how these problematizations, instrumentations, and legitimization of social reality have come about and institutionalized at scales that include the EU, but also the global and the national.

These points take on particular importance when one seeks to discover whether the EU makes a difference to the politics of economic activity. Research by neo-Gramscians and historical or sociological institutionalists is right to highlight that, at least since the mid-1990s, a discourse that the EU possesses a 'social' approach to economic policy has become increasingly hollow. Similarly, researchers using these approaches underline that there is less and less evidence that the EU is either a rampart against the effects of liberalizing world trade or a leader in the making of global institutions and organizations. This said, by focusing upon the value-driven decisions made over industries such as pharmaceuticals or policies concerning competition, those who have been at the heart of these processes can be identified with greater precision. Specifically, by targeting analysis upon the relationship between Freedom, Security, Equality, and Tradition that develops during the making of EU policies and their defence in global and national fora, one can identify more precisely when distinctive standpoints for the EU have been developed and by whom. Indirect evidence from a large number of research projects focused upon a range of EU policies, suggests that the EU has decreased its production of positions that are clearly different from those developed by member states or other world powers such as the US (e.g. Youngs, 2010). In reading this literature, Freedom appears to be increasingly trumping the other three values at this scale. Only new research calibrated upon values within policymaking could produce more compelling evidence on this point.

Notwithstanding the current lack of a strong evidence base on values in policy-making, the analysis presented in this chapter nevertheless highlights that one can and should stress that there has been nothing inevitable about the trends in value prioritization presented above, nor about them continuing in the future. Politics as the mobilization of values has produced the EU of today, just as recasting this politics could redirect the European government of economic activity towards new goals in the years to come. Distinguished scholars such as Robert Salais (2013) have gone so far as to consider that since the 1950s the European project has been hijacked (his word is 'raped') by neo-liberals to such an extent that 'social Europe' has all but disappeared (Denord & Schwarz, 2009). There is a great deal of truth in this reading of history and of the value hierarchies that have dominated it. However, this does not mean that the whole idea of co-operating politically to regulate the economic at a European scale is inevitably neo-liberal. Even Colin Crouch, a staunch critic of neoliberalism who has called for a relaunching of 'assertive social democracy' (2013), now concludes that 'we need the EU but cannot trust it in its present form' (2015: 67). Indeed, in the conclusion to his much cited book on the distribution of wealth in the contemporary western world, Thomas Piketty also argues strongly that 'only regional political integration can lead to the effective regulation of the globalized patrimonial capitalism of the twenty-first century' (2014: 573).

For such recasting of the EU to come about, major changes would have to be made not only in how this particular international region is designed as a scale of decision-making, but also in the very way it is thought about as a space for politics. Despite the unlikelihood of such changes taking place in the short term, it is analytically inaccurate and normatively stifling to rule out the possibility of such change happening over a longer period of time.

5

What's Left for the State?

INTRODUCTION

From the beginnings of political economy, the nation-state has been at the centre of research and academic debate. Indeed, particularly in Western Europe and North America, such research grew alongside the development of welfare states, national education systems, and, more generally, the greater public interventionism which marked the period 1880–1970. Since that period, however, and despite overall budgets for public expenditure remaining high, the practices of the interventionist state have tended strongly to be analysed from three angles.[1]

Firstly, and most obviously, they have been frontally attacked by neo-liberal practitioners, 'experts', and academics for being wasteful and inefficient. Indeed, frequently armed with the New Institutionalist Economics presented in chapter 1, the aim of this critique has been to make the state smaller and thereby 'unleash' the world of business from the excessive regulation from which it is deemed to be suffering.

Firmly opposed to this neo-liberal narrative, a second critique of the contemporary state concerns how it has been weakened by developments within capitalism that have not been adequately addressed by states themselves. In particular, authors such as Wolfgang Streeck (2014a & b), together with Regulationist (Boyer, 2015) and Keynesian economists (Stiglitz, 2012), highlight the 'fiscal crisis' experienced by most European states due to the refusal of governments to raise revenues derived from direct taxes in particular. In similar vein, Colin Crouch (2004 & 2011) has denounced the emptying of the state of its capacity and legitimacy to act in an era of 'financial capitalism', a mode of accumulation within which, he claims, large multinational corporations have become virtually uncontrollable.

Finally, a third set of literature considers that although more actors are now engaged in the 'governance' of western societies than in the period of interventionist state expansion (Pinson, 2015), in many cases states have actually

[1] A considerable part of the reflection developed here stems from work undertaken recently with Matthieu Ansaloni. In thanking him for this contribution, I nevertheless underline that what is presented in this chapter is my responsibility alone.

been strengthened by adopting modes of operating based upon law and norms. This has occurred through a wide range of public policies switching to problematizations and instrumentations within which the state sets the normative framework for economic activity, but contributes to it financially much less than hitherto (Le Galès & Scott, 2008). Frequently citing the case of the UK, such authors consider that 'a bureaucratic revolution' has revamped the powers of the state by encouraging more competition between socio-economic actors through state-imposed 'market mechanisms', notably indicators, audits, and inspections.

While many of the claims made in this literature will be addressed in this chapter, two of its confusing aspects need addressing from the outset. Firstly, publications within this debate often conflate all public authority with the state, whereas this term will be used here to denote only public bodies and their actions located and set at the national scale. Secondly, and more problematically, too much of this literature is biased from the outset by normative assumptions and claims. Although understanding the utopias of neo-liberals, social democrats or neo-Marxists is clearly important, here I seek instead empirically-grounded answers to the question of how politics at the national scale, and state activity in particular, still affects economic activity.

This line of questioning on the state within a national scale of politics will be pursued in two parts. Centred upon the example of state support for electric vehicles as a response to environmental and economic 'crises', the first of these developments examines whether public authorities at the national scale, and those of France in particular, still engage in 'economic patriotism'. More precisely, by defining this term with Clift and Woll (2012: 308) as 'a prism to investigate how actors negotiate compromises between abstract economic objectives and territorially bound political objectives', our aim is to tease out the value judgements and prioritizations which have caused and shaped state intervention in the production and commercialization of the goods and services produced by the car industry. As will be shown, the key tension revealed is between Security (of sales and employment) and Freedom (of carmakers, but also of their imagined drivers). Mediated around particular definitions of Equality, this tension has left conceptions of Security in terms of environmental protection firmly on the side-lines.

The second part of this chapter then tackles the question of what actors at the national scale still do to protect and develop employment within their respective frontiers. Although most aspects of welfare state provision have been castigated by neo-liberal critics, employment policies which actively seek to put people to work have generally been welcomed by actors from all political parties as important and legitimate levers for reshaping economic activity. Indeed, at least in the EU, employment policy has been jealously retained as a member state prerogative (Jullien & Smith, 2014). Given this strong level of legitimacy, the puzzle that remains is why actors at the national scale, and state representatives in particular, experience such difficulty in orientating workers into the sectors said to contain the best prospects for growth and employment. Illustrated by the contrasting cases of aquaculture in Norway and wine in France, the key value tension examined here is between Equality (of workers) and Freedom (of employers), a tension mediated around distinctly biased conceptions of Security.

Overall, this chapter thus seeks to contribute to analysis of the role of politics in economic activity by critically examining not just the 'authority' of states, but above all their capacity to make and implement public policies while infusing them with normative justification and legitimacy (Le Galès, 2014: 17; Muller, 2015).

5.1. EQUALITY RUN OVER BY FREEDOM AND SECURITY: ELECTRIC VEHICLES

At least in Europe and the US, the car industry has been associated with states for more than a century. During this period, automobiles clearly became central to transportation practices and, more fundamentally still, the organization and regulation of geographical and social space. In so doing, the Freedom of carmakers to produce relatively unregulated cars, as well as that of car-drivers to use them as they see fit, has been consistently defended in terms of values and thus politics (Gusfield, 1981). Just as importantly, however, this industry has long been associated with 'industrial' production and thence the generation not only of private and national wealth for owners of capital, but also of substantial numbers of jobs. Put succinctly, and as the massive public subsidies given to carmakers since the 1970s testify, the value of Security, defined as security of employment as much as of transportation and production, has long been mobilized to legitimize production in this industry. Moreover, alongside a progressive concentration of the industry which, paradoxically, has entailed many mergers and joint ventures that cross national frontiers, makes of car continue to be associated with one particular state: Renault with France, Volkswagen with Germany, Volvo with Sweden, etc. In this way the symbolism of each nation-state has permeated practices of finance, production, marketing, and consumption, and vice versa. Moreover, specific definitions of the values of Freedom and Security, as well as their mutually sustaining relationship, have been institutionalized throughout much of the world.

Notwithstanding the highly value-laden political significance attached to the car industry and the very usage of automobiles, the 1970s also saw the beginnings of a questioning of its dominant product: cars with internal combustion engines. Sparked by the first 'oil crisis', but also by increasing concerns over the environmental impacts of vehicles fuelled by hydrocarbons, for a short period carmakers and governments began to invest in alternative engines, and in electric vehicles in particular (Callon, 1979). However, when oil prices dropped, these initiatives quickly lost both commercial and public support. Indeed, due to reformulated concerns over 'climate change', energy provision in general, then the global financial crisis of 2007–08, it is only over the last decade that renewed and sustained interest in electric vehicles has re-emerged. Based upon original research conducted by Axel Villareal,[2] this section is devoted firstly to retracing more precisely how and why this type of vehicle came to be politically reinvented and, in France but also elsewhere, an object of 'economic patriotism' (Clift & Woll, 2012). Secondly, I then go on to explain why this reinvention has not brought about the reinstitutionalization of the car industry which looked a distinct possibility in 2008–09. The key analytical claim made here is that if some proponents of electric vehicles certainly worked intensely to both redefine and mobilize the value of Security from an angle of environmental sustainability and re-hierarchize Equality as an intervening (and thus equally important) value, they singularly failed to convince key sets of actors to share this political shift. Put bluntly, whereas the commercial failure of electric vehicles is generally ascribed to 'technical' or 'functional' issues (such as battery capacity or recharging), using Villareal's research, I show that the causes of this failure have been deeply political.

5.1.1. Fermenting a 'Second Revolution' for the Car Industry

Although the dominant business model for the manufacturing of cars has made three significant shifts over time—from artisanal production (1890–1910) to Fordism (1910–1960s) then to Toyotism, i.e. 'lean production' (the 1970s onwards)—specialists of this industry largely concur that it was only when sustained advocacy of electric vehicles emerged in the mid-2000s that deep change became a genuine prospect (Freyssenet, 2009; Jullien & Lung, 2011). The argument made was that a concerted switch to electric vehicles would change not only the productive and commercial strategy of each manufacturer, but also consumption of automobiles and thus driving and transportation practices. More profoundly still, this type of automobile was predicted to prompt a substantial remake of the industry's Institutional Order (IO) and relationship to the other IOs (e.g. that of the energy industry) with which it overlaps and interacts. Before grasping precisely which institutions were predicted to change by most informed commentators and many practitioners

[2] More precisely, Axel researched and wrote a PhD thesis on this subject under my supervision between 2009 and 2014 (Villareal, 2014). This dissertation drew heavily upon observation of actor meetings, analysis of press coverage, and more than 100 semi-structured interviews. Axel gave me permission to use his findings in this book and has kindly commented upon what follows. However, I bear total responsibility for the claims made here and the interpretation of his work upon which they are based.

alike, it is of course crucial to first unpack and explain the industry's IO as it stood at the last turn of the century.

The most obvious place to start is to briefly examine the car industry's Sourcing Institutionalized Relationship (IR) in terms of its values, rules, norms, and conventions, as well as the actors who have dominated their setting. Particularly since the 1970s and the emphasis laid upon 'lean production', this IR has been deeply structured by a relationship between a relatively small number of large car 'manufacturers' and a vast quantity of sub-contractor companies who are generally small. Rather than produce every component of 'their' cars, manufacturers have strongly tended to concentrate the work of their own employees upon vehicle design, assembly, and marketing. Meanwhile, sub-contractors have sought to diversify their respective clienteles by producing components for as many manufacturers as possible. Although this trend has largely developed independently of collective and public action, it is important to grasp that representatives of both have nevertheless been involved in generating frameworks for manufacturer–sub-contractor relations. Providing legal systems within which contracting can take place and be guaranteed constitutes the most obvious angle from which collective (e.g. national and European trade associations) and public (e.g. ministries of industry and commerce) actors have participated in the evolution of the industry's Sourcing IR. But the latter also includes a wide range of norms and rules concerning vehicle safety and performance around which commercial operators, interest group officials, and civil servants frequently negotiate. Revealingly, over both contracting and vehicle norms, tensions between the values of Security and Freedom constantly structure and condense the politics of this IR in general, and the definition of it as a public problem in particular. Crucially, Equality has effectively been silenced, while Tradition has merely been a supporting value for the continued hegemony of hydrocarbon engines.

Much of what has just been said about the car industry's Sourcing IR also applies to its Commercial counterpart. Just as manufacturers have developed dense, interdependent relations with sub-contractors in order to make their cars, they have also built similar linkages with garages in order to distribute, sell, and service them. Indeed, although some new cars are sold directly by carmakers and an increasing number by supermarkets, most sales continue to entail a direct exchange between a customer and a garage affiliated to a brand. Moreover, it is this relationship that is widely used to lock-in the provision of after-sales servicing, repairs, and even loans to buy the car in the first place. Garages are thus very much part of the car industry, as testified by the efforts made by their owners to aggregate their interests and participate in the making of institutions that structure the selling of cars. Large carmakers certainly tend strongly to dominate the updating of these institutions at national and EU scales (Jullien, 2008). But by sub-contracting much of their marketing and sales activity they have also helped create another tension between the values of Freedom and Security over which public authorities have frequently been called upon to arbitrate. Focused on issues ranging from accusations of cartelization to quotas on Japanese imports, this industry's Commercial IR, and the involvement of states therein, have therefore contributed significantly to shaping its IO as a whole.

If a steady shift in manufacturer–sub-contractor interdependence has deeply marked the car industry, this has been mirrored and often accelerated by a parallel displacement within its Financial IR. As in so many other industries, ownership of the larger firms involved has strongly tended to shift from families to shareholders. In so doing, the role played by banks has become less central and that of stock exchanges predominant. Just as important is the impact of mergers that have taken place since the 1960s and 1970s (e.g. Peugeot and Citroën in 1976), as well as deeply institutionalized 'joint ventures' such as the one developed by Renault and Nissan since 1999. A third and final dimension of this industry's Financial IR concerns the role played by public authorities. As we shall see more closely, throughout the world national governments, as well as the European Union (EU), have contributed to the capitalization of vehicle-making for decades. Peaking initially in the 1970s, these 'state aids' fell considerably during the period 1985–2005. Nevertheless, such subsidies never actually disappeared and have remained a set of key policy instruments for public authorities committed to 'economic patriotism', instruments which, moreover, have been regularly co-produced and recycled by carmakers themselves (Jullien & Lung, 2011). Put succinctly, although on the surface the 'problem' of financing the car industry appears to have been dominated by practices and discourse which mobilize the value of Freedom (of the entrepreneur), its irregular but constant dependence upon public intervention has meant that the value of Security has also been omnipresent. Indeed, struggles to reconcile Freedom and Security once again lie at the very heart of this IR.

Why have states accorded so much importance and social meaning to Security as a value in an industry which, after all, is not directly linked to life or death issues? A large part of the answer to this question of course lies in the jobs linked to the making and selling of cars, and thus to the Employment IR that structures them. Particularly during the period 1945–70, the making of vehicles became a major part of industrial activity and thus a source of jobs in many Western (and Soviet Bloc) countries. Even more importantly, during this period of expansion trade unions often became powerful actors who, together with the management of manufacturers and their opposite numbers within ministries of industry and of labour, developed longstanding neo-corporatist arrangements within which national negotiations took place, in particular to set wage rates, devise pension schemes, and develop professional training. Indeed, in many countries this institutionalization of the car industry's Employment IR not only shaped capital–labour relations within the industry, but also considerably beyond as part of arguments in favour of 'economic patriotism'. Notwithstanding the apparent strength of the institutions built prior to 1970, however, they have since been systematically challenged by actors within and without car firms who consider that the cost of employment has become a handicap for car production in developed countries, and thus a reason for reducing it or for relocating factories and jobs to countries where wages are lower and rules or norms are less constraining (e.g. Romania). Indeed, the contingent character of institutions in the Employment IR, as well as their subservience to the industry's other IRs, has revealed itself the most clearly in states such as the UK where public support for national car manufacturers has been virtually abandoned since the 1980s. In this extreme case, previous commitments to the value of Security in this industry were overturned in favour of the Freedom of consumers to buy products from anywhere in the world and of companies to divest nationally or invest internationally as a consequence. In most other car-producing European countries, as well as the US, a certain commitment to the value of Security continues to impact upon the Employment IR and thence upon the framing of problems and instruments for the industry as a whole. Nevertheless, even in these national cases, by the mid-2000s commitments to the value of Freedom began to have greater institutional impacts.

In summary, the period 1970–2005 generated a number of uncertainties which seriously challenged the cohesion of the car industry's IO, and this particularly because during these years (de)regulation at the global scale began to undermine the capacity and desire of certain public authorities to continue to govern car-making and selling at the national scale in the name of economic patriotism. Crucially, the importance that had been accorded to the value of Security lost considerable ground to that of Freedom. Indeed, this section has outlined the institutionalized relationships and practices against which many experts and actors deduced in the late 2000s that 'revolutionary change' would occur when sparked into life by the environmental and financial 'crises'.

5.1.2. Political Work to Prompt Deep Change

Identifying sources of uncertainty and reasons for change is of course one thing; actually transforming them into problem definitions, policy instruments, and legitimizing discourse and symbols is quite another. Indeed, the case of electric vehicles provides a particularly salient illustration of this maxim which, moreover, highlights the causal influence of values, and thus of politics, upon economic activity. In order to grasp how this political work played out, let's first examine the impressive range of actors who, as of 2008–09, sought to re-problematize, re-instrument, and re-legitimize the car industry from this angle.

Actors seeking to challenge elements of the IO via the promotion of electric vehicles most obviously centred their quest upon its Sourcing IR. By proposing a new form of motorization, they simultaneously sought to delegitimize and disempower departments within car-making firms, but also sub-contractors, who remained wedded to the internal combustion engine. Indeed, these challengers took the form of competing intra-firm organizational units (e.g. Renault's department entitled *Le programme voiture électrique*), entirely new carmakers (e.g. Tesla, a start-up based in California), or battery manufacturers (e.g. Bolloré). Indeed, given that batteries and their recharging were framed from the outset as the key problem—one of 'autonomy'—to be tackled both by producers and public authorities, considerable efforts were made to produce new relationships between firms (e.g. between Renault and Bolloré) and policy instruments in the form of national and EU R & D grants, or local subsidies for infrastructure provision.

More generally, the political work undertaken by challengers within the Sourcing IR sought to redefine transportation by car through aligning and allying themselves with like-minded challengers operating within the industry's Commercial IR. For the latter, the most obvious objective was lowering the price of electric vehicles. This aim was pursued initially by removing the high cost of each car's battery from its price, then charging a subscription for its rental (along the lines of the mobile phone model). This reduced the cost of a new basic vehicle to around $15,000, a figure that made it reasonably competitive with traditional cars. Meanwhile, an attempt was begun to encourage consumers to replace thinking in terms of purchase prices by the notion of 'Total Cost of Ownership'. Furthermore, when the financial crisis began to heavily impact upon the new car market in 2009, these commercial initiatives were supplemented by others financed by public authorities such as subsidized scrapping schemes for old cars, vehicle tax reductions, free parking for electric vehicles, or subsidies for infrastructures (e.g. recharging centres). In this way, a number of commercial and policy instruments were deployed to challenge the hegemony of conventionally powered vehicles.

Just as importantly, however, partisans of electric vehicles also began to advocate a new symbolism for cars based around the concept of 'mobility'. Instead of emphasizing performance in terms of speed and unconditional autonomy, attempts were made to 'green' the image of the car emphasizing how 'going electric' contributes to saving the planet (thus allying Security with Equality—in terms of equal rights to environmental protection), and by reminding drivers that their actual needs in terms of autonomy rarely exceed the 100km a day which electric vehicles readily cover (thus rejecting the anti-Freedom image often imposed upon them).

As emphasized by the involvement of public subsidies in the strategies presented above, no actor considered that significant changes in the Sourcing and Commercial IRs would occur without corresponding displacements within the industry's Financial IR. Accordingly, private investors in the form of shareholders and banks were encouraged to loosen and lower their institutionalized commitments to the production of conventional vehicles and switch instead to riskier, but potentially more lucrative, investment in electric vehicles. Meanwhile, various public authorities were brought on board using a more differentiated set of arguments. In non-car-producing countries like Israel, electric vehicles received public support in the name of increasing national security in the face of perceived growing uncertainties generated by oil-producing states. If such arguments were also mobilized elsewhere, in producing states like France, arguments about new markets opening up in the 'emerging' BRIC countries (Brazil, Russia, India, and China) were given equal if not greater prominence. From this angle, 'economic patriotism' inspired proponents of electrical vehicles who underlined the pressing need for 'France' not to be overtaken by new producers in order to obtain state support (Villareal, 2014: 256). Consequently, the French government granted low-interest loans to Renault and Peugeot that amounted to 6 billion euro in order to invest in 'technologies of the future'. In addition, EU funding for R & D on electric vehicles was also generated (Hildermeier & Villareal, 2011). Unsurprisingly, the awarding of subsidies was simultaneously legitimized in the name of safeguarding employment in countries like France where carmakers had been severely hit by fallout from the financial crisis (for instance in September 2008 Renault announced 4,000 voluntary redundancies). Indeed, political work within the industry's Employment IR was intensified to keep factories such as Sandouville in Normandy open, thereby reasserting both Renault's and the French government's commitments to economic patriotism. Throughout the processes described above, many actors thus sought to redefine the value of Security, reprioritize it as regards that of Freedom and harness to their cause an interpretation of Equality that contained the notion of environmental egalitarianism.

Overall then, throughout 2008 and 2009 public and private support for electric vehicles built up, a trend accompanied by impressive predictions of high market share—e.g. 23 per cent of all Chinese cars and 6 per cent of all French ones by 2020—and politicized discourse deployed by actors ranging from Renault's CEO to the then President of France, Nicolas Sarkozy.[3] In a word, building upon the reasons for abandoning conventional motorizations set out earlier and the arguments in favour of electric vehicles outlined here, by

[3] See in particular his speech made to the *Mondial Automobile* trade show in Paris on 6 October 2008.

late 2009 the stage looked set for the revolutionary change anticipated by pro-electric activists and most neutral commentators alike.

5.1.3. The Politics of Industrial and Societal Reproduction

How can one therefore explain that since 2009 the commercial objectives set have never remotely looked likely to be achieved? In 2013, only 112,000 electric cars were sold worldwide, i.e. a mere 0.14 per cent of total new car sales.[4] More profoundly, how, in the space of just a couple of years, did such widespread support for electric vehicles all but disappear? So-called technical issues have played their part. However, not only have these issues actually been political, the conflicts between values and value hierarchies they reveal have had deep and far-reaching effects considerably beyond the car industry itself.

An initial set of explanations of the resilience of this industry's pre-existing IO can be found around two uncertainties regarding electric vehicles—battery cost and vehicle autonomy—which their proponents had sought to reduce by developing new problem definitions, commercial and policy instruments, together with a legitimizing discourse within its Sourcing and Commercial IRs. The attempts made to reduce the cost of batteries for these cars have clearly proved insufficient. On the one hand, research has so far not managed to come up with a product that is both efficient and less costly. On the other, proponents of electric vehicles have not succeeded in spreading and popularizing a reasoning about costs in terms of 'Total Cost of Ownership' which, theoretically at least, includes the thorny question of resale value. This said, the lack of change noted here cannot simply be ascribed to commercial instruments that have yet to prove sufficiently attractive. More profoundly, for such instruments to stand a chance of gaining legitimacy in the eyes of private and collective customers, as well as public authorities, a significant shift in the definition of the very problem of transportation by car needed to be achieved. Unsurprisingly, opposition to this call for change was led by supporters of internal combustion-engine vehicles who have always taken great delight in asserting that an electric car 'is not an automobile because it is not autonomous' (Villareal, 2014: 276). Despite such predictable and powerful opposition, redefining the very problem of transportation by car has been sought for years by activists working for environmental interest groups and, much more recently, pro-electric vehicle units within carmakers themselves. Particularly in the case of the former, defending a right to a cleaner environment for all has been fuelled by an egalitarian take on equality. However, neither of these groups of actors have succeeded in linking their detailed arguments

[4] Figures cited in Villareal (2014: 346) taken from autoactu.com.

about economic and environmental costs to a convincing meta-narrative (or 'global referential', Muller: 2015) that would supplement their case with a layer of social or even societal meaning. Consequently, 'performance', 'prestige', and 'premiumization' (Jullien & Lung, 2011) have continued to dominate the industry's symbolic order (Flonneau, 2008). Overall, then, all the political work undertaken over this dimension of creating demand for electric cars has not managed to reframe Security as a private (manufacturers' and subcontractors') *and* public issue, i.e. one of sustainability in the name of Equality (protecting the environment for all), rather than a problem of simply sustaining the reproduction of car production.

This lack of change in the definition of the problem of vehicle cost has been accompanied by the absence of similar change occurring for the wider problem of transportation. As highlighted earlier, a range of environmentalists, car designers, and representatives of municipal authorities have argued throughout the 2000s that 'mobility' is the best way to frame today's relationship between transportation technologies and environmental protection. Alongside reinventions of public transport that have occurred in many cities, electric vehicles came to be seen by many such actors as a key means of satisfying needs not met by public transport, drastically reducing vehicle emissions and re-hierarchizing equality as a guiding value for public policy. Despite the discourse, rhetoric, and symbolism attached to the 'mobility' movement, however, it has thus far had relatively little impact upon the provision of new services to the public and even less upon their transportation practices.

One utilitarian explanation of this failure lies in the refusal of nearly all municipal (and national) authorities to impose restrictions upon the usage of conventional vehicles in cities, or to penalize this practice through taxes or tolls. In short, 'carrots' have been offered in the shape of incentives to buy or hire electric cars, but very few 'sticks' have been deployed alongside them. An additional explanation of this type would point to stabilized or even reduced petrol prices due to the evolving state of global supply, as well as the new sources of hydrocarbons discovered in the late 2000s via 'fracking'. Both these points need taking seriously because they impact on the Security–Freedom relationship. However, neither addresses why, despite clear evidence that penalties do work, that cheap fuel cannot last indefinitely and, in any case, has its own environmental costs, public authorities virtually throughout the world, and state representatives in particular, have failed to confront powerful vested interests in order to impose more constraining rules and norms upon them.

Tackling this question rigorously would require new research into the value systems of relevant politicians and civil servants, in particular to understand the inconsistent material and symbolic support they have given to electric vehicles over time. But such research would also need to dovetail with Villareal's existing results on the non-creation of demand for electric vehicles he ascribes more surprisingly to two other sets of actors: environmentalist movements and the very carmakers who ostensibly committed themselves to producing this type of car.

In the case of environmental pressure groups, it is relatively well known that they are often divided over electric vehicles because of the latter's dependence upon the generation of electricity—and in France, therefore, often upon nuclear power. What Villareal shows in addition, however, is that at least in France such groups have neither followed the electric vehicle debate closely, nor equipped themselves with the expertise and analytical tools that could have enabled them to do so. In short, the deep, value-driven commitments of environmentalists to Security as Equality-enhancing sustainability, have not been accompanied by a capacity and commitment to engage in the concrete processes of problematization, instrumentation, and legitimization concerning the creation of demand for vehicles powered by electricity. Indeed, their absence from these processes has strongly contributed to the non-creation of such demand. More fundamentally still, a linkage between the values of Security and egalitarian Equality has rarely been injected into these processes by any pro-electric vehicle actor.

Villareal's second stimulating finding is that carmakers themselves have shackled the creation of demand for electric vehicles by failing to invest in the actual selling of such cars to individual customers. Rather than develop a concerted campaign in favour of this new product that places manufacturers alongside car dealers, companies such as Renault have simply assumed that this link in the value chain would take care of itself, i.e. car salesmen and women would spontaneously become enthusiastic advocates of the new products. In practice, virtually all such dealers continue to highlight the uncertainties that concern these vehicles and encourage customers to invest instead in the traditional vehicles they know they can sell. The principal consequence of carmakers failing to strategize over electric vehicles from an angle that embraced their industry as a whole, and not just their own units of production, is that at the point of sale no autonomization of electric vehicles from the 'dominant design' of cars has taken place (Villareal, 2014: 347). This finding reveals not only that both car manufacturers and dealers now give primacy to Freedom, it also underlines that for these powerful actors Security has been diluted and reduced to the role of a supporting value: one that bolsters their own durability rather than that of the national industrial base and environment.

In conclusion, by applying the 'politics as values' approach this case study has revealed how the long-term aim of environmental protection has once again been subordinated to the short-term goals of reducing commercial uncertainty and rebuilding profitability for multinational corporations. Rather than simply stemming from the rational calculus of 'interests' so dear to liberal and neo-Marxist scholars, however, this subordination needs explaining instead as one of 'Security in the name of environmental equality' being dominated by 'Security as continuity of profits for shareholders'. Arguments in favour of reproducing the car industry's IO have not simply won out because the most powerful of its actors flexed their muscles, in particular by threatening national governments with massive job losses. Instead, this defeat for challengers to the status quo has been caused by the non-institutionalization of new problem definitions, policy instruments, and modes of legitimation. During attempts to launch these three processes, value choices and possible re-hierarchizations have been blurred and fudged by the very proponents of electric vehicles. Merely describing their domination by actors who possess massive material and symbolic resources therefore tells us nothing new. Analyzing how the dominated have failed to develop a politics that matches their economic, environmental, and social ambitions, and in particular their failure to harness state representatives to their cause by re-hierarchizing their respective values, provides a more fruitful avenue for research and reflection.

5.2. HOW SECURITY SUBORDINATES EQUALITY: LABOUR MARKET POLICIES OR THEIR ABSENCE

If social science has convincingly and rigorously refuted the 'common sense' and populist adage that the European welfare state is 'a corrosive drain' upon economic activity (Hay & Wincott, 2012), this has not stopped a raft of neo-liberals from denigrating and seeking to dismantle state intervention of this type. Generally, however, these actors make an exception for 'labour market policies' which, since the 1980s, have been radically reformed. In so doing, the role of the state has been reframed as one of actively seeking to ascertain the human resources needs of employers, then either orientating the qualified unemployed in the appropriate direction, or training the unqualified in order to fill the 'gaps' identified (Palier, 2002: 228). As Thelen (2001: 71) so cogently explains, this policy change corresponds to a shift away from a problematization in terms of the redistribution of wealth and the taming of trade unions (associated with the post-war period of sustained growth and labelled 'industrial relations'), towards a definition of the public problem in terms of meeting the 'firm-level' concerns of employers for productivity, efficiency, and higher value-added production (legitimized by the slowdown in Western growth rates and the increased competitiveness associated with 'globalization'). In so doing, throughout most of the developed world 'supply side' policies have been developed and promoted around the representation of 'a skilled labour force as a public good' (Culpepper, 2000: 223). Moreover, resources and hope have been invested in a theory of action within which private employers will co-operate in the production and enhancement of this upgraded workforce.

Notwithstanding that this generalized shift in the aims and instruments of labour market policies superficially looks very similar in a wide variety of countries, nor that the OECD has been a vociferous proponent of such convergence, Historical institutionalists have also shown that embedding 'active' labour market policies in different states has taken a variety of forms and stimulated differing levels of change. Analyses of reputedly 'Liberal Market Economies', such as the UK, have shown not only that relatively small sums of public expenditure have been devoted by states to such policies, but also that employers and employer associations in such countries have thus far largely failed to bolster policy change by supporting state representatives in their quest to identify collective labour needs (Martin & Swank, 2004; 2012). More counter-intuitively, Thelen has explained why even in Germany, a country generally depicted as a 'Co-ordinated Market Economy', active labour market policies have often failed due to low levels of 'employer solidarity' (2001: 76; 2004). Indeed, research in this area has produced considerable data firstly upon the attitude of employers' associations to active labour market public policies and, secondly, on how the latter have been interpreted, supported or ignored at the level of individual firms. In so doing, the self-interest of each firm (e.g. to retain the apprentices that it trains) and, more generally, the issue of sharing information amongst and between private and public actors (Culpepper, 2001), have often been highlighted as key factors which hamper policy implementation.

Whilst most of this research on shifts in labour market policies, and thus the supposedly 'new' role played by states in economic activity, is convincing and stimulating, two of its recurrent characteristics currently limit its heuristic value. Firstly, this scholarship often neglects to underline that quests for productivity and efficiency have always been at the forefront of employers' minds: within any industry, its Employment Institutionalized Relationship (IR) has never been less than a vital component.

This point leads to a second concerning the level of analysis preferred by specialists in labour markets. These researchers tend strongly to concentrate upon national, horizontal policies (the macro) or the level of the firm (the micro). Indeed, failures in macro policies are often attributed to negative practices at the micro level. My concern here is that in jumping over the level of each industry (the meso), research in labour market policies has neglected a crucial dimension of the institutionalization of the economy within which problems are shaped, instruments are translated into concrete actions, and policy as a whole is legitimized. Specifically, existing research rarely tracks with precision how representatives of the state have actually worked in and around meso-level (i.e. industry specific) active labour market policies. What follows is thus an initial probe into what research can discover about the state's role in labour market policies if one adopts a meso-level and 'politics as values' perspective which, moreover, directly combines analysis of

Employment IRs with their respective Financial, Sourcing, and Commercial counterparts.

Empirically, this probe will compare two examples of industries within which states have intervened in labour markets with sharply contrasting outcomes. Centred upon Norway's aquaculture industry, the first illustration provides a briefly sketched ideal-type of how, when acting in the name of certain values, states can still strongly re-orientate both their labour market and the Institutional Order of an industry. In this instance, labour market policies have indeed been what Crouch calls 'a central example of assertive social democracy' and thence of 'the social investment welfare state' (2013: 67 and 84). Taken from the French wine industry,[5] my second example of state intervention in labour markets deepens this analysis of why the outcome of state interventionism is so dependent upon an onerous set of scope conditions. Both cases are compared over time in order to highlight the contrasting changes in labour market policies that each have featured. Overall, the principal claim made is that the cornerstone of successful state intervention in this issue area is a conception of Security as a public good within which the value of Equality also plays a key role in the framing of problems and the setting of instruments.

5.2.1. What States Can Do when Security is a Public Good

Largely because of its small size, Norway is seldom mentioned when state interventionism is compared. Nonetheless, it is well known that since the late 1960s its state has benefited greatly from revenues generated by the oil produced within Norwegian waters, a source of wealth that has contributed greatly to the high standard of living of most of its population and the relative generosity of its social protection policies. What is less well known, is how the Norwegian state has deployed some of its oil revenues in order to diversify economic activity within its borders around a distinctive problematization of the politics–economics nexus. In particular, faced with a declining sea-fishing industry, over the last four decades, state representatives and other actors have consistently worked to create, then develop, an aquaculture that has attained the highest profitability and productivity levels in the world. Throughout, a state-led active labour market policy has been at the heart of this story, a positioning that stems from Security in this industry being couched as a public good linked to egalitarian principles.

Aquaculture in general is an industry that first expanded in the 1970s and 1980s, then accelerated over the following decade (Carter & Casales, 2014). In

[5] Fieldwork on this question was conducted with Thierry Berthet in 2011–12, a contribution for which I thank him profusely. However, this interpretation of our findings is mine alone.

Norway, the industry was initially dominated by a plethora of small, family-run companies whose capital essentially came from own resources and local banks. As of the 1970s, the state began to provide some financial support through regional development and 'innovation' policies, the latter in particular facilitating technological breakthroughs in production (e.g. cages) and processing (e.g. filleting and packaging) which paved the way for intensification of the industry as a whole (Wiig-Aselesen, 2007). Moreover, the Norwegian state also invested from the outset in the marketing of Norwegian Salmon as a collective brand while defending its producers in bilateral trade negotiations and at the WTO (Carter, Ramirez & Smith, 2014). In short, the Financial, Sourcing, and Commercial IRs of the industry were all affected to a significant degree by state intervention. Employment policy, at least in these early years, was largely neglected however.

As with Norwegian oil, it is also common knowledge that France contains the largest national vineyard in the world, an area within which not only the most prestigious wines but also the largest turnover and profits are made. Alongside the rest of European agriculture, most French wine production began centuries ago within smallholdings as part of either subsistence farming (wine for own consumption), or polycultural practices (excess wine to be sold through markets) (Dion, 1988). As elsewhere, many of these holdings were family-owned, whilst others were tenancies leased from large landowners. Indeed, from the point of the view of the French state, until the late nineteenth century, the question of who worked to produce grapes was simply part of a wider 'agrarian problem' concerning the relationship between rural and urban populations. As of the 1880s, this definition of the problem began to change, however, as the professions of grower and merchant organized themselves on a national basis in order to politically work in favour of more interventionist collective and statist action. The creation of a Ministry of Agriculture in 1881 channelled much of the state's responses to this development. More generally, the period 1875–1930 constituted the genesis of a neo-corporatist and highly interventionist approach to regulating the French vineyard underpinned by the value of Security (Warner, 1960; Smith, de Maillard & Costa, 2007). Although, employment questions were not at the forefront of this *rapprochement* between wine's professions and the state, one instrument in particular was favoured: as of the 1880s, a more systematic national approach to agricultural training was developed via specialized secondary schools (*lycées agricoles*), a policy whose legacy means that today there are still more than 800 of these schools in France, together with 500 specialized professional training centres and 19 higher education bodies.

Crucially, during the period of sustained growth in French wine production which, in general terms, lasted from the late nineteenth century until the 1970s (and indeed continued into the early 2000s for regions such as Bordeaux), the pedagogical orientations given to educational and training establishments in wine-growing regions were dominated by the 'needs' expressed by actors whose main preoccupations have been the industry's Sourcing and Finance IRs: i.e. product and capital-related issues. Indeed, these orientations became particularly explicit in the period of rapid production growth that marked the 1950s until the 1980s: young people wishing to remain on the land were trained in ever-increasingly intensive farming techniques, meanwhile those inclined to find employment in towns were expressly encouraged to do so. Indeed, although legitimized as being about Freedom to choose, the rapid urbanization experienced by France during these years was caused above all by how the values of Freedom and Security were translated into statist backing for the mechanization of agriculture and the concentration of farms into ever-larger, monocultural units (Muller, 1984). In a word, Security was defined both individually at the level of each farm and collectively at that of the agricultural industry as a whole. More generally, in this way the population of salaried farm-workers grew, but the overall number of people working in farming dropped sharply.

In summary, it is clearly difficult to rigorously compare the development and growth of the Norwegian aquaculture industry in the 1970s and 1980s with that of French wine in the mid-twentieth century. However, if one reduces the point of comparison to the role played by state actors in these processes, then clear similarities can be discerned. In both states, policy instruments were established by state actors in order to prompt expansion, encourage better quality products, and promote greater productivity. Moreover, in both cases, expansion of this kind was defined as a public good legitimized in the name of the state itself. Most fundamentally, in Norway and France the value of Security was mobilized as a means of not only accompanying the Freedom of private enterprises, but also working towards collective goals and more egalitarian outcomes for their workers.

5.2.2. State Intervention when Security is Privatized

Given that in general around 50 per cent of the cost of making a bottle of wine in France relates to labour, one could be forgiven for assuming that when, in the 1970s and 1980s, then again in the 2000s, market conditions became more difficult, the French state would have revitalized a strong employment policy for this industry. The enigma addressed here is that it very definitely has not. More specifically, if a range of isolated measures such as specialized agricultural high schools and databases on viticultural employment continue to exist, the French state has found it increasingly difficult to formulate an overall policy which attracts consistently high levels of support from the representatives of growers and merchants. On the contrary, despite state-produced warnings about the ageing of viticultural workers (at least

30 per cent are over fifty) and the consequences of a drop in the employment of family members on wine farms (down 30 per cent since 2000), these demographical statistics have thus far been downgraded by producer representatives to the status of an occasional issue for individual firms. For such actors, the labour market is no longer seen as a collective, let alone a public, problem.

In order to grasp this incongruous gap between an industry structured around a politically and economically powerful Institutional Order on the one hand and, on the other, denial of challenges to its Employment IR by its key representatives, a brief update of recent employer–employee relations in French wine estates will first be presented before zooming in on one regional vineyard: Bordeaux. The overall thesis developed here is that although the structuring of French grape production had previously been co-ordinated by a state-producer coalition in the name of Security and Equality, the value of Freedom has increasingly come to predominate. In the case of labour market issues, this emphasis upon the Freedom of wine estate owners and managers has obstructed their reproblematization and instrumentation. The overall consequence has been ineffectual political work on employment issues, together with asymmetric interdependencies which have left the industry's Employment IR subservient to orientations that have been developed instead within its Sourcing, Commercial, and Financial counterparts. In a word, an increasingly liberal approach to the labour market has eliminated the value of Equality from policymaking and left that of Tradition to take care of itself.

What first needs stressing is that since the 1980s the intensification of wine growing within ever-larger holdings has continued. Throughout, the state has accompanied this development with instruments designed for farmers and growers, such as early retirement schemes and incentives to encourage the 'installation' of young farmers. By contrast, however, salaried farmworkers have been paid far less attention. This can be exemplified first by examining the content of official reports on the wine industry. In 2002 the French Senate's 150 page *L'avenir de la viticulture française* makes no mention of employment questions. In 2008, the national Economic and Social Council made a similar report within which 5 of its 142 pages do mention employment statistics. However, no opinions whatsoever were expressed on this issue, not even by the four trade unions invited to do so. In short, at the national scale the question of who works for wine farms, together with their respective skills, has not been problematized.

In terms of political work aimed at actively shaping wine's labour market, it is essentially at the regional level instead that French state officials have been most active. Here the case of Bordeaux is particularly revealing since its vineyard alone employs no less than 25,000 workers, i.e. a third of the national total. Moreover, this wine region possesses the largest number of job vacancies within French agriculture. A third, even more revealing, reason for looking closely at state activity in this region is that its field office in Bordeaux has become a lone voice calling for greater attention to be paid to this issue. As one of its representatives declared in an interview:

> Since 2003 we have rung the alarm bells. We have said 'something needs to be done'. But until now the industry has eyes only for the price of a barrel of wine and China (May 2011).

Specifically, using the statistics systematically generated on a wide range of farming practices, the state's field services in Bordeaux have not only highlighted the dangers the industry is facing in finding skilled workers such as tractor drivers, but also the risks for the future manifested in the drop in interest in wine production shown by teenagers currently in secondary education (in 2000, 900 of the region's students specialized in wine whereas, by 2010, this figure had fallen to 290). Indeed, locally-based state officials have highlighted the extent to which classes are closing and schools are being forced to merge. More fundamentally, driven by a collective take on the value of Security, the concerns of the handful of state officials working on employment issues in Bordeaux are that a deep disregard for the labour market by dominant growers is actually getting worse:

> They don't understand anything about what is happening...All they do is present examples of misery and poverty in the sector;
>
> They simply don't care! They might make cosmetic or political statements. But it's just cheap talk. On a daily basis, this issue has no effect upon what they actually do;
>
> Immediate employability is their only criterion.
>
> (interviews, May and June 2012).

Fieldwork undertaken with the representatives of growers and merchants largely confirms these representations of grower priorities. For example, the region's key producer and merchant body—the *Conseil interprofessionel des vins de Bordeaux*—has no officer working on employment questions; moreover, in 2010 its 100 page strategic *Plan Bordeaux* contained just a few lines on this issue area. In addition, the region's Chamber of agriculture has great difficulty in getting growers and their staff to take their training courses at all. Put bluntly, the only employment questions that have resonance for the vast majority of growers concern the meeting of their own short-term demands, and this increasingly through private employment agencies. More deeply still, the persistence of stigmatizing terms like 'farm labourer' (*ouvrier agricole*) or the unskilled (*les petites mains*) locks-in and legitimizes a framing of viticultural employment which dissuades young people from choosing its career paths.[6]

[6] On this point see the report by ANEFA-Aquitaine, 'Une étude action sur la main d'œuvre saisonnier agricole en Aquitaine', <www.Anefa.org/regions/aquitaine>.

Faced with grower disinterest and faith instead in the liberalization of labour markets, representatives of the French state are currently disarmed and helpless. Despite the continued existence of some national policy instruments, the discarding of the value of Equality that has occurred over the last few decades, fuelled by a redefinition of Security in terms of market access, has ultimately left the state itself empty-handed.

This example of state (in)action in France contrasts sharply with how its Norwegian counterpart reacted to upheavals in the aquaculture industry in the mid to late 1990s. During this period, company ownership shrank drastically as international competition hit hard and an emphasis on productivity and efficiency suddenly came to dominate. Indeed, if sales increased threefold between 1994 and 2005, the number of persons directly employed in the industry fell from 7000 in 1990 to 3500 by the end of the decade, then to 2205 by 2005 (Wiig-Aselesen, 2007: 19–21). As so often when shareholders become the main financiers of companies, this drastic fall in job numbers was partly due to the emphasis these actors put on 'cost competitiveness'. Crucially, however, the Norwegian state and interest group leaders did not simply stand by and passively watch this trend. Instead, taking legitimacy from parliamentary legislation adopted in 1994, their reaction was to build specialized educational establishments, including at university level. Indeed, this action was framed as an integral part of national innovation policy involving a range of ministries which have contributed to a number of significant developments. First, by 2003 more than 1600 researchers in Norway were working on aquaculture (Wiig-Aselesen, 2007). Second, when one includes employees in the feed, vaccine, technical equipment manufacturing, and related sectors, Norwegian aquaculture featured 13,000 direct 'marine expertise' jobs in 2005 (Olafsen et al., 2006), a figure whose 'ripple effects' were calculated to have risen to 22,000 direct and indirect jobs four years later (SINTEF, 2009). Finally, to complete the picture, it is important to factor in the jobs in factories in the many other European countries where most Norwegian salmon is processed (SINTEF, 2005). In short, through implementing judicious national and corporate development strategies within which the values of Security (framed collectively) and Equality, thence purpose-built employment policies, have been central, state and private actors representing Norwegian aquaculture have not only reinforced a key branch of their country's economic activity (US$4.9 billion in exports in 2011, nearly five times that of Canada), but also relegitimized the very role of the interventionist state.

In concluding this brief comparison between state practices in Norway and France, it is important to confront it with the findings of labour market specialists who have looked in much greater detail at how states and employees can co-operate in this issue area. From this perspective, for example, Culpepper underlines that 'States are good at standardizing measures, not at assessing contextual information...Such policies can only be crafted if state policy-makers incorporate the private information accessible to employers' associations in the design of public policies' (2001: 278). Whereas my Norwegian example largely corroborates this claim, the case of the French wine industry underlines that in other instances the state possesses such data while it is the employers who have chosen not to act upon it. Crucially, figures do not speak for themselves. Indeed, here French wine growing elites have downplayed collectively defined values of Security and Equality in the name of the Freedom of individual estate managers to meet their labour needs as they see fit.

Culpepper also underlines the need not to blame either state or employer representatives but to focus instead upon the characteristics of their relationship. Although in general terms this finding is borne out by both of the case studies, it is equally important to address directly the value systems of each set of actors. In the Norwegian case the priority given to Security and Equality by both the state and employers caused and legitimized the placing of labour issues at the centre of aquaculture's development. In contrast, the obsession with Freedom of wine growers in France has reduced their relationship with the state to a one-way street that has left public officials feeling helpless and unwanted.

CONCLUSION

What the state still does is a vast question that obviously cannot be fully addressed in a single chapter. What this analysis has endeavoured to do instead is to refute the material determinism of both neo-liberal and leftist writings on the state, while proposing an alternative that also goes beyond analyses in terms of governance and Historical Institutionalism.

Neo-liberal accounts of the contemporary state obtusely ignore how sustained economic activity can only occur when publicly-backed institutions structure markets and firm behaviour. As my examples from the car industry and labour markets show, state intervention has been a decisive influence upon socio-economic outcomes, either favouring lasting practices or handicapping their development. Of course, both sets of examples also show the crucial role played by companies and their respective interest groups. Nevertheless, it is equally excessive to claim, as many neo-Gramscian opponents of neo-liberalism do, that representatives of businesses act consistently against state interventionism, or even manage to aggregate their own interests amongst themselves on a regular basis. As Cornelia Woll has shown clearly in research on other industries (2008), one should never underestimate the difficulties managers of firms have in defining and aggregating their own interests, let alone those of their respective industry as a whole. In short, material determinism of either liberal or post-Marxist types, be it ideologically driven or purely analytical, obscures the scope conditions that encourage or discourage state representatives from seeking to affect the course of economic activity. The major cause of this blind-spot is that such theories lack a definition of politics which places values at its heart. Little wonder then that both liberal economists and neo-Gramscians end up only seeing actors defending the goal of freedom without examining the value behind this quest, nor its dialectical relationship with the values of Security and Equality.

Historical institutionalists and certain theorists of 'governance' certainly provide a more solid basis for beginning research that identifies scope conditions for state intervention and the role of what they call 'ideas' in particular. The former rightly target institutions as the sets of rules, norms, and conventions which state representatives work upon in order to impact on economic practice. The latter provide heuristic means of capturing the relations between actors within which this work on institutions takes place. However, because such authors generally do not anchor their analysis in empirically grounded constructivism, both approaches accord insufficient importance to the role played by social representations in general, and values in particular. Indeed, the key claim defended in this chapter has been that what conditions a state's involvement in the economy are the hierarchies of values that structure the thought and action of its personnel. These hierarchies equip state actors not only with arguments and symbols with which to structure their respective arguments, but are also a key means of legitimizing their very involvement in economic activity. If, over the last forty years, representatives of the state have certainly supported the rise of Freedom as an organizing principle for public action in the economy, the case studies presented here show that the legitimacy and capacity of public actors to intervene in the economic is more likely to increase if the values of Security and Equality are given at least equal prominence. More precisely, by defining Security collectively in terms of Equality in order to emphasize that it is a public good to be shared by the widest possible cross-section of the population, state actors can provide themselves with a posture from which to convince other stakeholders that their role in economic activity is a positive one. In so doing, they can reinstate or augment their own legitimacy and indeed power.

6

Local Government

Economic Saviour or Gravedigger?

INTRODUCTION

Since the 1970s, throughout Western Europe and beyond, a great deal of hope has been invested in local government as a means of encouraging and supporting economic activity. Indeed, 'local economic development' involving a wider range of private and collective actors has frequently been promoted as a means of making up for cuts in national government involvement, geographical asymmetries of wealth, and even the so-called 'globalization of capitalism' discussed in chapter 3. More positively, the local has also been advocated because of the economic successes attributed to localities where 'endogenous', network-based development has predominated (e.g. the 'third Italy' in general and Emilia Romagna in particular: Bagnasco & Trigilia, 1993), or where intra-state authorities have been given greater autonomy (e.g. Scotland: Carter & Smith, 2009 or Wales: Cooke & Morgan, 1998). More generally, during the 1980s and 1990s in particular, a range of geographers and sociologists sought to show how and why local authorities were the most effective, efficient, and accountable sources of public support for economic growth (Storper, 1997).

As both western capitalism but also research has evolved, however, the faith once invested in the local level of government as a primary and efficient supporter of economic activity has been considerably shaken. As findings of 'regions that fail' accumulated, academics began to seek deeper reasons why certain localities 'won' whereas others stagnated or 'lost' (Crouch et al., 2001). Indeed, new research began to show that decentralizing the authority to intervene in the economy could at best lead to the duplication or scattering of public support, while at worst it could shore up counter-productive, and sometimes even corrupt, political and economic practices.

It is clearly beyond the scope of this chapter to present systematic evidence to show that increased interaction between local levels of government and economic activity have led to more or less efficient societal outcomes. As in previous chapters, instead my first goal is to discover the institutions affecting economic life that have been created, consolidated, changed, or abandoned through action at the local scale, whilst the second is to identify the causes. In keeping with the overall claim made throughout this book, I will show that these causes are deeply political. More precisely, through revealing the values that have been mobilized or suppressed at the local scale around economic initiatives in two French *départements*, the aim of this chapter is to pinpoint how prioritization of values has affected economic outcomes.

The first of these case studies concerns efforts to develop and promote local food chains in the area that surrounds the city of Bordeaux: the Gironde. Although on the surface this initiative, widely supported by local authorities, seems consensual, it has actually generated deep frictions between definitions of Tradition and Security and their defenders, frictions largely mediated around the values of both Equality and Freedom. The chapter's second study concerns local economic development more generally, this time in the neighbouring *département* of the Charente. Here I show that what looked initially like a more straightforward confrontation between the values of Freedom (of a firm to act in its own interests) and Security (framing those interests in collective and longer term ways), has entailed a deeper downgrading of Equality as a locally-held value.

Overall, this chapter not only challenges the simplistic notion that by regulating economic activity at the local scale, productive and commercial practices will become more efficient and in keeping with indigenous expectations and goals. By showing how the mobilization and prioritization of values to affect institutions is an omnipresent part of political work at this scale too, it also focuses attention more sharply upon the value-driven conflicts and contradictions which strongly structure its outputs and outcomes.

6.1. TRADITION AS A ROAD TO SECURITY? LOCAL FOOD CHAINS IN ACTION

As many readers will have experienced directly through shopping in 'farmers' markets' or purchasing food directly from farms, over the last two decades many citizens of Western countries have rediscovered a degree of direct contact with producers of food that had largely been lost over the twentieth century. Part of this trend has clearly been motivated by dissatisfaction with supermarket produce, concerns about the welfare of small farmers or the protection of the environment. Another part undoubtedly stems from the quest by some consumers for their food, together with the act of buying it, to reacquire social meaning. However, it is an illusion to think either that such consumer demands arose spontaneously, or that the producers concerned have done nothing to restructure and promote their 'supply'. Quite the contrary, local food chains are always the product of varying modes of collective action undertaken by farmers and retailers. Moreover, in many instances such action has been supported, and sometimes even sparked, by local public policies of varying kinds (Gomez & Itçaina, 2014). This support by local government for actors who have sought to shorten food chains is often presented as being a 'win–win' situation for all concerned: consumers get better food, farmers improve their livelihoods, environmental protection is enhanced, and local politicians gain legitimacy. Having first unpacked these assertions by showing how local food chains in the Gironde have actually impacted upon the Institutional Order of agriculture in this area, this section then proceeds to analyse the causes of these ambiguous effects by focusing upon the key value tension it has generated. As will be highlighted, in the case of local food networks in this area, as in others examined elsewhere (Ilbery & Maye, 2005a & b; Renting et al., 2003), efforts to reprioritize Tradition as regards Security have been mediated by particular conceptions of Equality. Specifically, this political work has generally subordinated egalitarian concerns to those of equal access, thereby bringing the value of Freedom firmly back into decision-making equations.[1]

6.1.1. Local Food: An Economic and Political No-brainer?

If economic life really was just about supply meeting demand, most Frenchmen and women would only eat local food. According to recent surveys, 71 per cent of this population consider that the geographical origin of what they eat is important to them,[2] while 46 per cent go so far as to claim they look at how far it has travelled before buying it.[3] Moreover, such surveys suggest that the reasons consumers prefer local food include a desire to support producers from their region (88 per cent), because local food tastes better (82 per cent), protects the environment (79 per cent), and is more 'authentic' (77 per cent).[4] One must of course take great care in interpreting surveys of this kind, in particular, when consumers are not questioned about their perceived financial constraints, nor observed actually buying a local product despite its price

[1] This section is based partly upon an on-going PhD thesis undertaken by Pierre Naves under my supervision. Despite his considerable indirect input to these pages, I of course take full responsibility for what is written below.

[2] BEUC—The European Consumers' Organisation, *Where does my food come from?* 2013, p. 16.

[3] Crédoc, 'Les Français avancent à grands pas sur la longue route écologique', *Cahier de recherche*, issue 272, December 2010.

[4] Observatoire Cetelem, 'Le consommateur européen en mode alternatif', 2013. <http://observatoirecetelem.com/publications/2013/observatoire-cetelem-consommation-2013.pdf>.

being higher than an equivalent produced elsewhere. Nevertheless, one can reasonably conclude from this data that today considerable latent demand for local food exists in France. How, then, can this be squared with actual consumption patterns revealing that most food consumed in that country is produced at great distances from where it ends up on plates? For example, only 4 to 7 per cent of fruit and vegetables sold in French retail outlets is 'local'.[5] Are distributors in general, and supermarkets in particular, simply not listening to calls to change their supply?

Understanding this gap between discursive expressions of demand and actual practice starts with putting the simplistic supply and demand formula to one side, then taking up instead analysis in terms of the institutions which structure not only food distribution, but the agricultural industry as a whole. In so doing, one not only grasps how the predominance of distantly produced food has come to be so pervasive in Western societies, but also the opposition proponents of local food chains have faced when seeking to challenge this domination of agriculture's Institutional Order.

When studying this Order, the most obvious place to start is with its Commercial Institutionalized Relationship (IR). Put succinctly, at least in France, until the advent of the railways in the 1830s, most food was consumed within a radius of 100 kilometres of its production. Hitherto, food was either eaten on the very place of production (subsistence farming) or transported relatively short distances to market. Of course, exceptions to this rule existed for the rich and for imported products such as sugar and spices. However, the revolution in transportation introduced by the railways was seized upon by food wholesalers as a means of achieving a step-level change in the supply of farm produce to towns and cities in particular. Consequently, these wholesalers built warehouses and worked to build and consolidate networks of retailers to whom they sold-on agricultural commodities in either processed (e.g. flour) or unprocessed (e.g. vegetables) forms. In so doing, national markets for different foodstuffs began to emerge, bringing with them greater convergence over retail prices in particular.

Simultaneously, these very same wholesalers also worked upstream of the distribution of produce in order to concentrate the supply of produce in larger lots, facilitate its delivery to railway depots in small market towns, and, more generally, standardize and intensify agricultural production. Indeed, as supply chains grew longer both physically and through acquiring more intermediaries, arguments emerged to modify institutions within agriculture's Sourcing IR. For example, whereas prior to the 1830s standards for farm produce remained informal and dependent upon local expectations, the lengthening of food chains generated support for national rules and norms (Stanziani,

[5] <http://agriculture.gouv.fr/circuits-courts>.

2005). The latter developed relatively progressively until the 1950s when, following the disruption of agriculture's Institutional Order as a whole (Muller, 1984), national, then European or international standardization of foodstuffs became a central plank in the intensification of farming that continued unabated into the 1990s. During this period, not only did farms tend strongly to merge into ever-larger units, to specialize in a limited number of products and produce them using inputs such as fertilizers and pesticides, France as a whole rapidly became a highly urbanized country. In so doing, a key counterpart to intensive agriculture was a system of food distribution based upon supermarkets and, as of the 1980s, hypermarkets.

Crucially, however, none of these overlapping developments in agriculture's Commercial and Sourcing IRs simply flowed automatically from technological innovations and spontaneous shifts in the structure of supply and demand. Rather these major displacements in socio-economic life were constantly shaped by political decisions concerning support for, or resistance to, technology, as well as to its likely impact upon population patterns and practices. Indeed, this point can be clearly exemplified by completing our analysis of French agriculture's Institutional Order through briefly examining the histories of its Employment and Financial IRs. As regards the former, the emergence of national, then international, food chains can only be fully understood by recalling its dependence upon an 'agrarian' displacement which brought subsistence farming to an end, normalized the large, family-owned farm, but also encouraged the emergence of co-operatives and contract farming as a means of pooling or vertically integrating production. In short, without institutionalized transformations of agriculture's Employment IR, 'long' food chains could not have come about in the way they did.

Just as crucially, the concentration of farmland in fewer hands, mechanization and recourse to costly inputs would also have been impossible without radical change within agriculture's Financial IR. In order for all these trends to take root and receive institutionalized support, sources of capital needed to emerge in the shape of banks willing to lend money to farmers and, indeed, extend them credit on a permanent basis. In the French case, this source of capitalization was largely generated by the creation of state-supported banks (notably *Le Crédit Agricole*), together with 'price support' systems based upon public subsidies (Muller, 1984).

To sum up a potted history of French agriculture, neither its trajectory towards intensification, nor the concomitant institutionalization of 'long' food chains could have occurred without the conversion of its Institutional Order, together with its dominant hierarchy of values, outlined above. Indeed, if other values were sometimes evoked (e.g. Equality around the supposedly lower retail prices for food set by supermarkets), this historically crucial development was above all driven by the values of Freedom (for producers and distributors) and Security in order to guarantee continuous flows of food supplies to the urban consumer. Indeed, for the purposes of this chapter, what is vital to retain is that contemporary calls and moves to develop local food chains constitute nothing less than a direct challenge not only to this Order based on 'long' food chains, but also to the priority it has given to the Security of urban populations and the Freedom of large distributors to become key players in markets as a means of achieving its goals. Before analysing how this confrontation between long and short food chains has played out within the Gironde, it is therefore necessary to explain in broad-brush terms the extent of this challenge to institutionalized practices and patterns of interdependence.

Local food's most obvious challenge to Agri-food's institutions and configurations of power has been located in the Commercial IR. Dominated by supermarket chains since the 1970s, at least in France, this IR has become largely shaped by compromises between these corporations and increasingly weak public actors. Putting to one side the influence supermarket owners have gained through financing political parties or contributing to local tax bases, their enduring power over commercial issues can be attributed to two sets of practices in particular. First, these corporations have restructured flows of foodstuffs around distribution networks that have become either highly centralized or based on large regional hubs. In both cases, most intermediaries have been eliminated in the name of logistical economies of scale, thereby increasing the dependence of farmers upon national or mega-regional buyers. Local food chains clearly seek to disrupt this dependent relationship and create more space for farmers not only to control the distribution of their products, but also to better influence the setting of its prices. The latter point relates to the second part of supermarket activity within the Commercial IR which concerns their 'rules of exchange' (Fligstein, 2001) with food producers. Increasingly this relationship has been formalized around contracts signed with either individual farmers or co-operatives. If such contracts can offer these actors some security (since the selling of their produce is guaranteed) it also affects price-setting in the industry more generally (Bernard De Raymond, 2013). The third and final part of supermarket activity structured by the Commercial IR concerns promotion and marketing. Armed with large advertising budgets and other such devices, supermarkets are well placed to control the image of a product. In the case of *foie gras*, for example, they have even used the symbolism of the peasant farmer for products that are now predominantly produced intensively by large farms (Jullien & Smith, 2008b). What local food chain proponents seek to do is to win back control over the imagery of extensive farming, thereby recuperating the value of Tradition as a source of legitimacy and social meaning.

In so doing, local food activists also of course seek to modify institutions and the balance of power within Agri-food's Sourcing IR. Structured around institutions that constrain and render possible the production and processing of food, most of these are set at national, European, and even global scales. For this reason, proponents of local food have sought in particular to influence reforms of the Common Agricultural Policy (CAP), for example to obtain derogations from some aspects of food hygiene laws (e.g. around the use of wooden containers in the making of Comté cheese). However, given that defenders of intensive and 'distant' food production built and have 'maintained' the CAP since the 1950s, modifying Agri-food's Sourcing IR in the name of local Traditions is always met with considerable resistance.

Finally, although Employment and Finance issues may seem less central to the local food agenda, it is important to grasp that the IRs which structure both also participate strongly in rendering change from these angles to Agri-food's Institutional Order an object of permanent struggle. Producing and distributing local food typically requires labour to be trained and organized differently to that of farms committed to longer value chains. Because, as we saw in chapter 5, representatives of the latter have dominated training and employment policies for more than half a century, again defenders of the status quo begin any negotiation in this domain with a head start over their local food adversaries. Similarly, converting a farm towards local food production and distribution necessitates capital which banks—i.e. the very financiers who since World War II committed themselves so wholeheartedly to intensive farming and 'distant' food—are often reluctant to lend.

In summary, actually challenging the Agri-food industry's Institutional Order from the angle of local food is thus anything but a 'no-brainer'. Although many good reasons can be expressed for doing so, at least in today's France, turning this list into a political project, armed with solid values and tooled up for battle with dominant actors and institutions, is a momentous undertaking. Indeed, just how big a task this is can be grasped even better by examining how it has fared in specific areas and food chains.

6.1.2. Picking up the Challenge of Local Food in the Gironde

Indeed, using Pierre Naves's research on local food initiatives over fruit and vegetables in the Gironde, the key role played within this area of economic activity by value prioritization can be clearly demonstrated. Surrounding the metropolis of Bordeaux and its 750,000 inhabitants, the Gironde's fruit and vegetables come partly from market gardening close to its major city, but mostly from neighbouring *départements*, in particular the Lot et Garonne. Indeed, since most agricultural activity in the Gironde is devoted to wine, local food products are relatively few and far between. Since the 1990s, this absence has increasingly been turned into an opportunity for farmers from further afield to sell part of their produce through a range of market stalls and Internet-assisted modes of direct producer–consumer distribution. Meanwhile, the perceived lack of local food in this area has been turned by actors within public authorities into a similarly wide range of policy instruments designed to encourage the development of local food chains. These now include subsidies for the holding of physical markets, others for managing the websites of 'drives' that use internet ordering, new local rules on public procurement of food, particularly for school canteens, as well as financial assistance for communication campaigns in order to raise general public awareness and promote specific initiatives. From the point of view of analysis, however, this apparent enthusiasm for local food raises two thorny questions: although there are now many policy instruments to support this trend, do they fit with a stabilized 'public problem' and its corresponding hierarchy of values? What overall impact has local food in the Gironde had upon the Agri-food industry's Institutional Order? In answering these questions, no less than five zones of friction prompted in this area by local food need explanation.

The first is definitional and concerns what actually constitutes local food. As many other examples from economic life testify (Dubuisson-Quellier, 2013), categorizing a product or range of products has strong effects upon the way it is perceived by distributors and consumers alike. Indeed, when such categories are loose or confusing (e.g. for many 'organic' products), both sets of actors can quickly become disenchanted and then abandon them as guidance for their purchases. In the case of local food, the French Ministry of Agriculture published an official definition in March 2009. In formalizing the category of *circuit court* (local food chain), its defining characteristic was essentially reduced to a combination of:

(i) 'proximity' between producer and consumer;
(ii) an absence of intermediaries between farmer and consumer.

If this definition seems clear on paper, in practice it is anything but. Many farmers in direct contact with consumers live considerable distances away from them (more than 100km for many fruit and vegetable producers in the Lot et Garonne who sell their produce in Bordeaux). Meanwhile, many farmers sell directly to nearby supermarkets, thus becoming eligible for local food status in the eyes of the Ministry despite these outlets generally being seen as part of long value chains. More generally, the category of intermediaries is also fuzzy. For example, do co-operatives fall into this category or are they classified as 'farmers' in this instance? Even without seeking an exhaustive list of definitional problems, one can immediately see that 'local food' in itself is very unlikely to spontaneously generate either a like-minded set of proponents, or an institutionalized label with which to promote its existence. In short, at least in France and in the Gironde in particular, the category of local food is currently seen by its own supporters as increasingly unclear. What most protagonists have lost sight of, however, is that that rediscovering clarity here can only be achieved by revisiting the values and value hierarchies local food is supposed to embrace and enhance. Specifically, the tension between promoting Traditions or fostering Security for producers cannot simply be avoided by considering that these are automatically complementary goals. If Tradition is the primary value, then the Freedom of farmers and distributors to sell products that meet this criterion ends up trumping the emphasis upon proximity and direct sales, the smaller farmer and environmental protection. Conversely, if the main aim is to enhance Security around these three phenomena, then Tradition slides to being a secondary goal and Freedom is pushed further down one's hierarchy of values. Leaving this hierarchy ambiguous may have certain advantages in the short term, but it may well end up undermining the social meaning and socio-economic worth of local food in the medium to long term.

A second zone of ambiguity surrounding 'local' fruit and vegetables sold in the Gironde concerns whether public authorities should support them in the name of territorial or sectorial logics. Choosing the former raises challenges because it necessitates the drawing of a frontier beyond which products are no longer seen as 'local'. Whereas a pure bureaucrat would have no problem with this, most local authorities are led by politicians who prefer not to create such clear distinctions between insiders and outsiders. Indeed, they are urged to resist such a practice by commercial operators who profit from situations where such 'borders' can shift. More fundamentally, the local food movement faces an even deeper challenge here because, at least over the twentieth century, activities such as the production of fruit and vegetables tend strongly to be structured in terms of sectors within which the Freedom and the Security of the individual producer or distributer have been prioritized, rather than territories where the values of Tradition and a collective take on Security once predominated (Muller, 1984). This means that many institutions located within the Agri-food industry's Commercial, Sourcing, and Employment IR have detached themselves from local decision-making bodies in order to operate on, and be regulated at, a national, European, or even global scale. One of the key consequences here is that policies and rules introduced by local government to favour 'their' producers may fall foul of policies set elsewhere designed to harmonize economic activity in a sector. Here competition policy most obviously aids and abets the construction and perpetuation of sectorial policies within which discrimination by territory is outlawed in the name of economic Freedom and Equality of opportunities. For the moment, local policies in the Gironde which, for example, favour public procurement from local farmers, have yet to be scrutinized or attacked by bodies such as France's *Autorité de la concurrence*, or the European Commission's DG Competition. Nevertheless, as elsewhere in Europe, the theoretical possibility that such attacks might eventuate does nothing to facilitate the building of a durable movement in favour of local food in this region, nor increase a feeling of solidarity amongst its members. Conciliating local food and competition is not seen as an issue so long as market share is low and supermarkets can also participate and use local food for their own image (i.e. if Equality as equal access between all firms is not challenged). But what happens if market share increases and is construed as a threat by powerful actors with clever lawyers? In short, finding a balance between supporting a territorial logic of action (based on Tradition and collective Security) and reconciling it with sectorial ones (based on Freedom, individualized Security, and Equality of opportunity) is a challenge local authorities in the Gironde have had a great deal of difficulty in framing, let alone instrumenting. Instead, the friction this generates between Security, Tradition, and the Freedom of farmers to continue to act 'sectorally' has tended to paralyse politicians and administrators and, subsequently, attenuate the ambitions for policy change they initially may have held.

Such hesitations are also strongly linked to a third characteristic of support for local food in the Gironde regarding the plethora of public bodies who, to different degrees of intensity, are engaged in this process. The Regional Council of Aquitaine's mandate not only encompasses both the Gironde and Lot et Garonne, but it is also explicitly mandated to support 'economic development' within its frontiers. On the basis of this legitimacy, in 2011 it created an officer responsible for local food, a series of instruments for fostering this practice and, with the Regional Chamber of Agriculture, an 'Observatory' charged with producing knowledge about the domain as a whole. However, its policies have frequently been in competition with those of the Gironde's *Conseil Général*, Bordeaux's municipal government, and that of other towns in the area. More precisely, sometimes these local policies supplement each other by sharing the same value definitions and prioritizations, whereas on other occasions they have resulted in duplication or even contradictions. Again, over and above the difficulties they create for the daily functioning of proponents of local food, such frictions sap the coherence and credibility of the movement as a whole and the values that underlie it.

Finally, a great deal of confusion also surrounds how farmers, co-operatives, distributors, and the local authorities listed above evaluate the impacts and costs of local food strategies. At the scale of the individual farmer or even co-operative, such evaluations entail the development of methods that most have never been trained to adopt and practice. Given that most farmers and co-operatives not only sell their produce via local food chains, but also participate in more 'distant' ones (Dubuisson-Quellier & Le Velley, 2008), distinguishing the added value of the former is often highly difficult. Similarly, those involved in distributing local food via 'drives', market stalls, or the Internet also have great difficulty in evaluating with precision their 'local food' activity. Indeed, the most challenging aspect here is often in aggregating data in a way that is both accurate and relevant to decision-makers. As Naves's research has encountered on many occasions (2016), although local food producers often claim to be part of 'networks', databases which include all such operators are yet to even exist in the Aquitaine region. Consequently, data produced on the economics of local food in this locality is always sketchy and often contested. Not surprisingly, this lack of systematic knowledge feeds into the uncertainties about value hierarchies flagged earlier in this section. Specifically, without data about the economic, social, and environmental outcomes of local food initiatives, actors find themselves ill-equipped to systematically discuss the different value priorities flagged earlier, let alone to move towards decisive action on this front. Crucially, however, the inexistence of such data cannot simply be ascribed to the inadequacies of local collective and public organizations. Instead, the lack of instrumentation this constitutes can only be fully understood in terms of the non-stabilization of local food as a public problem in this area, together with the absence of concomitant value-driven modes of legitimation.

Little wonder then that local food as a mode of commercialization and proto-social movement has had great difficulty in promoting and defending itself politically. More precisely, despite benefiting from a symbolism and a rhetoric which is highly favourable to it, local food in the Gironde has no solid foundations in terms of value prioritizations. Localized Traditions of farming and eating are of course constantly evoked, but without such references being either precise or suffused with deep social meaning. Security is a value believed in and deployed as part of arguments to keep small farmers in business and avoid the hegemonic control of agriculture by supermarket chains. However, the version of Security that prevails is so linked to individual producers that it ends up re-invigorating the values of Freedom and Equality (reduced to equal opportunities). Consequently, as in the Scottish borders (Ilbery et al., 2004: 343), a collective definition of Security has not been used more positively to link up with environmental protection and thence questions regarding the durability of certain farm practices as opposed to others. More fundamentally still, at least in the area and sector studied here, local food has singularly failed to meld together the values of Tradition and Security in a compatible way. Specifically, this movement has yet to formulate a problem, set of instruments, and modes of legitimation which could consistently counter arguments made by those who place the entrepreneurs' Freedom to sell their goods as they see fit above all other social goals. As a result, Freedom remains an intervening value which, invariably, supports an equal access approach to Security rather than one based on egalitarian or Traditional principles.

6.2. FREEDOM RULES AGAIN: LOCAL ECONOMIC DEVELOPMENT

My second example of how the local scale has recently been invoked as a means of maintaining or revitalizing economic activity concerns the collective and public interventions known as 'local economic development'. Following the crisis experienced in the 1970s by many large, vertically integrated, European and North American firms, at least in some localities, the following two decades witnessed both the rebirth of alternative forms of economic organization and its theorization within business studies and the social sciences. According to these specialists, the 1970s was a period of paradigmatic change within which 'Fordist' companies had increasingly been supplemented, and sometimes replaced, by more flexible networks of small and medium sized enterprises (SMEs). When writing about the 1980s, they saw this process as particularly well-illustrated by examples of regional dynamism such as 'the Third Italy' (in particular Emilia Romagna: Trigilia, 1986) and California's Silicon Valley (Piore & Sabel, 1984). The recipe for success theorized from these examples boiled down to local firms being strongly encouraged to envisage themselves as vital components of 'industrial districts' within which entrepreneurial SMEs could out-compete lower cost adversaries by emphasizing their collective capacity to innovate, transfer technologies, create synergies, and profit from their strong sense of local identity. Indeed, it was argued, such identity created meaningful symbols that not only deepened inter-enterprise trust, but also built positive ties with local politicians and administrations. To use the terms of this book, the political and academic message was that local solidarities founded upon durable reconciliation of Freedom, Security, and Tradition were well-placed to compete in the new capitalism.

Since the euphoria of the 1980s, however, specialists of local development admit that the faith invested in this model of economic activity has been shaken for two main reasons (Crouch et al., 2001; Trigilia, 2009). Firstly, they consider that the markets for many goods and services have been globalized which has meant that all North American and Western European local development areas have been exposed to intense competition from competitors from throughout the world (Asia and Eastern Europe in particular). Since companies from such countries pay their workers lower wages, have less fiscal and environmental constraints, and often benefit from governmental subsidies, they have gained market share and forced companies even in many fabled industrial districts to switch to 'low cost' business models. This in turn has reduced levels of local trust and co-operation in such areas. In short, the values of Security and Tradition have been decoupled from that of Freedom, leaving the latter as the principal guide for collective and public action.

The second reason specialists of local development have begun to play down the economic significance of industrial districts is a deep-seated debate within this very field of academic specialization. In some instances, those who made their names by theorizing the success stories listed above have linked the existence of strong industrial districts to a specific historical conjuncture. For example, as early as 1992, Trigilia hypothesized that, at least in the Italian case, productive systems of this type were just 'an interlude' in the development of capitalism (1992). More often, however, research has sought to go further in both mapping the variety of local economic development models and theorizing its causes. From the first angle, Le Galès and Voelzkow (2001) for instance highlighted the importance within many regions of 'network firms', i.e. large companies who influence local economic development through their web of sub-contractors and suppliers. This finding was then taken up by Crouch and Trigilia (2001) within a typology that distinguished regions dominated by industrial districts, network firms or simply by 'clusters' of firms operating in the same sector (e.g. the Formula 1-centred high performance motor industry in Oxfordshire, England). In terms of explanation, the role of public policy and authorities has been added to the initial set of variables for defining industrial districts. This has been done to show how local, but also national (Glassmann & Voelzkow, 2001) policy instruments, such as the building of science parks, infrastructures (roads, high-speed internet, etc.), and professional training, can provide levers and catalysts for greater integration within local productive systems. More generally, certain public authorities have also been seen as contributing to the development or maintenance of 'associational economies' such as South Wales (Cooke & Morgan, 1998), and this through encouraging identification with locality via discourse and symbolic action.

Notwithstanding the contribution of this research and theoretical development, since the early 2000s remarkably little scholarly attention has been given to local economic development within sociology and political science.[6] Indeed, this gap in scholarly investment is even more remarkable given that the changing institutions and markets flagged above, together with increasing promotion of Freedom as a guiding value, are likely to have impacted upon the practices and causes of localized productive systems. Having examined cases of local development closely myself in the early 1990s (Smith, 1995), I therefore took up an invitation received in 2015 to revisit this field of activity and the analytical debates it has inspired. This opportunity was to conduct a study of a local political economy commissioned by the employers' association of the Charente: *l'Union du Patronat de la Charente* (UPC).[7] Located in South-West France and with a population of 333,000, this *département* is roughly the size of a rural English county. What motivated the commissioning of our

[6] One explanation is that researchers in these disciplines have increasingly focused instead upon the development of cities and metropolitan areas. Another is that geographers have taken over this 'terrain' with different sets of questions and methods designed essentially to map local economic activity with precision, as opposed to explaining its socio-political causes.

[7] Although I was deeply involved in structuring, analysing, and writing-up this study, nearly all the empirical legwork was undertaken by Amandine Montagut and Yves Montouroy. In thanking them for their significant contributions to this research, I nevertheless take full responsibility for what follows. Moreover, I must underline that the organization of this study, the UPC, also has no responsibility for this analysis.

study was intense concern amongst leaders of the UPC that despite their territory possessing a relatively strong industrial heritage, as well as the continued expansion of its most famous product, Cognac, many of its companies were stagnating or even going to the wall. A lack of co-operation amongst local firms was spontaneously diagnosed as being a prime cause of this trend, alongside deep criticisms of the timidity or irrelevance of local public policies directed at the economy. Our study sought to test these claims, as well as others taken from the specialized literature listed above, through conducting over fifty interviews with local company directors and participating in debates over our findings. Here these results will be synthesized by focusing firstly upon what my 'politics as values' approach reveals about patterns of economic activity in the Charente, then upon the form taken by collective economic action in this area. As will be highlighted throughout, politics as I define it is omnipresent within this case of local development. Given what this book has argued so far, it will come as no surprise that the value of Freedom has played a determining role in its social and collective outcomes. Indeed, the primary importance given to this value has fuelled the remaining and new pockets of dynamism in this area, but also contributed to their fragility. However, the increased importance given to this value in local economic thinking and action can only be fully explained by delving deeply into the competition that has taken place between individualized and collective conceptions of Security, as well as how Tradition has rarely been mobilized in support of the latter.

6.2.1. From Business Logics to Firm–Locality Types

Rather than attempt from the outset to characterize the Charente's economy as an industrial district, as dominated by network firms, or as simply a range of sectorial clusters (Crouch & Trigilia, 2001), we strove first to capture how each firm's commercial practices fitted, more or less smoothly, with the local area. Our second challenge was to discover why some firms invested more deeply in their locality than others and, above all, why this level of development did not simply correlate to their respective business logic. To map these logics, the four recurrent economic practices examined throughout this book—financing, employment, sourcing, commercialization—were used as criteria with which to grasp the role played by the Charente within each firm's business activities. The following three types of 'firm-locality inscriptions' emerged from our interview data: the autonomous, the anchored, and the rooted.

A first range of firms are largely *autonomous* from this locality because although it obviously contains their offices and employees, the Charente is not where capital or raw materials are sourced, or goods and services are sold. Instead, these companies are financed either by the corporation to which they belong (and whose headquarters could be anywhere in the world), or by shareholders through national stock exchanges. Similarly, the 'ingredients' needed to manufacture their products come from outside the locality either as basic commodities, or as goods that have been initially processed by subcontractors who again are not based in the Charente. Finally, this locality is not where products are sold either as finished products to consumers (e.g. handbags made by Hermès), or as components for assembling companies (e.g. helicopter parts manufactured by Meggit). Consequently, purely in terms of business logics, for companies within this ideal type the Charente is essentially just a location for its plant and employees.

Parts of a logic of autonomy are also present in a second ideal-type I call the *anchored*, and this because the firms it describes also depend little upon the Charente in order to finance their operations and sell their products. For example, although companies such as a large manufacturer of machine tools (Leroy Somer) were founded and grew initially in the area, they are now part of multinational corporations who have their capitalization managed from afar. Moreover, like autonomous firms, they have few clients within the *département* itself because their markets are either European or global. Nevertheless, these companies are anchored to this locality firstly because their units of production and management are extensive, thus constituting sunk costs which would have to be written-off should any relocation of production take place. Additionally, these companies are more dependent than their autonomous neighbours upon a skilled labour force whose training they have often invested in considerably. For both these sets of reasons, it follows that leaving the Charente in order to seek lower cost employees (e.g. in Romania), or administrative economies of scale (by centralizing management practices at their corporate headquarters), would not be a straightforward process. Nevertheless, as several recent plant closures in the *département* have shown, ultimately these firms are only anchored within it. As with floating hotels, anchors can be drawn and the enterprise can thus be moved elsewhere, or simply 'sunk in deep water'.

Indeed, it is precisely over this point that the business logic of an anchored firm differs from one that is *rooted* in a locality. Within this third ideal-type, not only does the company source a significant part of its raw materials or components locally, but it also generates its finance via local banks, other credit organizations, and public policies. Moreover, a certain amount of its products are sold locally, typical examples being the brick and tile manufacturer Terreal, or the packaging company Hertus. More importantly still, rooted companies are far more dependent upon the skills and availability of a localized labour force than their autonomous and anchored counterparts. In short, these firms are virtually untransferable to other localities because at least three, and often four, of the basic planks of their business logics are deeply inscribed in the social fabric of their current location.

Like all typologies, mapping firms as autonomous, anchored, or rooted has its limits. For instance, some firms straddle two categories. In the Charente, the most obvious instances are its largest and best-known Cognac producers: Hennessy and Martell. Although both clearly depend upon the Charente for their raw material (all the grapes from which Cognac is distilled must be grown locally), their finance stems from multinational corporations (LVMH for Hennessy and Pernod Ricard for Martell). Moreover, their consumers generally live thousands of kilometres away (today mostly in Asia and the US). These firms thus appear to be deeply rooted but could conceivably reduce, or even theoretically abandon, their production of Cognac should their shareholders decide it would be more profitable to finance the production of, say, vodka in the UK instead.

A second limit of a typology such as this is that the business logic of a firm, and thus its categorization within a type, can change over time. For example, the numerous smaller distillers of Cognac that have progressively been taken over by Hennessy or Martell were more clearly rooted in the Charente due to the familial character of their finance and management. Similarly, when Leroy Somer was locally owned its business logic was turned more towards the *département*, in particular through an approach to employment that once contained many social, and often paternalistic, elements.

6.2.2. Embeddedness, Territory, and Values

More fundamentally, the limitation of this, and any other, typology is that it provides a descriptive list rather than an analytical tool. In order to capture both a fuller picture of the actual inscription of a firm in its locality and its causes, an additional set of sharper questions need to be asked. More precisely, those that concern us here entail going beyond describing the strictly business logic of each firm in order to understand the wider involvement of its management in the Charente and their reasons for investing in it, or not. Before providing empirical examples of such investment or its absence from our study of this *département*, three conceptual moves need to be made. First, I borrow the concept of 'embeddedness' from economic sociology, secondly I link it to the term 'territory' to include variables pertaining to public policy and politicians, finally I reassert the crucial role of values that overarches this analytical framework.

The principle advantage of the concept of 'embeddedness' (Granovetter, 1985) is that it guides research to discovering how the intra-business logics identified and illustrated above fit outside the firm within varying systems of social relations. Rather than being one-off interactions structured by short term, cost–benefit calculations, these are most often genuine, longstanding relationships within which different levels of solidarity or even trust can develop. In short, questions of research driven by embeddedness produce knowledge about how a firm's managers relate in very concrete terms to their respective 'environments'.

This brings us to a second conceptual move which consists in defining these relational contexts as either sectorial or territorial. If many of a firm's relations are located primarily within sectors that can extend their reach throughout the world, such as spirit drinks for Cognac producers, others are intersectoral and strongly linked to specific localities (such as those that concern infrastructures and basic professional training). Indeed, because localities are spaces of rules and public action, but also of social meaning, I deliberately switch to the concept of 'territory' in order to encapsulate them. More precisely, as Caitríona Carter and I have illustrated elsewhere with the example of Scotland (Carter & Smith, 2008 & 2009), studying economic activity around sector–territory mediations provides a heuristic means of deepening analysis of firm embeddedness.

Finally, and even more fundamentally, what I call here 'territorial embeddedness' needs to be studied from the angle of the 'Politics as values' approach deployed throughout this book. This approach refutes rationalist analysis in terms of constant cost–benefit calculations, while postulating instead that actors are driven by what they consider is 'the right thing to do'. Specifically, I hypothesize that the relationship between a firm and the territory within which it resides is ultimately caused by the hierarchy its managers establish, then apply in practice, between Freedom, Security, Equality, and Tradition.

Now that this set of definitions and claims are in place, let us return to the typology of business logics in the Charente in order to generate questions and findings about the politics of local economic development. Recall that a proponent of rational choice theory examining these logics would deduce that *autonomous* firms would not care about local development at all, *anchored* ones could care, but only about the specific issues that affect them directly (e.g. roads or internet access), leaving *rooted* firms as the only consistent 'rational' supporters of actions to support economic activity at the local scale. Crucially, however, our data frequently invalidates such predictions, thereby generating stimulating questions for both research and public policy. A first line of enquiry, not examined further here for reasons of space, concerns the relatively small subset of autonomous firms who do engage in local collective action. Instead, the two sets of questions dealt with below are:

(i) Why do so many anchored firms invest so much of their resources in attempting to orientate local collective and public policies that do not directly affect them?

(ii) Why, on the contrary, do a significant number of rooted firms refuse to participate in making these policies?

Explaining territorial commitment amongst anchored firms: given that the financing of these firms comes from outside the Charente, most of their products are sourced and sold elsewhere and the basic infrastructures enabling them to do so are already in place, it is counter-intuitive that the managers of many of these entities spend so much of their time co-operating with their counterparts in other companies in order to enact a wide range of collective and public interventions. In a word, although on paper these firms could be relatively footloose, in practice they are not. The first step in explaining what many commentators would see as an incongruous investment in local development is to consider that the embeddedness of these firms is not about commercial transactions per se. Rather decision-makers in these companies give priority to the medium- and long-term future because their underlying aim is to reduce uncertainty by making their ties with other actors as predictable as possible. As the owner of one such firm underlined to his counterparts during a meeting to discuss our findings, 'us business leaders need to understand that co-operating closely with public authorities is a win–win situation' (Angoulême, May 2015). This begs two further questions: why are mangers of such firms so driven by this approach to 'economic time'? And why does this translate into territorial rather than purely sectorial action?

At least in the Charente, answers to the former question are to be found in the importance given by managers of anchored firms to the value of Security. Our findings show firstly that these actors define the Security of their locality not only around projections into a relatively distant future, but also as a fundamentally collective goal that only sustained co-operation between a range of economic and social actors can attain. For example, managers from Lafarge, a large cement manufacturer, consider that the development of the local economy as a whole is important for their workforce, its training and, more generally, the image of industry itself within the Charente. Indeed, Security here is not given a purely individualistic meaning (that of their firm), but instead one that embraces collective, socio-economic interdependence.

Of course, collective action taken solely within the firm's sector of activity provides one avenue for both promoting the value of Security and enhancing the likelihood of its realization. For example, Leroy Somer's management closely follow how the French ministry of Research supports the engineering industry through subsidies. However, actors interviewed who work for anchored firms that invest in collective action, consider that sectorial political work alone is insufficient for two reasons. The first, and most obvious, concerns how such actors define territorialized 'collective competition goods' as essential to their competitiveness within sectors. They consider this can be achieved in part by intensifying knowledge exchange between local firms and plugging gaps in value chains by choosing to develop and work with neighbouring firms. Indeed, our interviewees from Leroy Somer underlined that precisely because the ownership of their firm was now based in Canada, they often had to make a case in-house for retaining their factories in the Charente which demonstrated its advantages over other territories such as South Wales or Romania (interview, Angoulême, March 2015).

The second reason managers of anchored firms have for investing in local development is that certain perennial challenges businesses face simply cannot be dealt with by adopting a purely sectorial logic. In the Charente, the most salient of such challenges concerns the capacity of its anchored firms to attract and retain skilled managers and employees. Contrary to popular belief, high salaries or the availability of cheap housing are not sufficient to attract and retain this category of worker in a predominantly rural area. Instead, special efforts need making both to generate jobs likely to interest the spouses of a firm's workers recruited from elsewhere and, more generally, to improve the local 'quality of life'. As regards spouses, other regions such as Brittany have been particularly active in creating local networks of human resources managers who systematically exchange information over job availabilities. However, in the Charente nothing formalized has ever been set up to tackle this dimension of employment challenges. Meanwhile, although 'quality of life' is clearly a vague notion whose definition varies greatly, at least for the category of managers and other skilled workers considered necessary for local development, in the Charente this has led to attempts to improve secondary schooling and subsidize municipal cultural policies in particular. Moreover, the shrinking distance of the *département*'s capital (Angoulême) from Bordeaux and Paris due to a new high-speed train link is currently being discursively turned into an advantage for families from certain social strata, whereas beforehand longer travelling times were presented as significant handicaps.

More fundamentally, however, the commitment of many managers of anchored firms to local development actions stems from them having striven to take 'ownership' of these problems (Gusfield, 1981). In the Charente, this quest is fuelled in particular by what company managers perceive as disinterest in industry by local politicians. Indeed, one of the reasons why calls for collective action amongst firms in the Charente has resonance for managers of anchored firms is a widespread perception that public actors are not looking after the public interest. In turn, and in contrast to other French *départements* such as La Vendée, this representation of reality is fuelled by the absence of a discourse by local politicians which, notably by mobilizing the value of Tradition, is reputed elsewhere to symbolize how the joint actions of local politicians and businesses possess social meaning and legitimacy. Indeed, in the Charente collective action amongst employers today takes strength from a belief that they can deepen an identification with the area, whereas those democratically elected to do just this have singularly failed in this respect. In a word, these employers today consider that they 'own' a significant part of the Charente's development problems.

Why do certain rooted firms reject territory?: If the participation of many anchored firms in the Charente's development can be explained through analysis in terms of embeddedness, territory, and values, this formula can also be used to understand why a large number of firms rooted in this area do not participate in territorialized collective action. Before beginning this analysis, however, it is first important to recognize that two other, simpler explanations are generally deployed by Charentais actors themselves. The first considers that firms which refuse to join local development initiatives are simply avoiding its costs and making the most of its benefits by 'free-riding' upon the efforts made by other actors. A second rationalist-type argument is that managers of such firms simply lack the time to engage in collective action. Needless to say, both of these analyses are generally insufficient and often completely wrong. There is no evidence in our interviews that managers of firms who do not believe in local development are cynics who want others to work for their benefit at no cost to themselves. Similarly, given that time is not universally perceived in the same way, what determines a manager's decision to invest in local development or not can only be fully explained by what they consider to be priorities and, therefore, by their respective hierarchy of values.

Stated more positively, when analysing the non-implication of actors from rooted companies in local development, the most fundamental driver is the prevalence of the value of Freedom, the rejection of Tradition as a motivation for acting collectively or publicly and a reduction of the value of Security to the short-term needs of each individual firm. The emphasis placed by such actors upon the value of Freedom explains not only how they perceive the future of their firm, but also reveals their lack of codes for understanding and getting involved in collective action. Such actors see their firm as isolated from others not because their business logic means they do not interact with local interlocutors, since they clearly do so. Rather, they cannot see how co-operation with other company managers will occur in a sustained manner so as to create solidarity and trust, nor do they have faith in the local organizations which claim to promote these goals. Indeed, part of the explanation of these representations lies in bodies such as the UPC rarely engaging in focused political work over the concrete issues that actually interest company managers (e.g. recruiting and retaining human resources).

However, these representations of the Charente as a hotbed of 'individualists' where collective action is nonexistent also stems from neglect by its elected elites of symbolic action that can foster identification with, and thus the legitimacy of, a territory. Rightly or wrongly, today these politicians are seen as cut off from 'the reality' of running a firm in today's conditions. A wide range of interviewees repeatedly told us that local politicians 'never come to see us' or, when they do, 'they are no good at understanding and transmitting our preoccupations'. More fundamentally still, unlike in other territories such as La Vendée or Emilia Romagna, Tradition as a value has not been updated by these politicians in a way that resonates with their business community and thence promotes identification, solidarity, and trust. On the contrary, the dominant attitude to public authorities amongst representatives of rooted firms who turn their backs on collective and public action is one of distrust, disdain, and defiance. Instead of envisaging leaders of collective or public bodies as allies, they are seen as living in a separate world. From this basic assumption, it is easy to understand why these managers of rooted firms restrict their conception of Security to purely sectorial and relatively short-term goals for their own companies. Moreover, in so doing they end up embracing Freedom more by default than by believing strongly in this value per se.

In summary, revisiting this recent study of the Charente from the 'Politics as Values' perspective has contributed to existing knowledge about local economic development in at least two ways. First, it has confirmed that the rational choice analysis in terms of cost–benefit calculus so dear to liberal political economy, insufficiently explains either investment in such development, or absences of commitment to this goal. One simply cannot deduce from the assumed business logics of individual firms why, in any locality, sentiments of solidarity or trust emerge between them, or fail to do so. Instead, the independent variable of political work provides essential tools for grasping the causality behind such processes. Second, and more fundamentally, I have also shown that it is values, and more precisely a hierarchy between those of Freedom, Security, and Tradition, that drive both political work and how it is interpreted by managers in firms that are only indirectly involved in it. As territories other than the Charente exemplify, such values can themselves be worked upon and given more or less social resonance. When such work is either not done or tackled 'inappropriately', local development itself soon becomes a meaningless term that has only negative effects upon economic activity and socio-economic outcomes.

CONCLUSION

More generally, as my case studies of both economic development in the Charente and local food networks in the Gironde underline, in itself the local is never a panacea. Producing positive effects through acting publicly or collectively at the local scale depends upon how representations of territory are mobilized to change or reproduce institutions that are relevant to an economic activity. More precisely, what needs to be ascertained is the extent to which a locality has an impact upon the value-fuelled problematizations around which institutions are challenged or defended, the policy instruments they maintain or modify and the modes of legitimation used to do either. From this perspective, the local scale can have an impact in at least two ways. Firstly, arguments of proximity can be mobilized to build or consolidate networks of actors, notably by promoting the value of security (from an angle of durable inter-firm relations). Secondly, the locality itself can be worked upon and mobilized as a mode of legitimation based upon the value of Tradition. By contrast, when given primacy that disconnects it from other values, Freedom-driven political work tends to negate references to the local by seeing them only as a constraint upon commercial action. This, for example, is what has occurred in many cities throughout the world over the last three decades. Armed with the value of Freedom and neo-liberal policy recipes, urban policies ranging from housing to culture have been transformed ostensibly in order to facilitate the growth of businesses and, perhaps above all, increase the wealth of the propertied upper and upper-middle classes.

From there, however, it is important not to reduce the causes of this trend to the hegemony of capital armed with neo-liberal ideology, as neo-Marxist or neo-Gramscian authors so often do (Harvey, 2003 & 2009). Although both these aspects of local politics clearly do need taking into account, as Pinson and Morel-Journel (2016) have convincingly shown, neo-liberalization has not been institutionalized in all cities and across all policy domains. Instead, resistance to value hierarchies dominated by Freedom continues to be mounted by many other actors. Moreover, in numerous cities struggles amongst the propertied and with other social groups have given rise to socio-economic practices and outcomes that are very different from those advocated by the neo-liberal purist's model. Once again, and as much from the point of view of the practitioner as that of the analyst, it is therefore vital to embrace the contingencies that have emerged in each local area and the value-fuelled politics that have caused each territorialized outcome.

7

Conclusion

This research essay has above all sought to build and propose a theoretically solid and sharply-drawn definition of politics, then to assess its heuristic worth against eight case studies of how contemporary economic activity is governed. Defined as *the mobilization or suppression of values in order to change or reproduce economic institutions*, this politics has been the causal influence behind the forms of economic government, co-operation, and conflict analysed in the preceding chapters. These analyses have also striven to contribute to debates about how economic practices are currently structured at or across four scales: the global, the EU, the state, and the local.

What now remains to be done is to deepen this analysis further by comparing the value frictions and hierarchies I have revealed in each case study. From there, more general lessons from the book as a whole will be synthesized before looking ahead to where, in my view, research in political economy, but also public debate in this issue area, could and should now be focusing its attention.

7.1. COMPARING POLITICS–ECONOMICS RELATIONSHIPS

Flagged from the outset, the first finding derived from comparing my case studies is that Freedom and Security are the values which are omnipresent within their respective governing. More precisely, in each issue area the principal tension that links or opposes actors lies in the relationship between and within these two values. This finding is not surprising given that capitalism in liberal democracies is theoretically grounded upon according autonomy to economic actors on the one hand whilst, on the other, controlling their actions in the name of the public interest. However, what my approach encourages research and reflexion to do is firstly delve deeper into the content of both Freedom and Security and, secondly, to include within analysis the role played by two other mediating values, Equality and Tradition.

Freedom is clearly a value that lies at the heart of liberal political thought in general and applied to economic activity in particular. Within this vast subject of scholarship, ideology, and practice, a basic shared assumption is that providing economic actors with a high degree of independence from external control is the best means of encouraging innovation, competition, positive usage of 'comparative advantages', and, consequently, optimal economic and social outcomes. This said, and despite rhetoric to the contrary, few renowned liberals have gone so far as to consider that the Freedom of economic agents should be completely unfettered by publicly set rules and norms. In the words of Isaiah Berlin, 'total liberty for the wolves is death to the lambs' (1990: 12). Instead, most liberals accept that Security is a value that needs integrating within the government of economic activity for at least two reasons. Firstly, rules in the name of Security limit negative externalities, such as environmental damage. Secondly, and more fundamentally, liberals acknowledge that durable economic activity can only take place if other Security-legitimated rules are also established and respected, notably property rights, contract guarantees and competition law. Indeed, as my case study of EU competition policy highlights, liberals frequently disagree strongly amongst themselves over how Freedom and Security should be balanced. Put succinctly, whereas those close to 'the Chicago School of economics and law' consider Freedom should trump Security in nearly all instances, 'Ordoliberals' believe more strongly in Security, as well as in the need for public administrations to be its guarantor (Denord, 2007).

Of course, Security itself is a value more spontaneously associated with the socio-democratic or 'centrist' political thought which has clearly also left its mark upon the way economic activity is governed in the polities that concern us here. Indeed, from this angle Security is generally thought about first and foremost from the point of view of the individual citizen, and the least well-off in particular, rather than from that of the firm and the entrepreneur. This value thus lies at the heart of the social protection and labour market regimes which impact upon the Freedom of owners, shareholders, and managers to run their respective businesses. But Security can also be defined from the angle of human safety, for example to legitimize constraints upon pesticide or vehicle pollution, or market authorizations for pharmaceuticals. Indeed, many critics consider that since the 1970s the value of Security has become so all-encompassing that the constraints placed in its name upon the Freedom of businesses have lost their 'bite' (Crouch, 2013; Schäfer and Streeck, 2013). To summarize such analyses using the terms of this book, if Freedom–Security is still seen as the key relationship within 'regulated capitalism', this couple has become increasingly tilted towards the concerns of Freedom's advocates at the expense of those of Security.

If the eight case studies in this book largely bolster this sweeping claim, they also enable analysis to go a stage further by identifying how the

Table 7.1. Mediating the Freedom–Security relationship

Case study	Equality	Tradition
Pesticide controls	Silent	Supporting stasis
Geographical indications for food	Intervening	Intervening
Pharmaceutical pricing	Intervening	Supporting stasis
Competition regulation	Intervening	Silent
Encouraging electric vehicles	Silent	Supporting stasis
Structuring labour markets	Silent	Silent
Promoting local foods	Intervening	Supporting change
Catalysing local economic trust	Silent	Supporting change

mobilization or suppression of Equality and Tradition have participated greatly in re-hierarchizing Freedom–Security relationships. Indeed, the second overall finding highlighted here concerns how actors have treated Equality or Tradition in their political work to either prompt change in the governing of economic activity or to conserve the status quo. As Table 7.1 sets out, in so doing, these values have played roles that range from supporting to silent, whilst in some cases 'intervening' more directly by providing the battleground within which conflict between Freedom and Security takes place.

Although there are obviously important differences between each of these cases, comparison of the roles played by Equality and Tradition enables better understanding of three types of socio-economic outcome: Freedom-dominated stasis, nascent incremental change, and paradigmatic gridlock.

The first of these types of outcomes is common to pesticide controls, electric vehicles, local foods, and labour market structuring. In each of these cases, proposals for radical change to economic practice and its governance have been formulated and, to varying degrees, injected into the definition of public problems, policy instruments, and acts of legitimation. For example, stricter rules on pesticide usage have been introduced throughout most of the Western world, just as encouragement for local food production has been given widespread public backing. However, in each of these four instances incumbent actors armed principally with the value of Freedom have won out. In the cases of pesticides and electric vehicles, Tradition has frequently been mobilized to support Freedom by legitimizing the status quo as anchored in longstanding economic and social practices. Contrastingly, and unsurprisingly, Tradition has been used by local food advocates as a means of legitimizing change but has had little impact upon consumer and producer practices.

More importantly still, in all four of these cases the value of Equality has either remained silent or been silenced. This is particularly obvious in the case of the French agricultural labour market where, in contrast to that of aquaculture in Norway, no sustained argument has been made for improving the lot of farmworkers, and this despite the difficulty farming in France now experiences in attracting employees into its ranks. Meanwhile, the silencing of Equality is also highly evident in the cases of pesticides and electric vehicles where arguments for greater environmental protection for all citizens in the name of collective goods have been drowned out by claims that individual producers 'need' to continue growing crops or making cars in ways that manifestly damage both the planet and human health.

If such debates within the value of Equality have largely been muzzled in the four cases just mentioned, they nevertheless have had a little more traction within the governing of two instances where the possibility of change has emerged: pharmaceutical pricing and inter-firm competition. In the case of medicines, chapter 4 related how since the late 1990s a sustained debate has emerged over how these products should be priced and, consequently, what degree of access patients should have to them. Here the 'incumbents' in the industry—large pharmaceutical producers—have been particularly active in arguing for the status quo by harnessing the value of Freedom (of patients and manufacturers) to that of Equality as equal opportunities. Meanwhile, a range of 'challengers', which includes some national regulatory agencies, ministries of health, and social insurance providers, have sought to develop a more egalitarian take on Equality as a means of legitimizing re-problematizations and instrumentations of pharmaceuticals in the name of both 'value for money' and the durability of national health systems. Mobilizing Freedom but also the value of Tradition (here of public support for scientific 'innovation'), many actors, notably in France, have thus far successfully worked politically in order to maintain high pharmaceutical prices. Nevertheless, as the English example highlights, this interpretation of Tradition has become increasingly challenged. Similarly, and over much the same period, the regulation of inter-firm competition has experienced deep debates over a Freedom–Equality based rationale for outlawing economic practices such as takeovers, abuse of market domination, and state aids. Here, 'Chicago'-inspired actors have advocated reasoning in terms of efficient outcomes for all consumers, whereas ordoliberals have remained wedded to both an equal opportunities problematization and instruments designed to favour Security.

The third and final type of socio-economic outcome witnessed in these case studies is that of stalemate between two competing and relatively evenly matched adversaries, each armed with their respective value hierarchy. The case that exemplifies this type concerns geographical indications (GIs) for foods. As related in chapter 3, producers and administrations in the EU are firmly in favour of these policy instruments because, they claim, GIs incentivize smaller producers to produce 'Traditional' foodstuffs by providing them with greater Security. Moreover, a certain egalitarianism pervades the EU's problematization of GIs, alongside denials that they seriously damage the Freedom of non-GI producers to compete within food markets. By contrast, stakeholders from the 'New World' are diametrically opposed to GIs precisely because, they claim, these policy instruments seriously restrict the Freedom of producers and consumers. In addition, the Security of both is best assured by trademarks and the free play of market forces, whilst Equality and Tradition are not seen to be at issue, and definitely not motives for institutionalized public problems. Indeed, to paraphrase Hobsbawn and Ranger (1983), New World producers are particularly distrustful of 'inventions of tradition' they perceive as locking in economic and political rents.

Overall then, much can be gained from studying the emergence and evolution of value hierarchies within industries and trans-industry regulations, then comparing them in order to deepen or refine analysis of their causes. Defining politics as the mobilization (or suppression) of values to affect institutions thus provides a heuristic means of analysing change and stasis within both economic activity and its governance. It does so by going beyond the 'interest' and 'power' centred political economies, notably those developed respectively by proponents of liberal Economic Institutionalism and neo-Marxist or neo-Gramscians, in order to identify how both these concepts are constructed within political work. Moreover, the analysis presented here also extends historical and sociological institutionalism, in particular by reframing institutions themselves as dependent variables whose change or reproduction can only be explained by conceptualizing political work as value-driven. Indeed, and ultimately, such analysis highlights the deep value-laden causes of social conflict regarding the economic in a way that many societal practitioners could find useful and 'actionable'. To go further in proposing a political economy of this type, however, a new agenda for research must first be mapped out then adopted.

7.2. THE ROAD AHEAD FOR RESEARCH AND REFLECTION

At this stage, at least two parallel paths now need to be taken in order to follow up on the propositions and analyses made in this book. On the one hand, inter- and intra-disciplinary cross-fertilization needs pursuing in order to bolster and renew the methodological dimension of the 'politics as values' approach advocated here. On the other, an equally demanding linkage needs building between the theorization of politics proposed and sophisticated, sociological approaches to the concept and study of power.

From the point of view of potential collaborations with other parts of the social sciences who have invested in the study of values, there are clearly a number of possibilities to pursue. Indeed, given their longstanding interest in values and the weakness of its treatment within political economy, specialists of the latter like myself obviously have much to learn from these sources.

The first and most evident of these other areas of social science is the history of political thought and philosophy. Sometimes labelled 'principles of justice', values are frequently at the heart of this strand of social science, and in particular its publications dedicated to the study of politics (see for example the life work of Quentin Skinner and, in particular his *Visions of Politics* trilogy, 2002). Here much inspiration can be taken from deep analysis of certain values in particular (e.g. Freedom), their roots and their evolution over time. Indeed, recent research in this vein has targeted the economic in ways that are concordant with the aims of this book (e.g. Denord, 2007). Moreover, given that much of the scholarship in this subject area is conducted by academics who, at least in part, identify themselves as historians, much can also be taken from their rigorous approach to documentary source material. Similarly, many of today's specialists in political thought frequently use computerized textual analysis, a research technique which could usefully be brought to bear upon questions of political economy (e.g. by analysing a time series of judicial decisions concerning inter-firm competition or speeches by politicians about labour markets).

Just as evidently, in order to pursue the 'politics as values' route, sustained exchange also needs to be built with specialists in contemporary political behaviour. Once again, values are at the heart of this field of research, and this whether the subject is studied using either quantitative or qualitative data collection techniques. Those who master questionnaire-based surveys tend to dominate the study of values within political science and sociology. Indeed, behind 'flagships' such as Ronald Inglehart (director of 'the World Values Series' and author of key books regarding post-modernist values—Inglehart, 1977—and the causes and effects of multiculturalism: Inglehart & Norris, 2009), an armada of colleagues have been engaged for several decades in tracking shifts in the values of individuals, as well as country-level and cross-national trends (Mayer, 2010). There is clearly much to be taken from this field, firstly in terms of conceptualizations of values and their links to politics and, secondly, as regards methodologically solid means of unpacking data and testing hypotheses on a large scale (e.g. questionnaire-based surveys of elites). More generally, and once again, those trained in political economy like myself therefore have much to gain from what has become a large research sub-discipline.

This said, such exchange must not become a one-way street. Although many specialists in political behaviour also deploy qualitative methods and study groups or organizations, to my knowledge combining this angle, their quantitative data and the constructivist and institutionalist approach advocated in this book has yet to be attempted. Indeed, there are three key aspects like-minded colleagues in political economy and I can bring to the table here. The first is the emphasis, underlined throughout this book, we place upon hierarchies of values and the mediations made between them. The second is detailed knowledge about, and careful theorization of, the institutions which structure the economic dimension of societies. As I have shown along with many other institutionalists cited over the course of the preceding pages, economic activity, and the co-operation or conflict that shapes it, do not occur in a random or arbitrary fashion. Instead, they are deeply structured by institutions that have been built, maintained, or changed through political work, i.e. the mobilization or suppression of values. Accordingly, (new) institutionalism's contribution to understanding contemporary 'regulatory' capitalism simply must be connected up with research on political behaviour in general. Indeed, as this book has demonstrated, it is precisely by melding compatible institutionalisms to constructivism that bridges can be built between theories of the state and capitalism, as well as other dynamic parts of the social sciences centred upon politics (Hay, 2006a & 2015).

The third contribution a melding of constructivism and institutionalism can make to dialogue with colleagues trained in these areas concerns the role of scale within contemporary politics. Although this was not their primary purpose, by focusing successively upon the global, the EU, the national, then the local scales of governing economic activity, chapters 3 to 6 have used a theorization of institutionalized configurations which pushes research beyond the excessively convenient focus upon the nation-state favoured by specialists of political behaviour. Yes, the national scale is still highly important and powerful and one can and should embrace the fact that valuable data sets have been constructed at this level. However, it is deeply misleading to start research from the assumption that the national scale is naturally the most revealing unit of analysis, just as it is intellectually lazy to interpret one's findings merely in terms of what they mean for the nation-state. Instead, it is more heuristic to consider that more pertinent units of analysis may, for example, be an industry that is regulated across the national, EU, global, and local scales of overlapping institutions and organizations (Jullien & Smith, 2014).

Indeed, these points on value hierarchies, institutions, and scale bring me full circle to a final debate that needs to be reframed within political economy itself, and thus within historical and sociological institutionalism more generally. This debate concerns the theoretical and methodological articulation between the type of conception of politics I advocate and a compatible definition of power. As I have asserted from the outset, it is extremely advantageous to analytically distinguish between *politics* (as the mobilization of values to affect institutions) and *power* (as the asymmetric relationships between actors who participate in the Institutional Orders which structure industries or trans-industry regulations). In this book, I have attempted to show how even within Institutional Orders that are so heavily skewed in favour of certain actors, such as those of the pharmaceutical or car industries, contingency, and thus scope for political work to engender institutional change, can and does still occur. Indeed, it is precisely through working to redefine or re-prioritize certain values that actors are able to widen (or shrink) this space of contingency. What now needs developing, however, is a means of theorizing how the structuring of asymmetries, and thus power, affect contingencies and how they can be politically worked upon.

In order to address this key challenge, with colleagues I have recently experimented with an adaptation of Bourdieu's Field Theory as a means of both achieving theoretical completion and coherence, whilst on the methodological front guiding research to produce appropriate sets of data (Itçaina, Roger & Smith, 2016a).

In terms of theory, much can be gained by engaging with economic sociologists who have also adopted the concept of fields in order to grasp the relational dimension of the economic, together with its asymmetries (notably Fligstein and McAdam, 2012). However, this interactionist variant of field theory nevertheless suffers from a number of weaknesses which sap its capacity to fully grasp the structural character of fields and thus of power distribution (Itçaina, Roger & Smith, 2016b). In particular, this approach theorizes state actors as being outside economic fields, and indeed in fields of their own, whereas we envisage them as intrinsic parts of the socio-economic. Consequently, for theoretical inspiration we have turned back instead to the founder of field theory, Pierre Bourdieu (1992). The reason for doing so has been to better guide our empirical research to discovering not only the regular interactions between protagonists within, for example, an industry such as wine, but also the underlying asymmetric sets of 'capital' which determine their respective position within such a space. Put succinctly, we have explored the analytical purchase of conceptualizing as fields the Institutional Orders theorized and illustrated in this book. In so doing, we have sought to include within our dependent variable—i.e. the institutionalized phenomena whose change or reproduction need explaining—an interpretation in terms of structural power. In order to avoid falling into a structuralism that minimizes the role of agency, however, the proposition this particular book has striven to formulate is to define an independent variable—the explanation—as being politics as values. More precisely, the challenge now is to show how the mobilization and prioritization of values reproduces or causes change not only within orderings of institutions, but how it also affects the relationship between each order and their respective 'fields of forces and struggles' (Bourdieu, 1992). Targeting how the mobilization of values can create contingency within and across fields is how I personally am now attempting to address this analytical challenge.

Meanwhile, in terms of methodological challenges, using Bourdieu-inspired field theory and detailed sociographical databases, other colleagues in France and Canada have already gone a long way towards studying power in a way that shows how asymmetric stocks of power affect societal outcomes. Indeed, this method of data production and analysis has proved extremely fruitful.

Moreover, these scholars have tackled this challenge in a way that increasingly encompasses the multi-scalar dimension of contemporary social, economic, and political life (Georgakakis & Rowell, 2013; Mérand, 2015). Overall, then, what now needs achieving is a seamless fusing together of constructivist institutionalism, 'politics as values' and what has too often been dismissed as an overly structuralist approach to fields and thence power.

These then are some key goals I consider now need to be reset for theory, methodology, and thus analysis. As important as they are, however, research must nevertheless not lose sight of the purpose of this exercise. To my mind at least, the aim is not just to make scholars, their students, and those listening outside academia better understand what structures economic activity. Nor should the objective simply be to clarify what politics is—although, as this book has underlined, this is clearly a vital step forward. Instead, the goal must be to discourage all fatalistic approaches to modern public life (Hay, 2007) which lead anyone to think that its socio-economics are set in stone and will always favour those that are currently at the top of the tree. We all have values and, at least in Western democracies, political work is open to us all if we really want to commit ourselves to it. Colin Crouch, for example, implicitly reformulates the value of Security when arguing that the time is ripe for a new political movement striving to found 'a social investment welfare state' (Crouch, 2013: 84). Similarly, Thomas Piketty has clearly sought to reassert the value of equality within his carefully documented call for 'putting the distributional question back at the heart of economic analysis' (2014: 15). Meanwhile, Colin Hay and Anthony Payne have implicitly encompassed both these proposals within their manifesto in favour of 'civic capitalism', a concept which, they argue, encourages us all to ask ourselves 'what capitalism can do for us and not what we can do for capitalism' (2015: 4).

Ultimately, over and beyond the precise arguments and propositions made by such scholars, what is vital to retain is that rethinking the politics that shapes the economic, and therefore all our lives, is the first step to reclaiming it. As Joseph Gusfield underlined thirty-five years ago, by championing 'sociological irony' social science can and must 'hold up that which is taken for granted, familiar, and commonplace as something strange and problematic', and then 'imagine that things can be otherwise' (1981: 191, 193). At the very least, this book has provided some pointers for each of us, each in their own way, to move assertively and confidently in the direction of repossessing the economic by embracing the politics that has been, and always will be, its cause.

Bibliography

Abbott, F., Dukes, G. (2009) *Global Pharmaceutical Policy. Ensuring Medicines for Tomorrow's World*, Cheltenham: Edward Elgar.

Abdelal, R., Blyth, M., Parsons, C., eds. (2010) *Constructing the International Economy*, Ithaca: Cornell University Press.

Allaire, G. (1988) 'Le modèle de développement agricole des années 1960', *Economie Rurale*, issue 184–6: 171–86.

Allaire, G., Boyer, R., eds. (1995) *La grande transformation de l'agriculture*, Paris: Economica.

Amable, B., Palombarini, S., (2009) 'A neorealist approach to institutional change and the diversity of capitalism', *Socio-Economic Review*, 7(1): 123–43.

Anand, N. (2011) 'The Retrospective Use of Tournament Rituals in Field Configuration: The Case of the 1976 "Judgement of Paris" Wine', in Moeran, B., Strandgaard, J., eds., *Negotiating Values in the Creative Industries: Fairs, Festivals and Competitive Events*, Cambridge: Cambridge University Press, pp. 321–33.

Ansaloni, M., Smith, A. (2014) 'Whither The State When it Acts Through Markets? The Case of Pesticide Reduction in the vineyard of Bordeaux', *Economic Sociology. European Electronic Newsletter*, 15(2): 34–40.

Armstrong, K., Bulmer, S. (1998) *The Governance of the Single European Market*, Manchester: Manchester University Press.

Aylward, D., Zanko, M. (2008) 'Reconfigured Domains: Alternative Pathways for the International Wine Industry', *International Journal of Technology, Policy and Management*, 8(2): 148–66.

Bache, I., Flinders, M. (2005) *Multilevel Governance*, Oxford: Oxford University Press.

Bagnasco, A., Trigilia, V. (1993) *La construction sociale du marché, le défi de la troisième Italie*, Paris: Les éditions de l'Ecole Normale de Cachan.

Baran, P. (1957) *The Political Economy of Growth*, New York: Monthly Review Press.

Barma, N., Vogel, S. (2008) *The Political Economy Reader: Markets as Institutions*, London: Routledge.

Bélis-Bergouignan, M-C, Montalban, M., Sakinc, E., Smith, A. (2014) *L'industrie pharmaceutique: règles, acteurs et pouvoir*, Paris: La Documentation Française.

Benjamin, B., Podolny, J. (1999) 'Status, quality, and social order in the California Wine industry, 1981–1991', *Administrative Science Quarterly*, 44(3): 563–89.

Benoît, C. (2016) *Les transformations de l'accès au marché des médicament en France et en Angleterre (1995–2015): une économie politique*, forthcoming PhD thesis, University of Bordeaux.

Benoît, C., Gorry, P. (2013) 'The scientific based institutionalization of Health Technology Assessment: a bibliometric & network analysis'. Paper presented at the 10th HTAI Annual Meeting, Seoul, June.

Benoît, C., Nouguez, E. (2016) 'La fixation du prix des médicaments en France: entre planification, valuation et régulation' (forthcoming).

Berlin, I. (1990) 'The Pursuit of the Ideal', republished in *The Crooked Timber of Humanity. Chapters in the History of Ideas*, London: John Murray.

Bernard De Raymond, A. (2013) *En toute saison. Le marché de fruits et legumes en France*, Rennes: Presses Universitaires de Rennes.

Besson, Y. (2011) *Les fondateurs de l'agriculture biologique*, Paris: Editions Sang de la Terre.

Bhattacharjea, A. (2006) 'The case for a multilateral agreement in competition policy: A developing country perspective', *Economic Law*, 9(2): 293–323.

Billig, M. (1995) *Banal Nationalism*, London: Sage.

Bisley, N. (2007) *Rethinking Globalization*, Basingstoke: Palgrave.

Blyth, M. (2002) *Great Transformations: Economic Ideas and Institutional Change in the Twentieth Century*, Cambridge: Cambridge University Press.

Blyth, M., ed. (2009) *Routledge Handbook of International Political Economy (IPE): IPE as a global conversation*, London: Routledge.

Blyth, M. (2013) *Austerity: The History of a Dangerous Idea*, Oxford: Oxford University Press.

Boudon, R. (1999) 'La rationalité axiologique: une notion essentielle pour l'analyse des phénomènes normatives', *Sociologies et societies*, 31(1): 103–17.

Bourdieu, P. (1992) 'The Logic of Fields', in Bourdieu, P., *An Invitation to Reflexive Sociology*, Chicago: University of Chicago Press, pp. 94–114.

Boy, L. (2003) 'Quel rôle pour la politique de la concurrence dans les négociations internationals?' *Economie rurale*, issue 277–8.

Boyer, R. (2015) *Economie politique des capitalismes. Théorie de la regulation et des crises*, Paris: La Découverte.

Boyer, R., Saillard, Y. eds. (2002) *Regulation Theory: The State of the Art*, London: Routledge.

Braithwaite, J. (2008) *Regulatory Capitalism*, Cheltenham: Edward Elgar.

Braithwaite, J., Drahos, P. (2000) *Global Business Regulation*, Cambridge: Cambridge University Press.

Braud, P. (1996) *Emotion et politique*, Paris: Presses de Sciences Po.

Broom, A. (2014) *Issues and Actors in the Global Political Economy*, Basingstoke: Palgrave.

Buchet de Neuilly, Y. (2013) 'Mais où se trouve "l'intérêt national"? Les diplomates français dans les arènes du Conseil de l'UE', in J-M. Eymeri-Douzans and G. Bouckaert, eds., *La France et Ses Administrations*, Bruxelles: Bruylant, pp. 437–59.

Busch, L. (2007) 'Performing the Economy, Performing Science: From Neoclassical to Supply Chain Models in the Agrifood Sector', *Economy and Society*, 36(3): 437–66.

Busch, L., Juska, A. (1997) 'Beyond Political Economy: Actor Networks and the Globalization of Agriculture', *Review of International Political Economy*, 4(4): 688–708.

Büthe, T., Mattli, W. (2011) *The New Global Rulers. The Privatization of Regulation in the World Economy*, Princeton: Princeton University Press.

Callon, M. (1979) 'L'Etat face à l'innovation technique. Le cas du véhicule électrique, *Revue française de science politique*, 29(3): 426–77.

Callon, M. (1998) 'Introduction: the embeddedness of economic markets in economics', in Callon, Michel (ed.), *The Laws of the Markets*, Oxford: Blackwell, pp. 1–57.

Callon, M. (2007) 'What does it mean to say that Economics is performative?' in MacKenzie, Donald, Muniesa, Fabian, Siu, Lucia (eds.), *Do Economists Make Markets? On the Performativity of Economics*, Princeton: Princeton University Press, pp. 311–56.

Callon, M., Méadel, C., Rabeharisoa, V. (2002) 'The Economy of Qualities', *Economy and Society*, 31(2): 194–217.

Carpenter, D. (2010) *Power and Regulation. Organizational Image and Pharmaceutical Regulation at the FDA*, Oxford: Oxford University Press.

Carson, R. (1962) *Silent Spring*, New York: Houghton Mifflin.

Carter, C. (2015) 'Who governs Europe? Public versus Private Regulation of Sustainability of Fish Feeds', *Journal of European Integration*, 37(3): 335–52.

Carter, C., Casales, C. (2014) 'The EU's Government of Aquaculture: Completeness Unwanted', in Jullien, B., Smith, A., eds., *The EU's Government of Industries. Markets, Institutions and Politics*, London: Routledge, pp. 84–114.

Carter, C., Ramirez Perez, S., Smith, A. (2014) 'Trade Policy: All Pervasive but to What End?', in Jullien, B., and Smith, A., eds., *The EU's Government of Industries. Markets, Institutions and Politics*, London: Routledge, pp. 216–40.

Carter, C., Smith, A. (2008) 'Revitalizing Public Policy approaches to the EU: Territorial institutionalism, fisheries and wine', *Journal of European Public Policy*, 15(2): 263–81.

Carter, C., Smith, A. (2009) 'What has Scottish devolution changed? Sectors, territory and polity-building', *British Politics*, 4(3): 315–40.

Charles, N. (2015) *Ce que éduquer veut dire*, Paris: La Documentation Française.

Chauveau, S. (1999) *L'invention pharmaceutique. La pharmacie française entre l'Etat et la société au XXème siècle*, Paris: Institut d'éditions Sanofi-Synthélabo.

Chauvin, P-M. (2010) *Le marché des réputations: Une sociologie du monde des vins de Bordeaux*, Bordeaux: Féret.

Clift, B. (2014) *Comparative Political Economy: States, Markets and Global Capitalism*, Basingstoke: Palgrave.

Clift, B., Woll, C. (2012) 'Economic patriotism: reinventing control over open markets', *Journal of European Public Policy*, 19(3): 307–23.

Coe, N., Dicken, P., Hess, M. (2008) 'Global Production Networks: Realizing the Potential', *Journal of Economic Geography*, 8(3): 271–95.

Cohen, B. (2008) *International Political Economy: An Intellectual History*, Princeton: Princeton University Press.

Cooke, P., Morgan, K. (1998) *The Associational Economy: Firms, Regions and Innovation*, Oxford: Oxford University Press.

Corsinovi, P., Begalli, D., Gaeta, D. (2013) 'Public choice theory as a tool for CMO wine reform analysis', *World Review of Entrepreneurship, Management and Sustainable Development*, 9(2): 216–29.

Cox, R. (1986) 'Social forces, states and world orders: beyond international relations theory', *Millenium*, 10(2): 125–55.

Crouch, C. (2004) *Post-democracy*, Cambridge: Polity.

Crouch, C. (2011) *The Strange Non-Death of Neo-liberalism*, Cambridge: Polity.

Crouch, C. (2013) *Making Capitalism Fit For Society*, Cambridge: Polity.

Crouch, C. (2015) 'The Next Steps', in Hay, C., Payne, A., *Civic Capitalism*, Cambridge: Polity, pp. 62–9.

Crouch, C., Le Galès, P., Trigilia, C., Voelzkow, H. (2001) *Local Production Systems in Europe. Rise or demise?* Oxford: Oxford University Press.

Crouch, C., Trigilia, C. (2001) 'Conclusions: Still Local Firms in Global Capitalism?', in Crouch, C., Le Galès, P., Trigilia, C., Voelzkow, H., eds., *Local Production Systems in Europe. Rise or demise?* Oxford: Oxford University Press, pp. 212–37.

Culpepper, P. (2000) 'Can the State Create Cooperation? Problems of Reforming the Labor Supply in France', *Journal of Public Policy,* 20(3): 223–45.

Culpepper, P. (2001) 'Employers, Public Policy, and the Politics of Decentralized Co-operation in Germany and France', in Hall, P., Soskice, D., eds., *Varieties of Capitalism*, Oxford: Oxford University Press, pp. 275–306.

Culpepper, P. (2003) *Creating Cooperation: How States Develop Human Capital in Europe*, Ithaca, NY: Cornell University Press.

Denord, F. (2007) *Néo-libéralisme version française. Histoire d'une idéologie politique*, Paris: Demopolis.

Denord, F., Schwarz, A. (2009) *L'Europe sociale n'aura pas lieu*, Paris: Raisons d'agir.

Didry, C. (2013) 'L'approche par les capacities comme registre de restructurations: un nouveau regard sur l'entreprise et le contrat de travail?', *Revue française de sociologie*, 54(3): 537–66.

Dion, R. (1988) *Histoire de la vigne et du vin en France. Des origines aux XIXe siècle*, Paris Flammarion.

Dobbin, F. (1994) *Forging Industrial Policy: The United States, Britain and France in the Railway Age*, Cambridge, MA: Cambridge University Press.

Drexl, J. (2004) 'International Competition Policy after Cancun: Placing a Singapore Issue on the WTO Doha Agenda', *World Competition*, 27(3): 419–57.

Drummond, M. (2007) 'NICE: a nightmare worth having?', *Health Economics, Policy and Law*, 2: 203–8.

Drummond, M., Sorenson, K. (2009) 'Nasty or nice? A perspective on the use of HTA in the UK', *Value in Health*, vol. 12, supplement 2.

Dubuisson-Quellier, S. (2013) 'A Market Mediation Strategy: How Social Movements Seek to Change Firms' Practices by Promoting New Principles of Product Valuation', *Organization Studies*, 34(5–6): 683–703.

Dubuisson-Quellier, S., Le Velley, R. (2008) 'Les circuits courts entre alternative et hybridation', in Gilles Maréchal (ed.), *Les circuits courts alimentaires. Bien manger dans les territoires*, Dijon: Educagri, pp. 105–12.

Duran, P. (2009) 'Légitimité, droit et action publique', *L'Année sociologique*, 59(2): 303–44.

Epps, T. (2008) *International Trade and Health Protection: A critical assessment of the WTO's SPS Agreement*, Cheltenham: Elgar.

Evans, P., Rueshemeyer, D., Skocpol, T., eds. (1985) *Bringing the State Back In*, Cambridge: Cambridge University Press.

Fanon, F. (1963) *The Wretched of the Earth*, New York: Grove Wiedenfeld (translated from the 1961 French original version).

Fligstein, N. (2001) *The Architecture of Markets. An Economic Sociology of Twenty-First-Century Capitalist Societies*, Princeton: Princeton University Press.

Fligstein, N., McAdam, D. (2012) *A Theory of Fields*, Oxford: Oxford University Press.

Flonneau, M. (2008) *Les cultures du Volant. Essai sur les mondes de l'automobilisme*, Paris: Editions Autrement.

Fourcade, M. (2009) *Economists and Societies: Discipline and Profession in the US, Britain and France, 1890s to 1990s*, Princeton: Princeton University Press.

Fox, E. (2009) 'Linked-In: Antritrust and the Virtues of a Virtual Network', *International Law*, 43(1): 151–74.

François, P., ed. (2011) *Vie et mort des institutions marchandes*, Paris: Presses de Sciences Po.

Freyssenet, M., ed. (2009) *The Second Automobile Revolution*, Basingstoke: Palgrave.

Frieden, J., Lake, D. (2010) *International Political Economy: Perspectives on Global Power and Wealth*, 5th edn, New York: W.W. Norton & Co.

Froud, J., Johal, S., Leaver, A., Williams, K. (2006) *Financialization and Strategy: Narrative and Numbers*, London: Routledge.

Garrier, G. (2002) *Histoire sociale et culturelle du vin*, Paris, Larousse.

Genieys, W., Hassenteufel, P. (2015) 'The Shaping of the New State Elites. Healthcare Policymaking in France Since 1981', *Comparative Politics*, 47(3): 280–95.

Georgakakis, D., Rowell, J., eds. (2013) *The Field of Eurocracy: Mapping EU Actors and Professionals*, Basingstoke: Palgrave.

Gereffi, G. (2014) 'Global Value Chains in a post-Washington Consensus World', *Review of International Political Economy*, 21(1): 9–37.

Gereffi, G., Korzeniewicz, M. (1994) *Commodity Chains and Global Capitalism*, London: Praeger.

Gill, S. (1991) *American Hegemony and the Trilateral Commission*, Cambridge: Cambridge University Press.

Gill, S., Law, D. (1988) *The Global Political Economy. Perspectives, Problems and Policies*, Hemel Hempstead: Harvester.

Gilpin, R. (1975) *US Power and the Multinational Corporation*, New York: Basic Books.

Gilpin, R. (1987) *The Political Economy of International Relations*, Princeton: Princeton University Press.

Glassmann, U., Voelzkow, H. (2001) 'The governance of local economies in Germany', in Crouch, C., Le Galès, P., Trigilia, C., Voelzkow H., eds., *Local Production Systems in Europe. Rise or demise?* Oxford: Oxford University Press, pp. 79–116.

Gomez, A., Itçaina, X. (2014) 'Utopiques alliances? La construction de la cohérence discursive des mobilisations autour des circuits courts en Pays Basque', *Lien Social et Politiques*, issue 72: 93–108.

Gourevitch, P. (2005) *Political Power and Corporate Control*, Princeton: Princeton University Press.

Granovetter, M. (1985) 'Economic Action and Social Structure: The Problem of Embeddedness', *American Journal of Sociology*, 91: 481–510.

Gusfield, J. (1981) *The Culture of Public Problems. Drinking-Driving and the Symbolic Order*, Chicago: University of Chicago Press.

Hall, P. (1986) *Governing the Economy*, Cambridge: Polity Press.

Hall, P., Soskice, D., eds. (2001) *Varieties of Capitalism*, Oxford: Oxford University Press.

Hall, P., Taylor, R. (1996) 'Political Science and the Three New Institutionalisms', *Political Studies*, 44(5): 936–57.

Hall, P., Taylor, R. (2009) 'Health, Social Relations and Public Policy', in Hall, P., Lamont, M., eds., *Successful Societies. How Institutions and Culture Affect Health*, Cambridge: Cambridge University Press, pp. 82–103.

Hall, P., Thelen, K. (2009) 'Institutional Change in Varieties of Capitalism', *Socio-Economic Review*, 7(1): 7–34.

Harvey, D. (2003) *The New Imperialism*, Oxford: Oxford University Press.

Harvey, D. (2009) *Social Justice and the City* (Revised edition), Athens, Georgia: The University of Georgia Press.

Hauray, B. (2006) *L'Europe du médicament. Politique-Expertise-Intérêts privés*, Paris: Presses de Sciences Po.

Hay, C. (2002) *Political Analysis. A Critical Introduction*, Basingstoke: Palgrave.

Hay, C. (2006a) 'Constructivist institutionalism', in Rhodes, R., Binder, S., Rockman, B., eds., *The Oxford Handbook of Political Institutions*. Oxford: Oxford University Press.

Hay, C. (2006b) 'What's Globalization Got to Do With It? Economic Interdependence and the Future of European Welfare States', *Government and Opposition*, 41(1): 1–22.

Hay, C. (2007) *Why We hate Politics*, Cambridge: Polity.

Hay, C. (2010) 'Introduction: Political Science in an Age of Acknowledged Interdependence', in C. Hay (ed.) *New Directions in Political Science*, Basingstoke: Palgrave, pp. 1–24.

Hay, C. (2015) 'Good in a crisis: The ontological institutionalism of social constructivism', paper presented at the congress of the *Association française de science politique*, Aix-en-Provence, June 22–24.

Hay, C., Payne, A. (2015) *Civic Capitalism*, Cambridge: Polity.

Hay, C., Wincott, D. (2012) *The Political Economy of European Welfare Capitalism*, Basingstoke: Palgrave.

Held, D., McGrew, A., eds. (2007) *Globalization Theory. Approaches and Controversies*, Cambridge: Polity Press.

Held, D., McGrew, A., Goldblatt, D., Perraton, J. (1999) *Global Transformations*, Cambridge: Polity Press.

Hellwig, F. Z. (2003) 'A way forward for geographical indications', paper given to World Intellectual Property Organization conference on GIs, San Francisco, 9–11 July.

Herrigel, G. (2010) *Manufacturing Possibilities. Creative Action and Industrial Recomposition in the United States, Germany and Japan*, Oxford: Oxford University Press.

Hildermeier, J., Villareal, A. (2011) 'Shaping an emergent market for electric cars: how politics in France and Germany transform the European automotive industry', *European Review of Industrial Economics and Policy*, issue 3 (<http://revel.unice.fr/eriep/?id=3329>).

Hobsbawn, E., Ranger, T. eds. (1983) *The Invention of Tradition*, Cambridge: Cambridge University Press.

Hobson, J., Seabrooke, L. (2007) *Everyday Politics of the World Economy*, Cambridge: Cambridge University Press.

Hollingsworth, J., Schmitter, P., Streeck, W., eds. (1994) *Governing Capitalist Economies*, Oxford: Oxford University Press.

Horn, L. (2009) 'Organic Intellectuals at Work? The High Level Group of Company Law Experts on European Corporate Governance Regulation', in Van Apeldoorn, B., Drahooupil, J., Horn, L., eds., *Contradictions and Limits of Neoliberal European Governance*, Basingstoke: Palgrave, pp. 125–41.

Ilbery, B., Maye, D. (2005a) 'Food supply chains and sustainability: evidence from specialist food producers in the Scottish/English borders', *Land Use Policy*, 22(4): 331–44.

Ilbery, B., Maye, D. (2005b) 'Alternative (shorter) food supply chains and specialist livestock products in the Scottish-English borders', *Environment and Planning A*, 37(5): 823–44.

Ilbery, B., Maye, D., Kneafsey, M., Jenkins, T., Walkley, C. (2004) 'Forecasting food supply chain developments in lagging rural regions: evidence from the UK', *Journal of Rural Studies*, 20(3): 331–44.

Inglehart, R. (1977) *The Silent Revolution*, Princeton, NJ: Princeton University Press.

Inglehart, R., Norris, P. (2009) *Cosmopolitan Communications*, Cambridge: Cambridge University Press.

Itçaina, X., Roger, A., Smith, A. (2016a) *Varietals of Capitalism. A Political Economy of the Changing Wine Industry*, Ithaca: Cornell University Press.

Itçaina, X., Roger, A., Smith, A. (2016b) 'Field Theory Recast', forthcoming.

Jas, N. (2007) 'Public Health and Pesticide Regulation in France Before and After Silent Spring', *History and Technology*, 23(4): 369–88.

Jas, N. (2010) 'Pesticides et santé des travailleurs agricoles en France. Questions anciennes, nouveaux enjeux', *Courrier de l'envrionnement de l'INRA*, issue 59, October, pp. 47–59.

Jessop, B. (2002) *The Future of the Capitalist State*, Cambridge: Polity.

Joana, J., Smith, A. (2002) *Les commissaires européens: technocrats, diplomates ou politiques?*, Paris: Presses de Sciences Po.

Jobert, B., Muller, P. (1987) *L'Etat en action*, Paris: Presses Universitaires de France.

Jordana, J., Levi-Faur, D. (2004) 'The Politics of Regulation in the Age of Governance', in Jordana, J., Levi-Faur, D., eds., *The Politics of Regulation*, Cheltenham: Edward Elgar.

Jullien, B. (2008) 'European Automobile Distribution: Globalization and Incomplete Liberalization', in Jullien, B., Smith, A., eds., *Industries and Globalization*, Basingstoke: Palgrave.

Jullien, B., Lung, Y. (2011) *L'industrie automobile. La croisée des chemins*, Paris: La Documentation Française.

Jullien, B., Smith, A., eds. (2008a) *Industries and Globalization. The Political Causality of Difference*, Basingstoke: Palgrave.

Jullien, B., Smith, A. (2008b) 'The transformation of the French Foie Gras Industry: Globalization, Intellectual Property Rights and Industrial Domination', in Jullien, B., Smith, A., eds., *Industries and Globalization: The Political Causality of Difference*, Basingstoke, Palgrave, pp. 182–200.

Jullien, B., Smith, A. (2011) 'Conceptualizing the role of politics in the economy: Industries and their institutionalizations', *Review of International Political Economy*, 18(3): 358–83.

Jullien, B., Smith, A., eds. (2014) *The EU's Government of Industries: Markets, Institutions and Politics*, London: Routledge.

Kalberg, S. (2010) *Les valeurs, les idées et les intérêts. Introduction à la sociologie de Max Weber*, Paris: La Découverte.

Keohane, R., Nye, J., eds. (1972) *Transnational Relations and World Politics*, Cambridge, MA: Harvard University Press.

Konefal, J., Hatanaka, M. (2010) 'Democracy, Justice and Sustainablity in an Age of Scientism, Marketism and Statism', *Journal of Rural Social Sciences*, 25(3): 1–17.

Kovacic, W. (1982) 'The Federal Trade Commission and Congressional Oversight of Antitrust Enforcement', *Tulsa Law Journal*, 17(4): 587–671.

Lagroye, J. (1997) *La sociologie politique*, Paris: Presses de la FNSP-Dalloz.

Langley, P. (2008) *The Everyday Life of Global Finance: Saving and Borrowing in Anglo-America*, Oxford: Oxford University Press.

Lascoumes, P., Le Galès, P. (2007) 'Introduction: Understanding Public Policy Through its Instruments', *Governance*, 20(1): 1–21.

Lawrence, T., Suddaby, R. (2006) 'Institutions and institutional work', in Clegg, S., Hardy, C., Lawrence, T., Nord, W., eds., *The Sage Handbook of Organization Studies*, Los Angeles, Sage (2nd edition), pp. 215–54.

Le Galès, P. (2014) 'Recomposition de l'Etat: changements d'échelle, normes extérieures, nouvelles organisations', in Le Galès, P., Vezinat, N., *L'Etat recomposé*, Paris: Presses Universitaires de France.

Le Galès, P., Scott, A. (2008) 'Une révolution bureaucratique britannique? Autonomie sans contrôle ou "freer markets, more rules"', *Revue française de sociologie*, 49(2): 301–30.

Le Galès, P., Voelzkow, H. (2001) 'Introduction: The governance of local economies', in Crouch, C., Le Galès, P., Trigilia, C., Voelzkow, H., eds., *Local Production Systems in Europe. Rise or demise?* Oxford: Oxford University Press, pp. 1–24.

Lebaron, F. (2000) *La croyance économique: les économistes entre science et politique*, Paris: Le Seuil.

Lehmbruch, G., Schmitter, P., eds. (1982) *Patterns of Corporatist Policy-making*, London: Sage.

Levi-Faur, D. (2006) 'Varieties of Regulatory Capitalism: Varieties of Regulatory Capitalism: Getting the Most Out of the Comparative Method', *Governance*, 19(3): 367–82.

Lewis, N. (2008) 'Constructing economic objects of governance: the New Zealand wine industry', in, Stringer, C., Le Heron, R., eds., *Agri-Food Commodity Chains and Globalising Networks*, Aldershot: Ashgate, pp. 103–19.

McClosky, H., Zaller, J. (1984) *The American Ethos. Public Attitudes toward Capitalism and Democracy*, Cambridge MA: Harvard University Press.

McDermott, G. (2007) 'Politics, Power and Institution Building: Bank Crises and Supervision in East Central Europe', *Review of International Political Economy*, 14(2): 220–50.

MacKenzie, D. (2006) *An Engine, Not a Camera: How Financial Models Shape Markets*, Cambridge, MA: MIT Press.

McKenzie, D. (2009) *Material Markets: How Economic Agents are Constructed*, Oxford: Oxford University Press.

Mahoney, J., Thelen, K. (2010) 'A theory of gradual institutional change', in Mahoney, J., Thelen, K., eds., *Explaining Institutional Change. Ambiguity, Agency and Power*, Cambridge: Cambridge University Press.

Mangenot, M., Rowell, J. (2010) 'What Europe constructs: towards a sociological constructivism', in Rowell, J., Mangenot, M., eds., *A Political Sociology of the European Union. Reassessing constructivism*, Manchester: Manchester University Press, pp. 1–22.

Manners, I. (2002) 'Normative Power Europe: A Contradiction in Terms?' *Journal of Common Market Studies*, 40(2): 235–58.

March, J., Olsen, J. (1989) *Rediscovering Institutions*, New York: Free Press.

Martin, C., Swank, D. (2004) 'Does the Organization of Capital Matter? Employers and Active Labour Market Policy at the National and Firm Levels', *American Political Science Review*, 98(4): 593–611.

Martin, C., Swank, D. (2012) *The Political Construction of Business Interests: Co-ordination, Growth and Equality*, Cambridge: Cambridge University Press.

Mayer, N. (2010) *Sociologie des Comportements Politiques*, Paris: Armand Colin.

Meltzer, E. (2003) 'Geographical indications and trademarks: Intellectual property any way you slice it', paper given at the WIPO 'Worldwide symposium on geographical indications', San Francisco, 9–11 July.

Mérand, F. (2015) 'Bourdieu: le champ, vecteur de la mondialisation', in G. Devin, ed., *10 Concepts Sociologiques en Relations Internationales*, Paris: Editions CNRS, pp. 49–70.

Molina, O., Rhodes, M. (2006) 'Conflict, Complementarities and Institutional Change in Mixed Market Economies', in Hancké, B., Rhodes, M., Thatcher, M., eds., *Beyond Varieties of Capitalism: Contradictions, Complementarities and Change*, Oxford: Oxford University Press, pp. 223–52.

Montalban, M. (2008) 'Shareholder value, political work and globalization in the pharmaceutical industry', in Jullien, B., Smith, A., *Industries and Globalization: The Political Causality of Divergent Responses*, Palgrave: Basingstoke.

Montalban, M., Ramirez Perez, S., Smith, A. (2014) 'Competition Policy: Ever Present but Far from all-Conquering', in Smith, A., Jullien, B., eds., *The EU's Government of Industries. Markets, Institutions and Politics*, Abingdon: Routledge, pp. 141–64.

Moore, K. (2011) 'Global Networks in Local Agriculture: A Framework for Negotiation', *Journal of Agricultural & Food Information*, 12(1): 23–39.

Mossialos, E., Permanand, G., Baeten, R., Hervey, T., eds. (2010) *Health Systems Governance in Europe: The role of European Union Law and Policy*, Cambridge: Cambridge University Press.

Muller, P. (1984) *Le technocrate et le paysan*, Paris: Economie et humanisme (republished in 2014 by l'Harmattan).

Muller, P. (1995) 'Les politiques publiques comme construction d'un rapport au monde', in Faure, A., Pollet, G., Warin, P., eds., *La construction du sens dans les politiques publiques*, Paris, l'Harmattan, pp. 153–79.

Muller, P. (2015) *La société de l'efficacité globale. Comment les sociétés modernes se pensent et agissent sur elles-mêmes*, Paris: Presses Universitaires de France.

Murray, D., Raynolds, L., Wilkinson, J. (2007) *Fair Trade: Transforming the Challenges of Globalization*, London: Routledge.

Muzaka, V. (2011) *The Politics of Intellectual Property Rights and Access to Medicines*, Basingstoke: Palgrave.

Naves, P. (2016) 'L'encadrement des circuits courts: du secteur agricole aux territoires?', *Economie Rurale* (forthcoming in issue 355).

Nicourt, C., Girault, J.L. (2011) 'La normalisation du travail viticole à l'épreuve de la réduction de l'usage de pesticides', *Économie rurale*, issue 321: 29–41.

North, D. (1991) 'Institutions', *Journal of Economic Perspectives*, 5(1): 97–112.

Olafsen, T., Sandberg, M., Senneset, G., Ellingsen, H., Almas, K., Winther, U., Svennevig, N. (2006) 'Exploitation of Marine Living Resources - Global Opportunities for Norwegian Expertise', report from a working group appointed by DKNVS and NTVA.

Ostrom, E., Ostrom, V. (2014) *Choice, Rules and Collective Action. The Ostroms on the Study of Institutions and Governance*, Colchester: ECPR Press.

Overbeek, H., van Apeldorn, B., Nölke, A., eds. (2007) *The Transnational Politics of Corporate Governance Regulation*, London: Routledge.

Palier, B. (2002) *Gouverner la sécurité sociale*, Paris: Presses Universitaires de France.

Parsons, C. (2003) *A Certain Idea of Europe*, Ithaca, NY: Cornell University Press.

Parsons, C. (2007) *Mapping Arguments in Political Science*, Oxford: Oxford University Press.

Permanaud, G. (2006) *EU Pharmaceuticals Regulation*, Manchester: Manchester University Press.

Picard, R., ed. (2015) *The Euro Crisis in the Media. Journalistic coverage of economic crisis and European Institutions*, London: I. B. Tauris.

Pierson, P. (2000) 'Path Dependence, Increasing Returns, and the Study of Politics', *American Political Science Review*, 94(2): 251–67.

Pierson, P. (2004) *Politics in Time: History, Institutions, and Social Analysis*. Princeton: Princeton University Press.

Pignarre, P. (2003) *Le grand secret de l'industrie pharmaceutique*, Paris: La Découverte.

Piketty, T. (2014) *Capitalism in the Twenty-First Century*, Cambridge, MA: Harvard University Press.

Pinson, G. (2015) 'Gouvernance et sociologie de l'action organisée. Action publique, coordination et théorie de l'Etat', *Année Sociologique*, 65(2): 483–516.

Pinson, G., Morel-Journel, C., eds. (2016) *Debating the Neoliberal City*, London: Ashgate (forthcoming).

Piore, M., Sabel, C. (1984) *The Second Industrial Divide: Possibilities for Prosperity*, New York: Basic Books.

Pollit, C., Bouckaert, G., eds. (2004) *Public Management Reform: A Comparative Analysis*, Oxford: Oxford University Press.

Posner, E. (2009) *The Origins of Europe's New Stock Markets*, Cambridge (MA), MA: Harvard University Press.

Radaelli, C. (1999) *Technocracy in the EU*, London: Longman.

Renting, H., Marsden, T., Banks, J. (2003) 'Understanding alternative food networks', *Environment and Planning A*, 35: 393–411.

Robert, C. (2010) 'Who are the European experts? Profiles, trajectories and expert "careers" of the European Commission', *French Politics*, 8(2): 248–74.

Rochefort, D., Cobb, R. (1994) *The Politics of Problem Definition*, Lawrence: University Press of Kansas.

Roger, Antoine (2010) 'Scholarly constructs and the legitimization of European policies. The circulation of knowledge on wine and the vine', *Revue française de science politique*, 60(2): 1–22.

Ross, G. (1995) *Jacques Delors and European Integration*, Cambridge: Polity Press.

Rousset, S. (2005) 'Les contrats entre récoltants et industriels dans la filière vitivinicole californienne', *Notes et études économiques*, issue 24.

Rousset, S., Traversac, J.-B. (2004) *Formes d'organisation des négociants en France et dans les Nouveaux Pays Exportateurs: l'effet de la qualité sur la structure des approvisionnements*. Dijon: Maison des Sciences de l'Homme de Dijon.

Saint-Gès, V., Bélis-Bergouignan, M.C., (2009) 'Ways of reducing pesticides use in Bordeaux vineyards», *Journal of Cleaner Production*, issue 17: 1644–53.

Saint-Martin, D. (2000) *Building the New Managerialist State*, Oxford: Oxford University Press.

Salais, R. (2013) *Le viol de l'Europe. Enquête sur la disparition d'une idée*, Paris: Presses Universitaires de France.

Saporta, I. (2014) *VinoBusiness*, Paris, Albin Michel.

Schäfer, A., Streeck, W., eds. (2013) *Politics in the Age of Austerity*, Cambridge: Polity Press.

Schmidt, V., Thatcher, M., eds. (2013) *Resilient Liberalism in Europe's Political Economy*, Cambridge: Cambridge University Press.

Schwartz, S. (2006) 'Les valeurs de base de la personne: théorie, mésures et applications', *Revue française de sociologie*, 47(4): 929–68.

Schwartz, S. (2012) 'An Overview of the Schwartz Theory of Basic Values', *Online Readings in Psychology and Culture*, 2(1). <http://dx.doi.org/10.9707/2307-0919.1116>.

Sen, A. (2009) *The Idea of Justice*, Cambridge, MA: Harvard University Press.

Shonfield, A. (1965) *Modern Capitalism*, Oxford: Oxford University Press.

Sil, R., Katzenstein, P. (2010) *Beyond Paradigms. Analytical Eclecticism in the Study of World Politics*, Basingstoke: Palgrave.

SINTEF (2005) 'Employment in the EU based on Farmed Norwegian Salmon', research report <http://www.sintef.no/globalassets/upload/fiskeri_og_havbruk/internasjonalt_radgivning/report_final.pdf>.

SINTEF (2009) 'The significance of the fishing and aquaculture industries for Norway in 2009 – a national and regional ripple effect analysis', research report.

Skinner, Q. (2002) *Visions of Politics* (Volumes 1, 2 & 3), Cambridge: Cambridge University Press.

Smith, A. (1995) *L'Europe au miroir du local: les fonds structurels et les zones rurales en France en Espagne et au Royaume-Uni*, Paris: l'Harmattan.

Smith, A. (2009) 'How the WTO matters to industry: the case of Scotch whisky', *International Political Sociology*, 3(2): 176–93.

Smith, A. (2010a) 'A Constructivist-institutionalist Approach to EU Politics: The Case of Protected Geographical Indications for Food', in Rowell, J., Mangenot, M., eds., *A Political Sociology of the European Union: Reassessing Constructivism*, Manchester: Manchester United Press, pp. 146–63.

Smith, A. (2010b) 'Industries as spaces for the politics of industry: the case of Scotch whisky', *Regional and Federal Studies*, 20(3): 389–407.

Smith, A. (2011) 'Multijurisdictional Regulation', in Bevir., M., ed., *Handbook of Governance*, London: Sage, pp. 300–12.

Smith, A. (2013) 'Transferts institutionnels et politiques de concurrence. Les cas communautaires français et britannique', *Gouvernement et action publique*, 2(3): 415–40.

Smith, A., de Maillard, J., Costa, O. (2007) *Vin et politique: Bordeaux, la France et la mondialisation*, Paris: Presses de Sciences Po.

Stanziani, A. (2005) *Histoire de la qualité alimentaire*, Paris: Le Seuil.

Stiglitz, J. (2006) *Making Globalization Work*, New York: W.W. Norton & Co.

Stiglitz, J. (2012) *The Price of Inequality. How Today's Divided Society Endangers Our Future*, New York: W.W. Norton & Co.

Storper, M. (1997) *The Regional World: Territorial development in a global economy*, London: Guilford Press.

Strasser, S. (1989) *Satisfaction Guaranteed. The Making of the American Mass Market*, Washington: Smithsonian Institute Press.

Streeck, W. (2014a) *Buying Time. The Delayed Crisis of Democratic Capitalism*, London: Verso.

Streeck, W. (2014b) 'The Politics of Public Debt. Neoliberalism, Capitalist Development and the Restructuring of the State', *German Economic Review*, 15: 143–65.

Streeck, W., Thelen, K. (2005) 'Introduction: Institutional Change in Advanced Political Economies', in Streeck, W., Thelen, K., eds., *Beyond Continuity. Institutional Change in Advanced Political Economies*, Oxford: Oxford University Press.

Tanaka, K., Juska, A. (2010) 'Technoscience in Agriculture: Reflections on the Contributions of The MSU School of Sociology of Food and Agriculture', *Journal of Rural Social Sciences*, 25(3): 34–55.

Teil, G., Barrey, S., Floux, P., Hennion, A. (2011) *Le vin et l'environnement. Faire compter la différence*, Paris: Presses des Mines.

Thelen, K. (2001) 'Varieties of Labor Politics in the Developed Democracies', in Hall, P., Soskice, D., eds., *Varieties of Capitalism*, Oxford: Oxford University Press, pp. 71–103.

Thelen, K. (2004) *How Institutions Evolve: The Political Economy of Skills in Germany, Britain, the United States and Japan*. New York: Cambridge University Press.

Thelen, K., Steinmo, S. (1992) 'Historical Institutionalism in Comparative Politics', in Steinmo, S., Thelen, K., Longstreth, K., eds., *Structuring Politics. Historical Institutionalism in Comparative Analysis*, Cambridge: Cambridge University Press, pp. 1–32.

Théret, B. (2003) 'Institutionnalismes et structuralismes: Oppositions, sustitutions ou affinities electives?' *Cahiers d'économie politique*, issue 44: 51–78.

Trigilia, C. (1986) 'Small firm development and political subcultures in Italy', *European Sociological Review*, 2(3): 161–75.

Trigilia, C. (1992) 'Italian Industrial Districts: Neither Myth nor Interlude', in Pyke and Sengenberger, eds., *Industrial Districts and Economic Regeneration*, Geneva: International Institute for Labour Studies.

Trigilia, C. (2009) 'Italy: rise, decline and restructuring of a regionalized capitalism', *Economy and Society*, 38(4): 630–53.

Van Apeldoorn, B., Drahokoupil, J., Horn, L., eds. (2009) *Contradictions and Limits of Neoliberal European Governance*, Basingstoke: Palgrave.

Van Waarden, F., Drahos, M. (2002) 'Courts and (epistemic) communities in the convergence of competition policies', *Journal of European Public Policy*, 9(6): 913–34.

Vauchez, A. (2014) *Démocratiser l'Europe*, Paris: La république des idées et les editions du Seuil.

Villareal, A. (2014) *L'industrie automobile à l'épreuve des voitures électriques. Entre changement et continuité*, PhD thesis, University of Bordeaux.

Vliegenthart, A., Overbeek, H. (2007) 'Corporate governance regulation in East Central Europe: the role of transnational forces', in Overbeek, H., van Apeldorn, B., Nölke, A., eds., *The Transnational Politics of Corporate Governance Regulation*, London: Routledge, pp. 177–97.

Warner, C. (1960) *The Winegrowers of France and the Government since 1875*, New York: Columbia University Press.

Weber, M. (1971) *Economie et société*, Paris: Plon.

Wigger, A. (2008) *Competition for Competitiveness: The Politics of the Transformation of the EU Competition Regime*, PhD thesis, Amsterdam: Vrije University.

Wigger, A., Nölke, A. (2007) 'Enhanced Roles of Private Actors in EU Business Regulation and the Erosion of Rhenish Capitalism: the Case of Antitrust Enforcement', *Journal of Common Market Studies*, 45(2): 487–513.

Wight, M. (1991) *International Theory*, Leicester: Leicester University Press.

Wiig-Aselesen, H. (2007) 'The Innovation System of Norwegian Aquacultured Salmonids', *TIK Working paper on Innovation Studies No. 20070606*.

Williams, R. (1973) *The Country and the City*, London: The Hogarth Press.

Williamson, O. (1975) *Markets and Hierarchies: Analysis and Antitrust Implications*, New York: The Free Press.

Williamson, O. (1985) *The Economic Institutions of Capitalism*, New York: The Free Press.

Wolfe, R. (2005) 'See you in Geneva? Legal (mis)representations of the Trading System', *European Journal of International Relations*, 11(3): 339–65.

Woll, C. (2008) *Firm Interests: How Governments Shape Business Lobbying on Global Trade*, Ithaca, NY: Cornell University Press.

Wright, A. (1990) *The Death of Ramon Gonzalez: The Modern Agricultural Dilemma*, Austin: University of Texas Press.

Young, A., Peterson, J. (2006) 'Introduction: The EU and the New Trade Politics', *Journal of European Public Policy*, 13(6): 795–814.

Youngs, R. (2010) *Europe's role in world politics: A retreat form liberal internationalism*, London: Routledge.

Index

The manufacturer's authorised representative in the EU for product safety is Oxford University Press España S.A. of el Parque Empresarial San Fernando de Henares, Avenida de Castilla, 2 – 28830 Madrid (www.oup.es/en or product.safety@oup.com). OUP España S.A. also acts as importer into Spain of products made by the manufacturer.

www.ingramcontent.com/pod-product-compliance
Lightning Source LLC
LaVergne TN
LVHW011803200926
848484LV00003B/767
* 9 7 8 0 1 9 8 7 8 8 1 5 7 *